Test Tube Envy

The Bucknell Studies in Latin American Literature and Theory
Series Editor: Aníbal González, Pennsylvania State University

Dealing with far-reaching questions of history and modernity, language and selfhood, and power and ethics, Latin American literature sheds light on the many-faceted nature of Latin American life, as well as on the human condition as a whole. This series of books provides a forum for some of the best criticism on Latin American literature in a wide range of critical approaches, with an emphasis on works that productively combine scholarship with theory. Acknowledging the historical links and cultural affinities between Latin American and Iberian literatures, the series welcomes consideration of Spanish and Portuguese texts and topics, while also providing a space of convergence for scholars working in Romance studies, comparative literature, cultural studies, and literary theory.

Titles in Series

Mario Santana, *Foreigners in the Homeland: The Latin American New Novel in Spain, 1962–1974*

Ronald J. Friis, *José Emilio Pacheco and the Poets of the Shadows*

Robert T. Conn, *The Politics of Philology: Alfonso Reyes and the Invention of the Latin American Literary Tradition*

Andrew Bush, *The Routes of Modernity: Spanish American Poetry from the Early Eighteenth to the Mid-Nineteenth Century*

Santa Arias and Mariselle Meléndez, *Mapping Colonial Spanish America: Places and Commonplaces of Identity, Culture, and Experience*

Alice A. Nelson, *Political Bodies: Gender, History, and the Struggle for Narrative Power in Recent Chilean Literature*

Julia Kushigian, *Reconstructing Childhood: Strategies of Reading for Culture and Gender in the Spanish American Bildungsroman*

Silvia N. Rosman, *Being in Common: Nation, Subject, and Community in Latin American Literature and Culture*

Patrick Dove, *The Catastrophe of Modernity: Tragedy and the Nation in Latin American Literature*

James J. Pancrazio, *The Logic of Fetishism: Alejo Carpentier and the Cuban Tradition*

Frederick Luciani, *Literary Self-Fashioning in Sor Juana Inés de la Cruz*

Sergio Waisman, *Borges and Translation: The Irreverence of the Periphery*

Stuart Day, *Staging Politics in Mexico: The Road to Neoliberalism*

Amy Nauss Millay, *Voices from the* fuente viva: *The Effect of Orality in Twentieth-Century Spanish American Narrative*

J. Andrew Brown, *Test Tube Envy: Science and Power in Argentine Narrative*

Test Tube Envy

Science and Power in Argentine Narrative

J. Andrew Brown

Lewisburg
Bucknell University Press

© 2005 by Rosemont Publishing & Printing Corp.

All rights reserved. Authorization to photocopy items for internal or personal use, or the internal or personal use of specific clients, is granted by the copyright owner, provided that a base fee of $10.00, plus eight cents per page, per copy is paid directly to the Copyright Clearance Center, 222 Rosewood Drive, Danvers, Massachusetts 01923. [0-8387-5613-1/05 $10.00 + 8¢ pp, pc.]

Associated University Presses
2010 Eastpark Boulevard
Cranbury, NJ 08512

The paper used in this publication meets the requirements of the American National Standard for Permanence of Paper for Printed Library Materials Z39.48-1984.

Library of Congress Cataloging-in-Publication Data

Brown, J. Andrew, 1970–
    Test tube envy : science and power in Argentine narrative / J. Andrew Brown.
      p. cm.—(The Bucknell studies in Latin American literature and theory)
  Includes bibliographical references and index.
  ISBN 0-8387-5613-1 (alk. paper)
    1. Argentine fiction—History and criticism. 2. Literature and science—Argentina. I. Title. II. Series.

PQ7697.B76   2005
863.009′36′0982—dc22
                                        2004027218

PRINTED IN THE UNITED STATES OF AMERICA

For Amy

Contents

Acknowledgments	9
Introduction	13
1. Butting Heads: Phrenology as Weapon in *Facundo* and *Amalia*	28
2. A Dandy New Scientist: Lucio V. Mansilla	55
3. Argentine Naturalism's Test Tube Anxiety	84
4. Test Tube Terror: Science and Society in Roberto Arlt	97
5. Borges's Scientific Discipline	125
6. Cortázar's Quantum Values	160
7. Test Tube Envy at the Turn of the Century: Convergences and Divergences	189
Conclusion	217
Notes	226
Works Cited	240
Index	254

Acknowledgments

THIS PROJECT SPENT MANY YEARS IN ITS OWN LABORATORY AND there have been many teachers, colleagues and friends who have made suggestions and given support at various points along its development. I would like to thank my undergraduate mentors Mary Davis and Pamela Gossin, both of whom contributed to the interests that resulted in this book. My professors at the University of Virginia all helped me greatly, regardless of their specialty or research focus. Fernando Operé, Donald Shaw, and Karen Parshall all read the manuscript at various stages and made substantial contributions to its quality. My adviser Gustavo Pellón played a special role in its creation and I cherish the many hours we spent together working through the project's early iterations.

My colleagues at Washington University in St. Louis have also helped a great deal. In general, the nurturing atmosphere of the Department of Romance Languages and Literatures has contributed enormously to my ability to write and revise and I thank all of my colleagues in Spanish, French and Italian who have helped make Washington University a great place to work. Elzbieta Sklodowska, John Garganigo, and Randolph Pope also read versions of the book and gave excellent suggestions for its improvement. Benigno Trigo made some helpful observations on the project as a whole and Anibal González and the anonymous reader for Bucknell University Press made invaluable suggestions that contributed greatly to the quality of the book. Rita Kuehler, Kathy Loepker, Helene Abrams, and Christine Hitchcock make up the best office staff a department could have and I thank them all for their help. Christine Hitchcock's talent with image design is on display on the cover of the book and I thank and recognize her for that especially.

Adria, Colin, and Eva have all made the work on this book much more enjoyable, their support and presence act as a backdrop to all that I have written, even if they are not particularly interested right now in the topic. Above all, Amy has made this project possible with her unflagging support and devotion from beginning to end.

A portion of chapter 5 appears as "Borges's Scientific Discipline" in *Hispanic Review*

A brief section of chapter 6 appears in "Reading *Rayuela* in the Rayuel-O-Matic" *Revista Canadiense de Estudios Hispánicos*

The section on Mempo Giardinelli in chapter 7 appeared as "Chaos in the Chaco: Ilya Prigogine and Mempo Giardinelli's *Imposible equilbrio*" in *Latin American Literary Review*

I would like to thank all three journals for the permission to publish these articles.

Test Tube Envy

Introduction

IN JUNE OF 2002, THE BUENOS AIRES NEWSPAPER *EL CLARÍN* PUBLISHED a series of articles and interviews lamenting the effect of the current financial crisis on the state of Argentine science. The articles shared themes of missed opportunities and unrealized potential, focusing on the personal and professional struggles of scientists in Argentina. The series was complemented, perhaps unwittingly, by the regular announcements of advances in Western science, from new discoveries in robotics to the progress of the Human Genome Project, that appeared weekly in *El Clarín* just as in many newspapers throughout the world. The conjunction of the reports of scientific advancement with those detailing the sad state of Argentine science is not new with the most recent Argentine financial crisis. From independence to the present day (with some important exceptions), the Argentine press has tended to trumpet the advances of science with great enthusiasm. This scientific fervor ranges from Bernardino Rivadavia's analyses of European science in his 1822 weekly *La abeja argentina* to *Crítica*'s eagerness at Albert Einstein's 1925 visit to Buenos Aires to the articles in *El Clarín* mentioned above. The attention paid to these advances in contemporary science and their popularizations, while serving to inform an interested Argentine public, also displays a tension in Argentine culture. This popular focus suggests, sometimes implicitly and sometimes explicitly, the construction of an authoritative scientific presence in Argentina that enjoys a certain cultural prestige even as it underscores the conspicuous absence of an indigenous scientific tradition. The Argentine biochemist Marcelino Cereijido has struggled with this tension in a series of books that consider the situation and history of science in Argentina with titles like *¿Por qué no tenemos ciencia?* and *Ciencia sin seso, locura doble*. In *¿Por qué no tenemos ciencia?*, Cereijido wrestles in particular with a similar dynamic of scientific presence and absence as he explores the question of the existence of renowned scientists from Latin America who are only able to be so when they leave Latin America for education and work in Europe and the United States. While Argentina and many other Latin American countries have many talented scientists and well-developed scientific programs, Cereijido, who works in Mexico, focuses on this perceived absence, attempting to understand why Latin Americans seem obliged to leave Latin America in order to enjoy success and why this situation does not seem likely to change. Cereijido, just as the newspapers, presents science as occupying a privileged space in society as a guarantor of modernity and cultural truth (in the Foucauldian sense). At the same time, he presents this Argentine space as relatively empty, in need of a discourse that imports the perceived cultural authority of science.

This dynamic, between the perceived absence of a scientific tradition and the need for a scientific presence to endow cultural and societal discourse with authority, serves as the focus of this book. Argentine narrative provides an important space in which these issues of scientific presence and absence can play out in a complex web of reference, appropriation, and reconstruction. Not only does narrative import scientific prestige as a kind of sociopolitical power play, it also creates and shapes the cultural discourses that will endow science with that prestige. With that in mind, the book asks the questions of how narrative, Argentine narrative in particular, navigates this tension, how popularized versions of science contemporary to narrative affect the production of a literary discourse and how narrative in turn influences the way science operates within a particular cultural context. I have suggested the phrase "test tube envy" to describe the phenomenon at the heart of these questions, attempting to evoke this very serious desire to appropriate an absent power even as I playfully allude to Freud's obviously flawed construction of feminine identity. Just as Freud's theory was more creative invention than objective description, the exercise of test tube envy creates and configures scientific discourse as much as it appropriates it.

The title of this book should at once invite and dismiss connections to the work of the French cultural historian Michel Foucault. In this late twentieth-century context, one can hardly speak of power without a concomitant self-positioning vis-à-vis Foucault's ideas on the operation of power within human culture. Indeed, Foucault's work on discourse, power, and science has proved invaluable to my conceptualization of the issue at hand, that is, how the discourse of science functions within the discursive fields we see constructed in various literary texts.[1] For example, how does phrenology as a science function within Sarmiento's *Facundo*? Does the presence of this science of the cranium provide structure to a text described by its author as having neither "feet nor head"? What is its relationship to what Carlos Alonso has described as Sarmiento's "desire for power" and how did it help Sarmiento establish real political power?[2] How did the use of phrenology in Sarmiento's text affect the way in which nineteenth-century Argentineans viewed and practiced the discipline? How do these elements relate to create real discursive power that can effectively discipline those against whom Sarmiento positions his text? Foucault's work has prepared an intellectual climate conducive to the framing of these questions as well as their possible answers.

However, to return to the title of the book, the phrasing "in Argentine Narrative" suggests an examination that seeks to unite several authors across some 150 years. Foucault, however, would at least claim to reject such a diachronic practice, seeking instead to study the synchronic relationships of discourse in what he has called an *episteme* in *The Order of Things*. The study of the development of an idea across time and paradigms of thought stands at odds to Foucault's described historiographical intentions, even if his own work violates those intentions from time to time. Contrary to Foucault's practice, then, I will use these Foucault-inspired questions to understand the development of the use of scientific discourse over an extended time. While the Argentine literary tradition is marked by obvious differences in conception and style, I hope that such a strategy will uncover enduring continuities. An engagement of Foucault's ideas on power as well as his rejection of continuity will serve as groundwork for the specific analysis of different examples of Argentine narrative. In this introduction, I will present my conceptualization of the relationship between the presence of science and the rest of the literary text, engaging many of Foucault's ideas on discourse and power as I construct the basis for the analysis to follow.

This method of studying the positioning of science within a given discourse is actually proposed by Foucault in *The Archaeology of Knowledge*, if in a slightly different context:

> In any discursive formation, one finds a specific relation between science and knowledge; and instead of defining between them a relation of exclusion or subtraction (by trying to discover what in knowledge still eludes and resists science, what in science is still compromised by its

> proximity to and the influence of knowledge), archaeological analysis must show positively how a science functions in the elements of knowledge. . . . it is a question of its existence as a discursive practice and of its functioning among other practices. (Foucault 1972, 185)

If Foucault chooses disciplines or modes of thinking as the object of his examination of discourse, in this study I propose to examine the literary text as a discursive field. My focus will then be the play of the various discourses and the method by which these interactions produce authority for the ideological or philosophical positions advanced in the texts. At the same time, I would resist the hermetic connotation that might accompany the identification of a single text as a complete discursive formation. I instead conceive of the literary work as a juncture of practices whose combinations involve relations of power that in turn produce both the literary text itself as well as the position of the text within society. The cultural authority enjoyed by a discipline, whether it be science or something else, has a direct impact on its rhetorical power within the text. Furthermore, the textual manipulation of that authority has a direct impact on the cultural norms that dictate both ideology and individual behavior. In this formulation, I both borrow and bend Foucault's ideas, using concepts that seem useful in a study that will, at times, violate (if such an action is possible when speaking of Foucault) his use of those concepts. David Shumway has suggested an "Add Foucault and stir" approach to how to use Foucault's ideas in different studies (Shumway 1989, 161). My intention is to proceed along those lines.

Foucault's work on sexuality also serves as an important model for understanding both the power of scientific discourse in the regulation of behavior as well as the ways in which literature can wield that power. Foucault's observation on the scientization of sex in the nineteenth century suggests an example of how scientific discourse can regulate behavior:

> It is easy to make light of these nineteenth-century psychiatrists, who made a point of apologizing for the horrors they were about to let speak, evoking "immoral behavior" or "aberrations of the genetic senses," . . . It [the nineteenth century] was a time when the most singular pleasures were called upon to pronounce a discourse of truth concerning themselves, a discourse which had to model itself after that which spoke, not of sin and salvation, but of bodies and life processes—the discourse of science. (Foucault 1990, 64)

Just as scientific discourse provided an uncomfortable mode for the expression of sexuality, the Argentine example shows how scientific discourse allowed for the enunciation of a range of political and philosophical objectives. For example, we will see that Sarmiento's use of phrenology to describe and control the textual bodies he ascribed to his gaucho enemies follows the same dynamic that we see in the scientific labeling of particular sexual expressions as "aberrations of the genetic senses." The subjugation and control implicit in that labeling display the possibilities for exercising political power over his opponents that Sarmiento sought. In a realm more philosophical than political, Julio Cortázar used the popular images of quantum physics to undermine the logical systems embodied by René Descartes, bringing to bear disciplinary force on the namesake of Cartesian reductionism.

Foucault's ideas serve this study as more than a theoretical model. His treatment of science both in the preceding citation as well as in other areas of his work illustrates a tendency in Western thought that will prove important in the works we will study presently. He positions science within an analysis of discourse as he conceives it, that is, a system of what is and can be said by a body of knowledge. For example, according to Foucault's conception, the discourse of medicine embraces all that can be conceptualized or spoken about medicine in a particular historical context. Foucault's analysis of medical discourse is instructive for the case at hand. In this project in particular, the French thinker affords science at once a privileged and a non-privileged space within his study. Initially, he privileges science by granting it a discursive power based on its rigorous ability to make observations, thus distinguishing it from other types of knowledge. His description of clinical medicine reveals just such a bias toward the particular nature of knowledge produced by a rigorous methodological scientific approach:

> Clinical medicine is certainly not a science. Not only because it does not comply with the formal criteria, or attain the level of rigor expected of physics, chemistry, or even of physiology; but also because it involves a scarcely organized mass of empirical observations, uncontrolled experiments and results, therapeutic prescriptions, and institutional regulations. And yet this non-science is not exclusive of science: in the course of the nineteenth century, it established definite relations between such perfectly constituted sciences as physiology, chemistry, or microbiology. (Foucault 1972, 181)

By describing what clinical medicine is not, Foucault provides an example of what he envisions science as; a rigorous discipline based on organized experimentation. He notes the relations between the two, but by so doing only further describes science's privileged position not only in Western culture but also in his own thought. The phrasing used to indicate that clinical medicine fails to satisfy the cultural criteria for science because it lacks the organized empirical data and experiments is especially revealing. By separating the idea of formal criteria from the "scarcely organized mass of empirical observations," Foucault's language suggests a rejection of clinical medicine's scientificity on both a cultural and a personal level. Science becomes, then, the touchstone for comparison, a discursive model against which other modes of thinking can be judged.

Many of Foucault's specific historical studies center on these "non-sciences," a focus that carries with it an inherent privileging of the hard sciences. By exposing the discursive formations of disciplines that enjoy (apparently undeserved) cultural prestige as scientific, he elevates the sciences he does not analyze. Foucault's subsequent relation of the nonscientific medicine to the scientific disciplines physiology, chemistry, and microbiology suggests the beginning of a reconciliation. Nevertheless, by founding that relationship on elements that produce "perfectly constituted sciences," he again deepens the dichotomy between hard and soft sciences even as he purports a kind of rapprochement. A clearer reduction of scientific prestige generally in Foucault's thought occurs as he relegates science to the position of one discipline among many that occupy a discursive field. Science is removed from its cultural pedestal and becomes one object of study among many. In the former quotation we see that attitude especially, but in the latter as well, when he begins to relate the non-science to science. Even so, by labeling the scientific and nonscientific elements, he again rescues knowledge produced in a rigorous manner. Through such a differentiation Foucault shows why these non-sciences are just that, not science, and therefore perhaps not worthy of the prestige granted them within a particular culture. For, even though Foucault claims to be interested only in the operation and description of these discourses, the demystification that his descriptions automatically provide questions the cultural authority they wield.

Foucault's privileging of scientific knowledge is a telling cultural decision that is reflected in literature as well. Referring to the second quotation, when Foucault writes of physics, one can almost sense the reverential tones with which Enlightenment thinkers spoke of Science with a capital S. As he does so, he not only invests hard science with cultural authority but also constructs science in a way that does not necessarily reflect its practice. That is, Foucault not only taps the cultural prestige of hard science, he constructs it, proposing the concept of "rigor" as a definition of what is scientific and therefore privileged. His subsequent analysis of clinical medicine depends upon this construction and provides an excellent example of how writing not only responds to cultural configurations of knowledge but also participates in their invention. Foucault's adoption of such an attitude indicates the cultural importance of what science and literature say within a given discourse and suggests a similarity between the rhetorical strategies of Foucault's text and those of the texts we will examine in this study.

While Foucault's definition of what is "scientific" hinges on the empirical nature of the data generated by the discipline, for the purpose of this study, the rigor or even the so-called truthfulness of the science is not nearly as important as the cultural prestige the science possesses both in the historical milieu of the text as well as within the text itself. The criteria I will use for science, then, hinge on historical and textual context. Those disciplines perceived by society contemporary to the text as able to generate scientific truth about reality will be considered to be science in this study, regardless of their current status. For example, to my purpose it is immaterial that phrenology now occupies the domain of circus performers because it was, as we shall see, once as well known and as well accepted as Darwinian evolution or Freudian psychoanalysis.[3] Borrowing, then, from Foucault's technique, I am much more interested in the function of a science as a discourse of power and control than in its ability to enunciate an objective truth about nature.

By focusing on the construction of discursive power within a single text or even within several texts, I necessarily limit the scope of the technique. Even so, by taking what science says as a bearer of cultural power in a Foucauldian sense we can illuminate certain rhetorical dynamics within the texts. Throughout the book I will refer to this narrative situation as "test tube envy" because of the relationship I see between science as a discourse of power and literature as a discourse that exhibits a perceived lack of that rhetorical power. The literary text, at least in many of the cases I have chosen to examine, becomes a space intersected by several discursive strategies, some more culturally powerful than others, that all interact as they combine to produce the text. In this textual production, we will see a flow of cultural authority as political and philosophical ideologies become associated with scientifically produced knowledge through a system of references to science. That flow then provides the tools that Argentine writers can then apply in their attempt to shape political and philosophical viewpoints, bringing their "aberrant" enemies into line with what is presented as scientific fact.

Studying literature in this fashion represents a slight departure from methods used by Foucault in his study of art and literature, particularly in *The Order of Things*. David Shumway has described Foucault's approach in this context, citing the French thinker's own words at the end of the quotation:

> in *The Order of Things* . . . art and literature are presented as having privileged access to the *episteme* of their time. Literature and art are not knowledges and thus are not ordered by the episteme of their era. An *episteme* in not a worldview or a *Zeitgeist*, but a configuration that structures thought and knowledge only of a particular group of disciplines. But literature may articulate the limits of this configuration, and thus "is about it as a whole . . . Arts are meta-epistemic, allegories of the deep arrangements that make knowledge possible." (Shumway 1989, 60)

As I analyze the texts in the pages that follow, I am more interested in the operation at the surface of the text, the interplay between science as a discourse of power and the other elements of the literary text. Rather than an object outside of discourse that offers a privileged perspective into one of the *epistemes* of the time as Foucault sees it, I conceive of the literary text as very much a participant in the various discourses of that historical context. For that reason, I limit my analysis to a consideration of the cultural and literary forces that create the text rather than one that takes the literary text as a broad description of the culture of the time. It is when we place several texts in constellation that we begin to perceive possible discursive rules for the continuing production of usable truth in society.

While I sidestep the truth value of certain disciplines, the question of how the author joins practitioners of those disciplines in generating knowledge about the text is of utmost importance. In speaking of discourses of power, Foucault uses medicine to illustrate the importance of the enunciator in the production of cultural truth, and therefore the ability to wield cultural power.

> Medical statements cannot come from anybody; their value, efficacy, even their therapeutic powers, and, generally speaking, their existence as medical statements cannot be dissociated from the statutorily defined person who has the right to make them, and to claim for them the power to overcome suffering and death. (Foucault 1972, 51)

While in his work Foucault examines and uncovers the construction of that authorial guarantee, he reserves an important position for the speaker in the wielding of discursive power. The works I will study here are then confronted with the problem of the perceived need to make scientific statements about their subjects without the appropriate authority to make such statements. The creation of such authority to speak of science as a scientist will form an important theme in the consideration of these texts. Indeed, the changing strategies for such a construction will help distinguish and unite texts across 150 years. For instance, we will see a literary preoccupation with the creation of an authoritative scientific persona in nineteenth-century texts as a method for gaining rhetorical privilege. In the twentieth century, we see more attempts to privilege ideas and concepts directly through association with popular scientific theories.

In both centuries, however, we will see how scientific discourse has influenced the constitution of Argentine society's "régime of truth." Foucault describes this term on a general level.

> Each society has its régime of truth, its "general politics" of truth: that is, the types of discourse which it accepts and makes function as true; the mechanisms and instances which enable one to distinguish true and false statements, the means by which each is sanctioned; the techniques and procedures accorded value in the acquisition of truth; the status of those who are charged with saying what counts as true. (Foucault 1980, 131)

As the authors incorporate scientific discourse into their various political, cultural, philosophical, and narrative situations and concerns, we will be able to appreciate the power dynamics that rule the production of truth. The process by which a literary text claims a place in this "régime of truth," both in its presentation as scientific as well as its reconfiguration of what is scientific and how science should operate will be the focus of this study. This power to define, a manifestation of Foucault's concept of "power-knowledge," is also a disciplinary one that will authorize and deauthorize both ideas and the bodies of those who hold those ideas. In that sense, many of these writers will create textual situations analogous to Foucault's argument that "the carceral network constituted one of the armatures of this power-knowledge that has made the human sciences historically possible" (Foucault 1977, 305). As the authors in our study call upon the authority of science, they simultaneously participate in a discursive system that creates textual prisons around political and philosophical figures as well as the ideas that they represent. We will see this dynamic in the will to control political figures that appears most clearly in nineteenth century texts and in the oblique control of philosophical ideas that occurs with the twentieth-century appropriations and constructions of scientific authority.

At the same time, we should not fall victim to the assumption that cultural power and authority flow in one direction from a complete science to a needy literature. N. Katherine Hayles has shown the flaws of that assumption convincingly:

> The premise that influence flows from science to literature implicitly valorizes science as the source of truth to which literature responds. Such an approach ignores the ways in which scientific theories, no less than literary theories and literature, are social constructions that reflect the prevailing concerns of the culture. Science is not a monolithic "source," but a complex field of discursive and experimental activities that has its own dissonances, fault lines, and convergences. (Hayles 1993, 317–18)

The texts that we will study use what could be termed raw materials of scientific reference and language in the creation of a discourse that presents the text as a participant in the same experimental activities that form the field of science. That is, the test tube envy that these texts seem to exhibit acts as evidence of the attempt to move from a perceived margin to a cultural center, not by aping blindly a "monolithic" science but by constructing a discursive field that subsumes the authority of a similarly constructed science. Argentina's particular situation complements this interaction further as it attempts to move from marginal to central positions in both literature and scientific discourse.

To engage Foucault's ideas while analyzing the power relationship between science and literature in a Latin American context calls to mind an important Hispanist whose valuable work on the novel in Latin America serves as another organizing principle for this study. I refer, of course, to Roberto González Echevarría and specifically his book *Myth and Archive*. Indeed, as I begin the study in chapter 1 with Sarmiento's *Facundo* it will become important to delineate the differences and similarities between my study and González Echevarría's influential work on the importance of scientific travel literature not only in Sarmiento but in nineteenth-century Latin American narrative in general. As we trace the rhetorical use of a literary discourse modeled on scientific theories, it will also be necessary to revisit and rethink the framework of "masterstories" González Echevarría constructs in his book.

I also find that we can appreciate this dynamic best by considering texts that are not included within the science fiction genre. Argentina certainly has one of the best-developed science fiction traditions in the Hispanic world as the introductions to a half dozen recent anthologies attest.[4] However, the dynamic at work in traditional science fiction is different from that considered here. In science fiction, scientific detail and reference serve as a motor for the plot, functioning as a jumping off point for a futuristic consideration of particular themes. By examining the role of scientific discourse in texts that do not share that dynamic, we appreciate better the way in which Argentine literature shapes and is shaped by contemporary popular science in the present. Indeed, such a focus is almost a necessity when we also remember that Argentine science fiction has as a principal characteristic the tendency to avoid scientific detail. In his study of Argentine science fiction Pablo Capanna notes that "una característica general de la cf argentina es su carácter escasamente 'científico,' pese a contar con varios autores de formación científica en sus filas" (Capanna 1995, 29). A study of the use of science, and particularly detailed scientific reference is almost obliged to look outside science fiction. Even so, one finds certain intersections between science fiction as a genre and the study of the relationships between science and fiction. I will examine those relationships in more detail in the final chapter.

In chapter 1, then, I investigate the several threads of scientific discourse that run through Sarmiento's *Facundo*, using González Echevarría's and Mary Louise Pratt's work on scientific travel writing as a point of departure. I have found a particularly important thread in the incorporation of references to physiognomy and phrenology. I first examine the function of those references in *Facundo* and then turn to José Mármol's *Amalia* for further evidence of the importance of a phrenological discourse in the writing of the generation of 1837. In both cases we see the writers fashioning themselves and their characters either as knowing phrenologists or as the objects of phrenological study. I will argue that this fashioning imbues their statements about political figures and situations with an air of scientific authority that serves to further their ideological goals. Of particular interest will be how these disciplines strengthen the way in which *Facundo* becomes a grab for political power.[5] Simultaneously, the cultural prestige enjoyed by *Facundo* after the fall of Rosas creates a situation in which the authority that seems to flow from science to narrative reverses, producing situations in which later scientific texts imitate the phrenological descriptions Sarmiento employed as a way to arrive at psychological truth. It is in that situation particularly that we see the exercise of real disciplinary power as Sarmiento's text becomes a source of diagnostic authority for subsequent treatises that pose as wholly scientific.

In chapter 2, I examine Lucio V. Mansilla's appropriation of the scientific model of literary discourse set by the generation of 1837. Mansilla's cultivation of references to phrenology and the evolving discipline of anthropology fashions the author as one who can wield Sarmiento's discourse of choice better than Sarmiento himself. Mansilla depends on science for rhetorical help in a textual self-fashioning that positions him and his ideas within the tradition of Sarmiento and others of the generation of 1837 even as he attacks their political decisions and values. To do so, we can observe a process by which Mansilla uses narrative to revive a phrenology that has fallen from scientific favor in order to then use its then new found authority. To continue in the vein of playful allusions to Freud's theories first developed in "test tube envy," one might argue that what we see in Mansilla's work is an Oedipal struggle for the cultural power that the test tube represents in this book.

If Mansilla embraced science as the model for his ideological and political agendas, Argentine naturalists like Eugenio Cambaceres grow uncomfortable in the embrace that they nevertheless continue. While they indeed cultivate and develop a medical discourse in their narrative that has been studied extensively by Gabriella Nouzeilles, they simultaneously distance themselves from the scientific discourse that they present in their fiction. What we see in chapter 3 is, then, the clear narrative use of various scientific models designed to privilege a xenophobic, anti-immigration agenda. Simultaneously and paradoxically, we see the presentation of these models combined with strategies that create a textual space between their use of science and the social uses of science Emile Zola describes in his model of the naturalist novel. I have called this wary construction of scientific discourse "test tube anxiety" and it is in this anxiety that we also see more clearly the way in which literature can work to control what Argentine culture accepts as scientifically authoritative.

We find the next case of test tube envy in the work of Roberto Arlt and Ernesto Sabato. In chapter 4, I study the continuity of this practice as it manifests itself in a narrative that is marked by profound thematic and metaphysical differences from the texts of Sarmiento, Mansilla, and Cambaceres. Arlt exhibits what I have termed a "test tube terror" in which he warns of the dangers of future technology and science, especially in the case of chemistry and poison gas. Paradoxically, Arlt garners authority for his condemnation of chemistry through his ability to employ that discipline's own language in his novels *Los siete locos* and *El lanzallamas*. We also see a more traditional (along the lines of Sarmiento, Mármol, and Mansilla) manifestation of test tube envy in Arlt's use of references to Darwin in his construction of a competitive, alienating world that lacks overarching meaning in *El juguete rabioso*. In both cases, Arlt uses science in the same rhetorical function as his nineteenth-century predecessors even as he uses that function to privilege his metaphysical concerns rather than political aspirations. I also examine Ernesto Sabato's work in the light of Arlt's example, appreciating Sabato's similarly designed critique of science. As an academically trained physicist, Sabato employs scientific terminology and authority in a demolition of positivistic thought first appreciated in Arlt's bleak view of scientific progress.

Arlt's combination of test tube terror and test tube envy appears in more discrete sections in the work of Jorge Luis Borges. In "Borges's Scientific Discipline," I examine Borges's trajectory from the use of mathematics and thermodynamics as specific supports for his critique of Nietzsche to his rejection of science as a workable system of knowledge. If a sense of "test tube disdain" predominates in his work, it is instructive to recognize that he employed strategies of scientific reference and the appropriation of scientific authority in early essays like "La perpetua carrera de Aquiles y la tortuga" and "La doctrina de los ciclos." Borges's example shows two important aspects of twentieth-century Argentine writing. First is its continuing use of the nineteenth century's rhetorical strategies and second is the struggle to free narrative completely from any kind of power dependence on science. I conclude the chapter noting the ironic situation in current Borges criticism where his rejection of scientific thought is undermined by a critical tendency to assign value to Borges's work because of a perceived ability to anticipate scientific advances like quantum mechanics or chaos theory. Borges's work responds to science, then, in three ways. Initially he uses it to discipline, or correct, particular modes of thought. Secondly, he disciplines science itself, criticizing its ability to describe nature completely. Finally, Borges himself is subjected to the power dynamics of science as some critics reinsert his work within a value system in which science continues to exercise authority.

Arlt and Borges's ardent admirer Julio Cortázar, with his development of a narrative based on quantum physics, provides the material for chapter 6. In much of his fiction, both short and long, we find a playful development of the narrative implications of the new physics, exploring particularly the fantastic pattern by which quantum mechanics might reveal truths about the visible world. Then, in his novel *Rayuela*, Cortázar extends beyond his exploration of science and the fantastic to a complex pattern of reference to scientists, using specifically the authority of Werner Heisenberg as a rhetorical and philosophical tool in an attack on Cartesian rationality of the past and present. In that attack, we see a further kinship with Arlt and Borges. That is, Cortázar unleashes a ferocious criticism of scientific methodology throughout his work as he mocks rational and logical thought, as does Borges, while depending upon the authority of science to do so, as did Arlt. Of course, Cortázar uses references to an idea of quantum mechanics that he bases on a constructed popular imagination and that many physicists would fail to recognize. Even so, the dynamic of the appropriation of the symbolic authority of scientific authority continues to manifest itself in Cortázar's work, linking nineteenth-century practice with the mid-twentieth century.

I finish the book with a glance at several contemporary authors and a longer look at Mempo Giardinelli's *Imposible equilibrio*, a novel that starts with an epigraph from the Nobel Prize winning chaos theorist Ilya Prigogine. Initially, I examine the way in which writers like Ricardo Piglia, Angélica Gorodischer, and Ana María

Shua choose to participate in the well-developed Argentine tradition of science fiction as an alternative to the tradition of test tube envy. In their case, this response can be seen as an answer to and a subversion of the power structures at work in previous texts. I then turn to Giardinelli's novel where I find that test tube envy continues as an organizing principle along side those alternative power structures appreciated in the work of the other three writers. I study the manner in which Giardinelli employs Prigogine's ideas, both as a rhetorical support for his view on postmodernity and as a model for the narrative reality Giardinelli creates. Prigogine's theories, already widely appropriated by postmodernist critics, serve the novel both as a scientific analogy for the chaotic reality described in *Imposible equilibrio* and as a pattern for the chaotic bifurcations in the structure of the novel as the plot unfolds along different lines. Giardinelli's meditation on Argentine postmodernity serves, ironically, as one of the clearest links with Sarmiento's work, not only with its evocation of chaos theory as proof of his view of postmodern existence, but in the very use of scientific epigraphs that evoke Sarmiento's use of quotations from Alexander Von Humboldt.

What I hope to show in the chapters that follow is the enduring nature of a relationship between Argentine literature and science that survives the momentous shifts in philosophy and narrative technique that have occurred in the 150 years since the publication of *Facundo*. This endurance of narrative strategy will help us to understand better the texts in question, appreciating an important cultural dynamic that unites them. It will also allow us a new critical lens that can help us appreciate the role of science in Argentine and Latin American literature, and its place in the construction of cultural power in Latin American society as well as the role of literature in the construction of scientific power. The historical span of the study will also teach us more about the process by which contemporary Argentine and Latin American narrative has come to be, simultaneously breaking out into new territories while holding fast to strategies already developed in its nineteenth-century antecedents.

1

Butting Heads: Phrenology as Weapon in *Facundo* and *Amalia*

ONE CAN HARDLY OVERSTATE THE IMPORTANCE OF DOMINGO F. Sarmiento and his best-known work, *Facundo: Civilización y barbarie, Vida de Juan Facundo Quiroga* (1845) in Latin American literature. The introduction to a recent volume of criticism dedicated to Sarmiento's work provides just such an example of the extent of the Argentine president's influence in his country and in Latin America:

> As the great nineteenth-century statesman and the dominant figure of a generation of nation builders, Sarmiento has earned a venerable yet polemical place in Latin American history. Architect of a nation, with a plan so far-reaching in design and scope that its consequences are still visible today, Sarmiento serves as a model of the triumphant romantic mind, linking projects of state with a radical feast of originality and selfhood traceable through his histories, biographies, and creative expressions. (Kirkpatrick and Masiello 1994, 1)

Sarmiento and his work have occasioned hundreds of critical articles and books dedicated to understanding their historical, political, and literary value. The concepts of *civilización* and *barbarie* that Sarmiento presents in *Facundo* have exercised an especially profound influence on the formation of Latin America's thought about itself. The impact of Sarmiento's political biography of Juan Facundo Quiroga continues to affect the intellectual arenas of Latin America and especially Argentina. The Argentine novelist and journalist Mempo Giardinelli, in a recent critique of Argentine culture, argues for the continued importance of Sarmiento's critique of Argentine culture and politics over 150 years after its publication:

> Hoy tiene tanta vigencia todo aquello que hería a Sarmiento, que revisitar el *Facundo* 150 años después francamente impresiona. Hoy también

el poder es bárbaro, aunque ande en limusina y cambie de corbata y de peinado todos los días. Y lo es porque—cito el *Facundo*—se trata de un poder "falso, helado, espíritu calculador que hace el mal sin pasión y organiza el despotismo con la inteligencia de Maquiavelo." (Giardinelli 1998, 199).

[Everything that bothered Sarmiento has such importance today that revisiting Facundo 150 years later is frankly impressive. Power is barbaric today as well, even though it may go around in a limousine and change its tie and hairstyle everyday. And it is because,—I cite *Facundo*—it is a power that is "false, cold, calculating spirit that does evil without feeling and organizes despotism with the intelligence of Machiavelli."][1]

That a leading Argentine intellectual would propose again the applicability of Sarmiento's *Facundo* in his recent best-selling book on Argentine culture, *El país de las maravillas* [Wonderland], suggests the enduring qualities of the text. Yet *Facundo*'s influence extends beyond the powerful ideas that form such an integral part of the text. Sarmiento's rhetorical strategies continue to affect the production of the literary text in Argentina. This strategy of "linking projects of state with a radical feast of originality" referred to by Gwen Kirkpatrick and Francine Masiello has endured in several works of the Argentine literary canon. One of the goals of this book is to suggest the *vigencia* of *Facundo* in one area of this "linking": that of the incorporation of scientific models, metaphors, and references in the creation of political and philosophical ideologies that are then expressed in literary form.

While Alexander Von Humboldt's 1801 expedition in South America was one of many in which European natural historians came to catalog and examine previously unknown flora and fauna, the success of his subsequent publications served as a watershed moment for Latin American thought. Humboldt's descriptions of the wonders of Latin America in a prose that was at once narrative and scientific in form became one of the models for writing about Latin America in the nineteenth century, as Roberto González Echevarría and others have argued so effectively. Indeed, just as Humboldt had used this scientifically based travel narrative to present his construction of Latin American nature, so too would the Latin American intellectuals intent on constructing their own version of Latin America. If one hoped to "tell the truth" about Latin America, its land, its governance, or its people, one told that truth in the same way that Humboldt had, or in a way that evoked the truths already created by Humboldt and accepted by Europeans and Americans alike. As Alonso has argued, Sarmiento exploited the scientific model as a means for garnering European recognition for a political authority he did not as yet possess (Alonso 1979, 118).

The contribution of Sarmiento's *Facundo* to this phenomenon is at once clear and debatable. While González Echevarría uses the work as the model of the nineteenth-century practice of modeling texts on those of the scientist-explorer, Mary Louise Pratt argues that Sarmiento only makes gestures toward Humboldt before setting off on what is to be a political treatise against *Federalista* Argentina (Pratt 1992a, 596). González Echevarría ultimately agrees that *Facundo* is marked by passages of a very nonscientific bent that ultimately make the text literary rather than scientific. This mixture of discourse notwithstanding, both Pratt and González Echevarría are in agreement as to the rhetorical importance of imitating the scientific travel writing of the eighteenth and nineteenth centuries as a way to establish textual authority. González Echevarría concludes, then, that these scientific travelers and their writings formed the basis for his Foucault-inspired concept of an archive that formed the cultural standard of truth for the nineteenth century. He argues that just as a legal paradigm ruled Latin American narrative through the colonial period, with independence came a shift to a paradigm of writing modeled after the scientific travelers of the late eighteenth and nineteenth centuries. González Echevarría further strengthens his argument by proposing a counter-canon of texts like *Facundo* and *Una excursión a los indios ranqueles* whose form imitates scientific travel literature alongside the canonical nineteenth-century literary tradition that favors novels like *Amalia* by José Mármol and *María* by Jorge Isaacs (González Echevarría 1990, 12).

I concur with this description of the importance of these scientific travel books for Latin American literature. As both González Echevarría and Pratt have argued, the European traveler/scientists who had come and written scientific truth about Latin American nature established a format for further writing about all kinds of reality in Latin America. In the case of Sarmiento, if he wanted to bestow truth value on his description of the physical, sociological, and political nature of Argentina and specifically that of Juan Manuel Rosas's dictatorship, he would need to imitate the structure of those travelers that had provided the model for truth telling and scientific description in Latin America. Owing, then, to the work undertaken by both González Echevarría and others on the importance of travel literature, especially in the creation of *Facundo*, the following analysis of Sarmiento's best-known work will examine, rather, the use of a specific scientific discipline in his construction of both Quiroga and Rosas. This focus does not diminish the importance of the work done on scientific travel writing; instead, it recognizes that we can now go farther in a direction indicated by this previous work. Such a strategy should enrich our reading of *Facundo* while revising many of the statements made by González Echevarría about the importance of science in *Facundo*. As we study Sarmiento's political treatise as a site of interwoven discourses rather than as the product of one determining archive, we can better appreciate the specific influences of individual scientific discourses on the formation of Sarmiento's political arguments.

Indeed, Humboldt did not serve as Sarmiento's only model of science in Argentine political discourse. The generation preceding Sarmiento also attempted to develop a political and societal discourse that availed itself of scientific models. Bernardino Rivadavia's 1822–23 newspaper, *La abeja argentina*, included a section on scientific discovery and theory in each issue. Rivadavia's explanation for the presence of this section in a newspaper whose aim was to wage rhetorical war against the Spanish empire makes clear the role the early Argentine statesmen saw for science as a cultural entity: "Las ciencias son como las plantas parasitas. Ellas no pueden nacer, y propagarse sin bajo el influjo del gobierno. El despotismo marchita y consume: la libertad las perfecciona y aumenta" [The sciences are like parasitic plants. They cannot be born nor can they propagate without the influence of government. Despotism withers and consumes them, liberty perfects and increases them] (Rivadavia 1822, 71). Science, for Rivadavia and the early political elite, served as evidence of a liberal government, the ability to talk about science a sign of political sophistication. *La abeja argentina* proceeds, throughout its short history, to report on all types of science, from curiosities to medical advances, to discoveries in physics. The model of Humboldt's scientific travel writings was complemented by the growing construction of science as an integral part of liberal society, essential to the conceptualization of an Argentine nation separate from the Spanish empire. When Sarmiento evokes Humboldt in *Facundo*, he is simultaneously evoking his political predecessors. With the initial example of Rivadavia and the repetition of Sarmiento, a demonstration of familiarity with scientific concepts has become a kind of password for Argentine intellectuals and statesmen who define themselves as against a perceived dictatorship. Rivadavia's example serves, then, both as earlier example of the importance of the scientific travel narrative and as evidence of the much broader influence of scientific discourse in Argentine political discourse. The much broader embrace of science that we see in Rivadavia's writing also invites us to reconsider the role of scientific travel narrative and science in general in Sarmiento's later text. This relation of science and political theory established by Rivadavia could also provide a system of power relations that Sarmiento could then tap as he attempted to establish his own political authority. González Echevarría's consideration of the text is instructive in this case, not only for what it uncovers, but also for what it leaves covered.

González Echevarría ends his discussion of the influence of scientific travelogues in *Facundo* with an analysis of the episode in which Quiroga narrates his killing of a jaguar.[2] The critic marks this episode as pivotal within the discursive framework of Sarmiento's text as it (for him) indicates the breaking free from the scientific models of the first part of the book: "Facundo Quiroga's penchant for brutality is an expression of his freedom. As an origin in the present, he validates Rosas's inclination to violence, and Sarmiento's own escape from the model furnished by the scientific travelers" (González Echevarría 1990, 116–17). He argues specifically that the language employed in the telling of the story exemplifies this movement away from scientific discourse, providing Sarmiento with the literary option inherent in the act of creating a narrative about Quiroga. "The language of the text is not that of the scientific travelogue but the accidental language of literature, a subliminal language, whose system is that of breaking the system, and whose aim is to be unique, like the gaucho and the tiger, to partake of their violent beauty" (124). González Echevarría sees *Facundo* as a book that does not or cannot maintain a purely scientific discourse. Instead, it employs a "language of literature" in instances that presumably qualify the entire text as literature rather than as a scientific text that does not quite get the science right.[3] The critic associates the jaguar with Sarmiento's wild discourse that first evokes and then subverts the scientific models. However, one could propose another connection in González Echevarría's critique of *Facundo*. The jaguar, for González Echevarría's understanding of *Facundo*, could be scientific discourse itself, nature as described by those European travelers who wrote it. Just as the gaucho kills the jaguar, the individuality that the gaucho represents for González Echevarría disrupts Sarmiento's cultivation of a discourse based on science. Indeed, he marks the episode in which the gaucho kills the jaguar as a point of separation where *Facundo* the text departs from its scientific model. For González Echevarría *Facundo* is a text that incorporates both the scientific model of the nineteenth century and the literary concepts and images of the twentieth century:

> This vertiginous sense of time will remain in Latin American fiction in the endings of novels like Carpentier's *El reino de este mundo* and García Márquez's *Cien años de soledad*, narratives in which the action is brought to a close by a violent wind that blows everything away. That wind first swept across the pampas in Sarmiento's *Facundo*. (125)

The Janus-faced discourse Sarmiento uses acts, then, as an important structuring element in *Myth and Archive*, as it produces a pivotal nineteenth-century text that reveals the literary tradition from which it descends and to which it proceeds. González Echevarría's use of *Facundo*, then, hinges on its ambiguity vis-à-vis the scientific discourse that it attempts to employ, employing it in one moment, only to allow it to blow away in the next. And yet the ambiguity collapses in the argument that Sarmiento abandons the scientific discourse in favor of the literary by suggesting clear-cut steps rather than subtle mixings of strategy and objective. Notwithstanding the critic's persuasive version of the work, this ambiguity is considerably more complicated, the connections and interconnections between literature and science continue to be at play, especially in the episode González Echevarría relates.

While the analysis of the jaguar episode is persuasive, the claim that it marks the departure from or disruption of Sarmiento's scientific strategy is somewhat troubling. González Echevarría ends his citation of the jaguar episode on the following sentence about Facundo Quiroga: "También a él le llamaron *Tigre de los Llanos*, y no le sentaba mal esta denominación, a fe" [He too was called the "Tiger of the Plains," and in truth, the designation was not a bad fit] (González Echevarría 118). This is obviously done for effect as the episode clearly concludes in the previous paragraph with the final sentence, "'Entonces supe lo que era tener miedo,' decía el general don Juan Facundo Quiroga, contando a un grupo de oficiales este suceso" (Sarmiento 1845, 46). [At that point I knew what it was to be afraid, said General Juan Facundo Quiroga, relating the event to a group of officers.] The story Quiroga tells certainly depends upon traditions of storytelling and literary construction; it is, after all, a narration. However, if we examine the entirety of the paragraph whose first sentence González Echevarría uses to end Quiroga's story, we see an important additional element of Sarmiento's description and presentation of Quiroga:

> También a él le llamaron Tigre de los Llanos, y no le sentaba mal esta denominación, a fe. La frenología o la anatomía comparada, han demostrado en efecto, las relaciones que existen entre las formas exteriores y las disposiciones morales, entre la fisonomía del hombre y de algunos animales a quienes se asemeja en su carácter. . . . Facundo, pues, era de estatura baja y fornido, sus anchas espaldas sostenían sobre un cuello corto una cabeza bien formada, cubierta de pelo espesísimo, negro y ensortijado. Su cara, poco ovalada, estaba hundida en medio de un bosque de pelo, a que correspondía una barba igualmente crespa y negra, que subía hasta los pómulos bastante pronunciados para descubrir una voluntad firme y tenaz. (46)

> [He too was called the "Tiger of the Plains," and in truth, the designation was not a bad fit. Phrenology and comparative anatomy have, in fact, demonstrated the relationship that exists between external form and moral disposition, between the physiognomy of man and that of some animals similar to him in character. . . . Facundo, then, was of short and well-built stature; his broad shoulders supported, on a short neck, a well-formed head covered with very thick, black, and curly hair. His face, slightly oval-shaped, was sunk in the middle of a forest of hair, matched by an equally thick, equally curly and black beard that went up to his rather pronounced cheekbones, to disclose a firm, tenacious will.] (2003, 93)

Sarmiento then continues with a description of Facundo Quiroga's physical appearance and habits that closely follows the model of phrenological and physiognomic writing. The beginning of a later paragraph furthers the analysis we saw in the earlier passages, "La estructura de su cabeza revelaba, sin embargo, bajo esta cubierta selvática, la organización privilegiada de los hombres nacidos para mandar" [The structure of his head revealed, nevertheless, beneath its jungle cover, the privileged organization of men born to rule] (46–47). If, as González Echevarría argues, Sarmiento's text unleashes the accidental language of literature in Quiroga's tale, he immediately contains the episode, converting it into a literary example of the scientific theory upon which Sarmiento bases his critique of Quiroga and the *Federalistas*. The story suggests the textual link between Quiroga and the jaguar that Sarmiento concretizes not with literary discourse but with references to the science of phrenology. Contrary to what González Echevarría argues, the literary remains subjected to the scientific in the form of phrenology. Indeed, rather than rejecting the scientific discourse that allows Sarmiento entrance to Foucault's "régime of truth," Sarmiento merely broadens the scientific structures that will qualify his statements as "true."

Furthermore, Sarmiento applies this authoritative knowledge to Quiroga's cultural body, that is, to Quiroga as a historical individual in Argentina's history. Phrenology allows Sarmiento to contain Quiroga, and by extension Rosas, by converting him into a body that can be explained and subsequently demystified by scientific means. Foucault has argued that taxonomy is one of the foundations in the discipline of "docile" bodies:

> They [organizations and taxonomies] are mixed spaces; real because they govern the disposition of buildings, rooms, furniture, but also ideal, because they are projected over the arrangement of characterizations, assessments, hierarchies. The first of the great operations of discipline is, therefore, the constitution of "tableaux vivants," which transform the confused, useless or dangerous multitudes into ordered multiplicities. (Foucault 1977, 148)

Phrenology afforded Sarmiento the kind of table that he could use to transform Quiroga, with all of his apparently dangerous possibilities into the animal that Sarmiento's version of phrenology said he was. By so doing, he attempted to trap the historical Quiroga in a kind of textual zoo where he could be observed safely in a cage rather than run rampant in the national imagination. Foucault argued that phrenology was used in the formation of "semiologies of crime" that tied outward appearance to specific criminal behavior; Sarmiento's use follows along those lines as he uses it to convert Quiroga from mysterious legend to knowable (and thus, controllable) subject (Foucault 1977, 259).

In the first half of the nineteenth century, phrenology enjoyed a popularity unmatched by the sciences of that time. *On the Constitution of Man* (1835), George Combe's popularizing handbook of phrenological thought, was the fourth-best selling English book in the nineteenth century after the Bible, *Pilgrim's Progress* and *Robinson Crusoe*.[4] In London in the 1820s and 1830s one could scarcely walk down a street or read a newspaper without encountering a notice for a meeting of a phrenological society or for a public lecture on the subject. Phrenology's impact on popular thought in Western society was similarly widespread. John Quincy Adams's complaint only serves to reveal the extent of phrenology's influence among the literary figures of the time:

> A young man, named Ralph Waldo Emerson, and a classmate of my lamented son George, after failing in the everyday avocations of a Unitarian preacher and schoolmaster, starts a new doctrine of transcendentalism, declares all the old revelations superannuated and worn out, and announces the approach of new revelations and prophecies. Garrison and the non-resistant abolitionists, Brownson and the Marat Democrats, phrenology and animal magnetism, all come in, furnishing each some plausible rascality as an ingredient for the bubbling cauldron of religion and politics. (Colbert 1997, 1)

Novelists and poets generally were also quick to react to and then incorporate phrenological principles. Edgar Allan Poe lent his support to the burgeoning discipline in 1836, "Phrenology is no longer to be laughed at. It is no longer laughed at by men of common understanding. It has assumed the majesty of a science, and, as a science ranks among the most important which can engage the attention of thinking beings" (286). Indeed, the twentieth-century historian John Davies has observed that knowledge of phrenological principles opens a new dimension on the reading of Poe's "The Fall of the House of Usher" (Davies 1955, 122–23). Sally Shuttleworth has produced an excellent study of phrenology in Charlotte Brontë's work as well as its impact in Victorian thought. In each case, Poe and Brontë incorporated phrenological principles in descriptions of characters as a way to establish scientifically the truth of such description. A character with reprobate tendencies would be more believable in the nineteenth-century context if his/her cranium confirmed such traits.

There is also evidence of phrenology's impact in the Hispanic world. Spain's best known phrenologist, Mariano Cubí y Soler, published a series of phrenological guides and handbooks in the mid-nineteenth century and embarked on a nationwide campaign to popularize Gall's science.⁵ Cubí y Soler's work was accompanied in the 1830s and 1840s when we see published a series of translations of phrenological treatises, including Georges Louis Bessières's 1836 *Introduction à l'étude philosophique de la phrénologie, et nouvelle classification des facultés cérébrales* published the following year in Valencia. Phrenology's presence in Spanish culture provoked a series of literary responses as well, with Manuel Bretón de los Herreros's 1845 play *Frenología y magnetismo* the best-known example. Another case, where a negative comment about phrenology only serves to prove its popularity in Spanish culture, is found in Ramón de Mesonero Romanos's satirical article "Romanticismo y los románticos," where the Spanish author pokes fun at the black-clad romantics engrossed in their reading of Franz Joseph Gall, the founder of phrenology (Mesonero Romanos 1993, 301). While phrenology arrived in Spain a little later than it did in other parts of Europe and in the United States, it was clearly on the lips of both supporters and detractors, further suggesting an important cultural presence.

While the presence of phrenology in early nineteenth-century Latin American culture has not been studied as widely, there is every indication that it enjoyed a similar level of popularity. Mariano Cubí y Soler traveled in Mexico and the Caribbean, teaching the discipline widely. As in Spain, we see both original and translated treatises on phrenology published throughout the nineteenth century and especially in the 1830s and 1840s.⁶ Even before Cubí y Soler's proselyting, phrenology was well known enough for Rivadavia to mention Gall in the science section of *La abeja argentina* in 1823, using the report of a scientific oddity to confirm the phrenologist's theories. He explains in his description of an eighteen-month-old male who has already experienced puberty: "Si los límites de un periódico no fueran tan estrechos, podríamos con este motivo hacer lagunas observaciones sobre la relación, que según el doctor Gall, parece existir entre el cerebelo y el aparato genital, relación que este niño confirma justamente: sobre el grosor notable de su cuerpo, y sobre la relación que quede haber entre él las partes de la generación" (Rivadavia 1823, 157). Rivadavia here uses Gall in a manner that suggests a familiarity with the theories even as he confirms their scientific value with further evidence. As Argentine literature in particular continued, we see the concept appear in several key texts. As we have seen in the passages quoted above, Sarmiento uses the term *frenología* as a scientific basis for his politically motivated description of Juan Facundo Quiroga as a jaguar. Some critics have noted the appearance of phrenology and more specifically the related science of physiognomy in Esteban Echeverría's "La cautiva" and in the writings of the Generation of 1837 generally.[7] We also see phrenology and physiognomy serving as a guiding force behind José Mármol's characterizations in *Amalia,* in addition to several references to that discipline in Lucio Mansilla's *Una excursión a los indios ranqueles.*

Despite its fame and generally widespread acceptance in the nineteenth century, phrenology is currently recognized only as a pseudo or quack science. Indeed, in the various scholarly books studying phrenology in the context of the history of science, one notices several pages justifying the identification of its subject as a science.[8] Phrenology's status as a pseudoscience also, apparently, causes many critics of literature and science to overlook the importance of references to phrenology in an overall rhetorical pattern of scientific references and allusions and thus exclude it from discussions on scientific discourse in Latin American literature. Given this state of affairs, it seems important to explain the theoretical underpinnings of the discipline. Its beginnings are often tied to Johann Lavater's theories on physiognomy. Knight argues, for example, that phrenology quickly subsumed physiognomy's tenets to become the established science of the brain and character in the first half of the nineteenth century (Knight 1986, 71). However, the creators of phrenology were adamant in their differentiation of the two theories. Indeed, Franz Joseph Gall, the inventor of phrenology, begins the account of his science with careful distinctions of his theories from those of Lavater, criticizing the latter's lack of scientificity. Gall, a Viennese physician, suggested a theory of the brain based on the following principles: first, that the brain is the seat of the mind; second, that the brain is not one but a combination of several mental organs; third, that these disparate organs have distinct functions and occupy specific areas in the brain; fourth, that the size of these organs can generally indicate the power of the organ's function in the character and disposition of the individual; and fifth, that the cranium of an individual will be shaped in a manner that corresponds directly to the size of the different internal mental organs of the brain (Cooter 1984, 3). As Cooter later notes, phrenology was best known for the fifth principle while its scientific authority rested more on the first four (3). Indeed, the logical and methodical nature of these assumptions as well as the methods and practices Gall used in his arguments helped phrenology (or craniology, Gall's preferred term) to acquire a scientific authority that has since been forgotten. The emphasis on the study of anatomy, already an accepted science, also added to the mystique of scientific rigor that surrounded phrenology, if not in all circles, at least in many.[9]

In this sense, phrenology was able to surpass Lavater's physiognomy as a science. Lavater's theories, while based on a similar correlation between outward appearance and inward propensity, focused also on the spiritual in human beings. Shuttleworth characterizes Lavater's thought in the following manner: "[according to Lavater] God had inscribed a language on the face of nature for all to read. It necessarily followed, then, that an absolute correspondence existed between outer human form and inner moral quality" (Shuttleworth 1996, 59). While phrenology may seem similar to physiognomy, and the two were conflated often in popular versions as we shall see, their assumptions were quite different. Gall was interested in the physiological functioning of the mind and in its craniological manifestation. In Gall's phrenology there was no place for a body/spirit dichotomy, everything was body. Both the outside and the inside were seen in physiological terms. While this approach drew fire from theological circles, it tapped into Enlightenment rationality and the growing materialism in contemporary science.[10]

Phrenology, then, enjoyed a scientific rigor that physiognomy could not and did not match. However, phrenology could and did enjoy the promise and attraction that physiognomy held for the masses, that is, the ability to read and divine the character and disposition of another. Cooter explains this dual cultural authority of phrenology:

> Under any circumstances his [Gall's] was the kind of doctrine to excite popular interest on the one hand and to bring down the weight of conventional authority on the other, and in the late eighteenth century and early nineteenth century this response was virtually guaranteed. By its aspiration comprehensively to explain human nature on the basis of a mapped-out hierarchical division of mental labor, by its promise to provide at a stroke practical solutions to the mysteries of character, personality, talent or its lack, crime and madness (hence, potentially, directly to manipulate and control behaviour); and by its ready comprehension to even the meanest intellect, Gall's doctrine beckoned into its orbit

every one of the social, psychological, intellectual, political and religious concerns that had been aggravated and heightened by the conditions of rapid and pervasive social and economic change. (Cooter 1984, 6)

Because of this combination, phrenology could tap into the popular appeal of physiognomy while maintaining its status as a serious science. This combination, in turn, inspired two of phrenology's most influential missionaries, Johann Spurzheim and George Combe. Without their proselytizing efforts, phrenology's impact on nineteenth-century society would have been much more limited.

Spurzheim was a former student of Gall's who later broke with his teacher over differences in opinion as to the use of phrenology. Gall preferred to leave the discipline at a level of scientific inquiry while Spurzheim saw potential for societal reform through the application of phrenological principles. Spurzheim then traveled to Great Britain, bringing phrenology along with him. His lectures created quite a fervor and established the tradition referred to earlier of widespread phrenological lectures. George Combe, a Scottish physician, attended one of Spurzheim's lectures and quickly became one of phrenology's leading proponents. The aforementioned success of Combe's book, *On the Constitution of Man*, was in large part responsible for the spread of phrenology through Great Britain and the United States. The reformist nature of the book, with its advocacy of phrenology as a method for the betterment of self, also entrenched the view of phrenology as a scientific tool for societal improvement. Combe's comments in the preface of his book explain his goal:

Accordingly, the laws of nature have formed an interesting subject of inquiry to philosophers of all ages; but, so far as I am aware, no author has hitherto attempted to point out, in a combined and systematic form, the relations between these laws and the constitution of Man; which must, nevertheless, be done, before our knowledge of them can be beneficially applied: nor has any preceding author unfolded the independent operation of the several natural laws, and the practical consequences which follow from this fact. The great object of the following Essay is to exhibit these relations and consequences with a view to the improvement of education, and the regulation of individual and national conduct. (Combe 1835, iv)

Combe here lays claim to the status of serious scientific discipline for phrenology as a body of knowledge that can chart the laws of nature. At the same time, Combe's connection of phrenology with society creates a science that has a direct impact on popular culture. Phrenology could then operate in two spheres as both a science and as a popular credo. The success of the efforts of Combe and others along these lines is what established phrenology as a widespread force in the popular culture of the time.

As I noted earlier, phrenology seems to have enjoyed an equal success in Latin America, with evidence of a familiarity with its concepts as early as 1823 and probably much earlier. While there has yet to be undertaken a study of the entrance of phrenology in Latin America, we know much of the mechanisms that allowed phrenology to take hold as a scientifically authoritative description of the human body and its nature. The interest paid to European and North American culture by the nation builders of Latin America in general and by Argentina's Generation of 1837 in particular help suggest one such conduit for the spread of the discipline.[11] We also have the appearance of physiognomy as a metaphor for the presentation of the Argentine land in both Esteban Echeverría's "La cautiva" and in *Facundo* as noted by Silva Gruesz. She remarks specifically on the friendship between Sarmiento and Horace Mann, a North American proponent of phrenology that suggests one possible contributor to Sarmiento's expressed interest in Gall's science (16).[12] A knowledge of phrenology and its prestige could easily have reached the Latin American intellectuals not only through the growing number of phrenological texts appearing in Spanish, but through friendships such as Sarmiento and Mann's, travels, and foreign newspapers and journals as they searched for models they could use in the development of the social and political models for statehood. Sarmiento's own journalistic writings in the period immediately preceding the writing of *Facundo* constantly make reference to newspapers from Great Britain and the United States that would have provided ample reference to phrenology.[13] The large British trading presence in Buenos Aires during the first half of the nineteenth century would have complemented Sarmiento's personal study with a large supply of information about the science that was all the rage on the other side of the Atlantic. Combined with the familiarity with which Rivadavia uses phrenological principles in *La abeja argentina*, we can be assured of its importance in the nation's culture. In fact, Sarmiento's usage of *frenología* in his description of Quiroga attests to just such an importance. Rather than a long explanation of the science, he uses the word as shorthand for readers, an understood tag-word that marked his description as scientific. Evelyn Fishburn supports such a reading in her book on portrayals of immigration in Argentine literature where she places Sarmiento's description of Quiroga within the "current vogue of physiognomy" (Fishburn 1981, 23). In much the same way these writers picked up on the cultural authority of scientific travelers like Humboldt, they recognized the power of phrenology and physiognomy as sources of rhetorical authority for their own projects.

The applicability of phrenology's unique cultural authority to the political and societal aims of the Generation of 1837 also makes it clear that Sarmiento's inclusion of phrenology in his description of Quiroga is no passing reference. Cooter notes that phrenology gained acceptance among the young intellectuals in Great Britain who had been disenfranchised by the landed scientific and intellectual elite who controlled the leading scientific societies and universities (Cooter 1984, 41). Phrenology became a discipline accessible to the disempowered young intellectual who then used it to wield scientific authority within a society that had denied him such power. With its description of the mental organs and propensities of individuals the discipline also held the promise of reform that could transform even the structures of English society (72).[14] Such promise could hardly be ignored by the young intellectuals in Argentina, looking to Europe and the United States for models that would help them displace the landed *caudillo* elite that denied them access to political power. The analogy between the Generation of 1837 and Great Britain's phrenologists is not perfect. The struggle in Argentina was not between intellectuals, at least in the eyes of the *Unitarios* who feared instead the power of the lower classes as harnessed by the *Federalistas*. Indeed, some of Sarmiento's pessimism about the possibilities of educating the Argentine gauchos would certainly not be shared by the English phrenologists.[15] However, the similar situation of a struggle between the more traditional, land-rich group in power and young intellectuals does suggest a certain ideological affinity between the two situations, an affinity that is confirmed by the use of phrenology in *Facundo*.

Another factor that could account for the attraction of phrenology would be its incorporation into European and North American romanticism. Cooter explains the attraction of phrenology to European romanticism:

> Epistemologically and socially this doctrine could be worked in a number of different ways. Certainly all did not endorse the radical material-

ism espoused by some supporters of the doctrine. Throughout the nineteenth century, in fact, phrenology was to have links with immaterialist traditions—occult, hermetic, Neoplatonic, and romantic. Indeed, Gall himself has sometimes been considered as a representative of the "Romantic school" and of having produced a hybrid "Romantic psychology expressed in positivist language and methodology." It was the romantic Johann Herder, apparently, who convinced Gall that he should study comparative anatomy and . . . it is true that Gall's ideas were to hold a certain fascination for Goethe and other German Naturphilosophen. (40)

The connection between phrenology and social dissent as well as its promise of a new understanding of human nature likely acted as important factors in the kinship the romantics felt between phrenology and their philosophy. The earlier description of the hybrid positivist/romantic nature of phrenology is especially important for our analysis of Latin American thought as romanticism there experienced a similar hybrid nature. Indeed, *Facundo* with its positivist language and romantic evocations seems to repeat that connection. The romantic convictions of the Generation of 1837 and especially of Sarmiento suggest yet another conduit for the introduction of phrenology into a privileged place in Argentine *Unitario* thought.

At this point, Sarmiento's comment upon finishing his analysis of the gaucho and the Argentine pampa seems appropriate. "He necesitado andar todo el camino que dejo recorrido para llegar al punto en que nuestro drama comienza" (Sarmiento 1845, 35). With the "camino recorrido" of phrenology and its cultural situation, the textual analysis of *Facundo* can begin. In fact, the function of phrenology in *Facundo*, while significant, can be described in a brief amount of space with the critical and historical context described. The dynamic between political and phrenological discourse exists on three distinct planes. First, Sarmiento uses a conflation of physiognomy and phrenology as a model for his analysis of not only Facundo Quiroga but the gauchos and the Argentine pampa as well. Second, he uses phrenology as a rhetorical term that serves to tag his analysis as scientific and therefore authoritative. Finally, he develops phrenological assumptions about humans and their environments as a basis for his description of Argentina and its inhabitants.

Many critics have remarked on the scientific taxonomies that Sarmiento employs in his description of the Argentine countryside, but only recently have any noted the peculiar scientific stance he occupies in this naming and description of the pampa.¹⁶ While we have already discussed the position of critics like González Echevarría who hold that Sarmiento's model is that of the scientific traveler, we see even more recently critics such as Silva Gruesz who have refined that position by including the importance of the physiognomic metaphor for the Argentina land. Sarmiento's model, then, is not just that of Humboldt, but that of the phrenologist/physiognomist as well. Sarmiento bases his descriptions of the pampa on a physiognomic model in which the scientist is able to divine inner qualities through a privileged reading of outer characteristics.¹⁷ Indeed, this model serves as the basis for Sarmiento's analysis as he characterizes it: "Estudiemos ahora la fisonomía exterior de las extensas campañas que rodean las ciudades, y penetremos en la vida interior de sus habitantes" [Let us study now the exterior physiognomy of the extensive fields that surround the cities, and let us penetrate the interior lives of their inhabitants] (16). The language Sarmiento employs as an accompaniment to his colloquial use of *fisonomía* creates a linguistic environment that activates the authority the term also carried in nineteenth-century science. While Silva's analysis focuses on Echeverría's "La cautiva," her remarks on Sarmiento's work introduce a previously unstudied aspect of *Facundo*, one that expands upon the theories of scientific influence in Sarmiento's text.

While we should not underestimate the power of physiognomy as a model for Sarmiento's adopted scientific stance, we must also admit that such a stance is implied and insinuated rather than stated outright. Certainly Sarmiento suggests Lavater and physiognomy, but he only alludes to them through his purely colloquial use of *fisonomía* and similarities between his project and that of the physiognomists. Sarmiento never directly invokes Lavater nor his science in the same way he does Humboldt or even phrenology itself.¹⁸ Indeed, his physical description of Facundo Quiroga, while largely based on physiognomic principles rather than Gall's more rigorous phrenology, is nonetheless identified as specifically based on the more scientifically authoritative phrenology. The use of the term at that point serves both to privilege his reading of his political adversary and cast a phrenological hue on the physiognomic practices used earlier in the text. Even twentieth century critics combine the two in analyses of the disciplines' effect on the text, and while Sarmiento's phreno-physiognomic conflation would seem to suggest the appropriateness of that critical strategy, it simultaneously underlines the need to recognize the historical distinction between Lavater's discipline and Gall's. Sarmiento's inaccurate naming of his science as phrenology exposes his clearly rhetorical use of science in constructing his politically motivated attack. Indeed, the introduction of Quiroga in his "zoo" depends on the conflation of the two theories.

Nevertheless, the specific impact of phrenology extends beyond its role as a privileging mechanism within ideological discourse. Many of the ideas Sarmiento advances on the ties between geography and individual characteristics as well as his position on civilization and barbarism find support in popular phrenological texts, especially Combe's *On the Constitution of Man*. A comparison of some of the ideas presented in the text with ideas developed in *Facundo* highlights immediately the similarities between the two. For example, in his introduction, Combe ponders the question of why certain people turn out civilized and others barbaric. The answer lies, he decides, in a person's surroundings. He also highlights the importance of education in an individual's environment that can determine the civilization of the person. The following quotation from Combe is especially significant if read with Sarmiento's position in mind:

> Man, ignorant and uncivilized, is a ferocious, sensual, and superstitious savage. The external world affords some enjoyments to his animal feelings, but it confounds his moral and intellectual faculties. External nature exhibits to his mind a mighty chaos of events, and a dread display of power. . . . Man, when civilized and illuminated by knowledge, on the other hand, discovers in the objects and occurrences around him, a scheme beautifully arranged for the gratification of his whole powers, animal, moral, and intellectual. (Combe 1835, 9)

Combe's uncivilized man bears a striking resemblance to Sarmiento's uncivilized gaucho, a similarity that is especially pronounced in Sarmiento's remark on the influence of the Pampa on the gaucho's abilities: "La vida del campo, pues, ha desenvuelto en el gaucho las facultades físicas, sin ninguna de las de la inteligencia. Su caracter moral se resiente de su hábito de triunfar de los obstáculos y del poder de la naturaleza" (Sarmiento 1845, 20) ["Country life, then, his produced physical facilities in the gaucho without any intellectual facilities. His moral character consists of his habit to triumph over obstacles and the power of nature."] Initially, Combe clearly outlines the same civilization/barbarism dichotomy that serves as the central concept in Sarmiento's text. The points of contact between the two texts, however, do not end on that level. Sarmiento's concept of "la vida del campo" [country life] exercises the same effect on the human being as Combe's "external nature." Both forces tend to encourage the evolution of the physical in human beings while ignoring a corresponding development in their moral faculties. "External nature" disrupts the moral and intellectual abilities of the uncivilized man, while "la vida del campo" impedes the intellectual ability of the gaucho. Combe further anticipates Sarmiento in his section entitled "Man Considered as an Organized Being" in which he outlines the effect of different geographical regions on the development of human beings and their specific faculties (Combre 1835, 46–51). In the comparison of the two passages, one can perceive the influence of Taine's ideas on race, milieu, and moment, with an emphasis on the effect of the milieu in the development of the human being.[19]

We should recognize, however, the very different motives of the two writers even in the face of their similar sociological ideas. In the quotations cited above, for example, important differences appear amidst the several similarities. In Combe's passage, nature is a more neutral entity, either positive or negative depending on whether its observer is civilized or uncivilized. The outside surroundings still act as an important element in the development of the human being, but their menace is tempered by the power of the civilized gaze. Sarmiento describes nature as a more threatening force, actively corrupting the intellectual facilities of the gauchos that make their living in the *campo*. Generally, Combe wrote of the dichotomy between civilized and uncivilized with the hope that his work would contribute to the civilization and betterment of those who had yet to attain such a state. His book on phrenology formed part of his attempt to educate and improve the impoverished masses. Sarmiento expresses a much more pessimistic view of the dichotomy, using phrenological principles to identify a negative situation and then denying any easy possibility of civilizing the uncivilized. Despite these differences in motive and in ideological goal, Sarmiento is still able to employ phrenology and physiognomy as rhetorical tools in his text. Sarmiento uses phrenological terminology and theory to increase the cultural authority of his text even as he sidesteps much of the social ideology that accompanied phrenology in Europe. The physiognomic model proposed by Silva Gruesz only begins, then, to explain the textual dynamics between Sarmiento's political goals and his use of the rhetorical power of phrenology.

The phreno/physiognomic model in Sarmiento's *Facundo*, in fact, allows us to reevaluate earlier studies of scientific discourse in Sarmiento's text, especially that of González Echevarría. As noted, Sarmiento's phrenologically based description of Quiroga resituates the romanticized story of the jaguar not only within a general scientific context in which phrenology contributes to the same textual environment as references to Humboldt, but because it specifically includes the description of Quiroga within the phrenological model instituted in the description of the Argentine countryside. Sarmiento gains authority not only as an Argentine Humboldt, but also as the phrenologist who can simultaneously read Argentine land and Argentine people. His self-fashioning as an Argentine Tocqueville in the introduction to *Facundo* seems to hint at this phrenological model for understanding nature and sociology:

A la América del Sur en general y a la República Argentina sobre todo, le ha hecho falta un Tocqueville, que presumido del conocimiento de las teorías sociales, como viajero científico de barómetros, octantes y brújulas, viniera a penetrar en el interior de nuestra vida política; como en un campo vastísimo y aun no explorado ni descrito por la ciencia, y revelase a la Europa, a la Francia, tan ávida de frases nuevas en la vida de las diversas porciones de la humanidad, este nuevo modo de ser que no tiene antecedentes bien marcados y conocidos. (Sarmiento 1845, 2)

[South America in general, and the Argentine Republic above all, has lacked a Tocqueville who, previously equipped with a knowledge of social theory just as a scientist travels with barometer, compass, and octant, would have penetrated the interior of our political life as a vast field still unexplored and undescribed by science, and revealed to Europe and France, so eager for knowledge of new phases in the lives of different segments of humanity, this new way of being that has no well-marked or known precedent.] (2003, 32–33)

This Argentine Tocqueville is not just the "viajero científico," but the kind of scientist that can "penetrar en el interior de la vida," that is, a scientist who can read the outside of the subject to understand the inside. Phrenology and physiognomy form, then, an important part of Sarmiento's project. The role of the two disciplines in nineteenth-century science and Argentine narrative also calls into question González Echevarría's dichotomy between the "traditional" Latin American literary canon represented by a text like Mármol's *Amalia* and the "real" canon he proposes, represented by *Facundo* and *Una excursión a los indios ranqueles*. If we take *Amalia* as an example, we see that many of the phrenological and physiognomic principles first seen in *Facundo* are repeated and developed in this novel of *Unitario* resistance against Rosas.

Mármol's novel has been read generally as part of Argentina's literary foundation. It has received critical attention from scholars like Doris Sommer who have examined the interplay between its romantic characteristics and its intent of forming a part of the Argentine literary tradition. She and others have also examined its political position within its historical context. As González Echevarría has argued, the novel belongs to the nineteenth-century Latin American canon of novels that closely follow European models of genre and style (González Echevarría 1990, 12, 103). While this focus on *Amalia* has produced excellent criticism, it has, to date, ignored the subtle incorporation of physiognomy and phrenology within its political condemnation of Rosas.

Initially, Mármol uses wording and images in his descriptions of different characters in the novel that suggest strong phrenological and physiognomic influences. These descriptions tend to focus on the construction of the characters' heads and faces, with one example appearing in Mármol's comment on Amalia's perfect head. "El cabello de sus sienes levantado, la naturaleza parecía hacer alarde de las perfecciones de aquella cabeza, de quien la imaginación no halla modelo sino en las imágenes bíblicas" [The hair lifted off of her forehead, nature seemed to brag of the perfection of that head, of whom the imagination could find no model save in biblical images] (Mármol 1991, 39). This description only adds finishing touches to a series of descriptions throughout the novel in which the *Unitarios* all enjoy well-proportioned visages and craniums with spacious foreheads. On the other side of the struggle, nearly all the *Federalistas* suffer from particularly narrow foreheads and otherwise unappealing skulls.[20] Indeed, in Mármol's descriptions of the villains, he makes the explicit connection between the features of the Federalistas' faces and heads and their own abilities, tendencies, and talents. Here are three examples:

> Rosas quedó cara a cara con un mulato de baja estatura, gordo, ancho de espaldas, de cabeza enorme, frente plana y estrecha, carrillos carnu-

dos, nariz corta, y en cuyo conjunto de facciones informes estaba pintada la degeneración de la inteligencia humana, y el sello de la imbecilidad. (Mármol 1991, 36–37)

[Rosas was face to face with a mulatto short of stature, broad of shoulder, enormous head, a flat, narrow forehead, short nose, and in whose features was painted the degeneration of human intelligence and the seal of imbecility.]

Su cabello desgreñado caía sobre su tostado semblante, haciendo más horrible aquella cara redonda y carnuda donde se veían dibujadas todas las líneas con que la mano de Dios distingue las propensiones criminales sobre las facciones humanas. (1991, 42)

[His messy hair fell over his toasted face, making more horrible a round and fleshy face where one could see the lines the hand of God had drawn that distinguish criminal propensities in human features.]

Era entonces como de treinta y cinco años, de estatura regular, rubio y de una fisonomía gatuna y siniestra, donde estaban dibujados francamente los instintos del mal y del vicio. (1991, 39)

[He was then around thirty-five years old, normal stature, blond, of a sinister and catlike physiognomy, where the instincts of evil and vice were drawn.]

In each, the face and the head of the character are described as a paper or canvas upon which are inscribed the signs that reveal his interior nature. Mármol activates the assumptions of physiognomy in his descriptions of the evil *Federalistas*, using the scientific (and apparently religious) authority of the discipline to prove his arguments. While such descriptions lack the specificity of phrenological descriptions of the organs of the mind, they effectively evoke the strategies espoused by the discipline.

This vagueness is interesting in itself. Mármol seems to be playing the science both ways, clearly alluding to the practices of physiognomy and phrenology in his descriptions while avoiding the specific terminology that would identify his descriptions as phrenological or physiognomic. Nevertheless, as we shall see ahead, Mármol specifically refers to the "ciencia of fisionomías" that does ground much of these descriptions within physiognomy (1991, 127). Mármol's use, then, looks back to the model provided by Sar-

144–45). Daniel appears as the one who knows where to look for the answers about an individual's personality. Mármol further emphasizes the image of Daniel as physiognomist in a conversation between Daniel and Eduardo where Daniel exclaims, "Pero ¿quieres que yo te enseñe a profundizar el corazón con una sola mirada, o a interpretarlo a una sola palabra que pronuncian los labios?" [But, do you want me to teach you to plumb the depths of the heart with a single glance, or to interpret it with a single word that lips pronounce?] (1991, 150). While Daniel's portrayal as the scientific observer of human beings is more tenuous than that of Eduardo, he nevertheless occupies a similar position in that he too can look at the exterior to determine the interior. The strength that such an ability gives becomes more clear when we consider the power that their ability to look affords them. Foucault's discussion of the panopticon explains how the actions of watching and being watched exercise real control over behavior (Foucault 1977). By affording the Unitarians the ability to observe scientifically, Mármol bestows their position with real power over the individuals that they observe, their ability to penetrate the exteriors of their subjects allowing them a more complete control. Eduardo's ability to evade the watchful eyes of the Federalistas accentuates this power, suggesting a situation in which Eduardo can employ panoptical power without being subject to it.

In both cases, Mármol strengthens the *Unitario* position by attributing to them a prestigious science that is then used as a tool to highlight the supposed depravity of the *Federalistas*.[23] We see, therefore, a double operation in the Unitarios' propagandistic use of phrenology and physiognomy. Phrenology is presented as the scientific basis of descriptions that depict the *Federalistas* that are either subhuman or very close to it. It is also used to portray the *Unitarios* as almost superhuman because of their knowledge of phrenology and physiognomy. Together, these two positions develop and widen the dichotomy of civilization and barbarism that *Unitarios* like Sarmiento and Mármol seek to cultivate. When we recall the image used by Rivadavia, calling science a parasitic plant that survives only on freedom, we can also appreciate the importance of this scientific have/have-not dichotomy. If the Unitarians are familiar with science and the Federalists are not, then the Unitarians inherit the status of the Argentine heroes of independence and the Federalists become the hated Spanish tyrants. In the light of Foucault's work, they effectively turn the tables, at least textually, on the repression suffered under the Rosas regime. While their phrenological savvy may be of scant comfort to those who suffered physical torture, it did offer a system through which they could participate in a kind of underground vigilance.

While science and, particularly, phrenology serve, then, as evidence of enlightened political thinking as well as a source of discursive authority for political attacks, at least according to the thinking of Rivadavia, Sarmiento, and Mármol, we should not overlook the effect that this literary discourse exercised on the practice of science in Argentina. Indeed, the cultural power of the phrenological method inherent in their texts can be seen to recur in other manifestations of nineteenth-century Argentine thought. For example, José Ramos Mejía, in his later work *Las Neurosis de los hombre célebres en la historia argentina* [*The Neuroses of the famous men from Argentina history*] (1882), gives a description of Rosas's cranium that bears a striking resemblance to Mármol's descriptions of the *Federalistas*: "El ángulo facial es tan agudo que basta un examen superficial para comprenderlo. La frente poco espaciosa, es deprimida, estrecha y cerrada, signo incontestable de inferioridad mental" [The facial angle is so sharp that one only needs a superficial examination to understand it. The less than spacious forehead is depressed, narrow and closed, an irrefutable sign of mental inferiority] (Ramos Mejía 1882, 182). Ramos Mejía presents this portrayal of Rosas in a book that attempted scientifically based descriptions of "los hombres célebres" of Argentina. His depiction of Rosas's forehead clearly exhibits the influence that phrenological principles of appearance and character exercised in Argentina, even thirty years after Rosas's removal. *Facundo* and *Amalia*, then, form part of a continuing effort by the *Unitarios* to use the cultural authority of phrenology and physiognomy to construct an unassailable scientific portrayal of the *Federalistas* as subhuman. Such was the authority of this construction that it shaped the way aspiring scientists in Argentina thought about psychology. One could say that *Facundo* used phrenology to create a kind of national zoo, where political enemies could be displayed and controlled.

While *Amalia* as a text suffers from none of the generic controversy we find in *Facundo*, that is, *Amalia* is clearly a novel while the jury is still out on what *Facundo* might be, both adopt a similar strategy in their inclusion of references both explicit and oblique to phrenology and physiognomy. The difference lies more in the placement of the scientific authority created by the references to phrenology. In *Facundo,* Sarmiento claims the status of phrenologist for himself. In *Amalia,* Mármol creates the scientific authority for his narrator but also for his protagonists, an extension made necessary by *Amalia*'s status as novel. Both texts, however, employ similar strategies to create that authority and establish scientific truth. The creation of this textual authority links the texts with the cultural discourse of science, presenting the political and narrative situations as expressions of scientific fact as it is perceived popularly. By so doing, each text exhibits the strong tendency in Latin American literature to imitate science on one level or another.[24] González Echevarría is correct in underlining the important difference between *Facundo* and *Amalia* in that the former hides its status as literature, choosing to imitate instead scientific writing. Nonetheless, the implication that such a difference keeps a novel like *Amalia* from employing the scientific discourse of the time is incorrect. To be sure, González Echevarría argues that the focus on novels like *Amalia* hinders the study of the influence of scientific travel writing generally on Latin American literature (González Echevarría 1990, 103). This argument notwithstanding, the effect of the critic's study is to reverse the hierarchy he assumes between novels like *Amalia* and texts like *Facundo.* Phrenology and physiognomy act as touchstones that erase such a dichotomy.

The case of phrenology and physiognomy shows, then, the considerable impact of scientific discourse as a model in Argentine literature, from political essay to political novel. If Rivadavia first proposed its importance within Argentine political discourse in 1823, it is in its elaboration by Sarmiento and Mármol that we see its establishment as a culturally authoritative mode of writing. Furthermore, literature also shaped the discourse of science and phrenology in the twentieth century, serving as the mode by which a widely recognized (in its time) work of science like that of Ramos Mejía would attempt to express judgments on psychology. The impact of the dynamic between narrative and science on both disciplines becomes all the more evident as we trace its continuing presence and development through the course of the nineteenth and twentieth centuries.

2
A Dandy New Scientist: Lucio V. Mansilla

As SARMIENTO AND MÁRMOL MOVED FROM THE POSITIONS OF REBELlious youth to those of authoritative leaders, their use of scientific rhetoric became a continuing model for the way many Argentine intellectuals would describe their reality. Lucio Mansilla's most widely read work, *Una excursión a los indios ranqueles* (1870) provides one such example of the continuing use of science as a model for writing in the nineteenth-century Argentine intellectual community. A recounting of the Argentine military officer and self-styled dandy's visit to the Ranquels as part of a mission to negotiate a treaty between the Argentine government and the indigenous groups of central northern Argentina, *Una excursión* appeared initially as a serial in *La Tribuna* and then as a book in 1870.[1] The book enjoyed enough popularity to warrant a second edition a few years later and to receive an award from Paris's International Geographic Congress in 1875.[2] As Mansilla relates his travels, he incorporates a variety of linguistic and cultural registers, describing the Argentine countryside one moment, the properties and peculiarities of Ranquel language and customs the next. Throughout these relations, Mansilla presents a series of ideological goals combining a campaign for his own political and social promotion with an impassioned call for the assimilation of the Ranquels and the other indigenous peoples of Argentina.

It ultimately failed in its ideological goals. After a long and complicated debate on the *cuestión del indio*, Roca's blitzkrieg against the indigenous peoples of Argentina helped to make much of Mansilla's argumentation moot. Enrique Poplizio characterized the shifting debate as one that moved from the Spanish example of Christianization and acculturation to one based on the United States example of "death to the Indian" (Popolizio 1985, 154). The ultimate failure of his aims notwithstanding, Mansilla's call for the pacification of the Ranquels rather than their extermination formed an important part of the political climate. While the issues were different from Sarmiento's attack on the *Federalistas*, the need for culturally authoritative discourse that led Sarmiento and Mármol to the use of scientific reference remained keen.

The text itself has enjoyed some popularity throughout the years despite Ezequiel Martínez Estrada's complaint that, although it was the best, it was also the most under-read work of Argentine literature of the second half of the nineteenth century.[3] In just the past fifteen years, *Una excursión* has experienced a sharp increase in critical attention. These recent studies have highlighted its extrageneric qualities as a text that extends far beyond the bounds of a straightforward travelogue. Critics have discussed its use of ethnographical practices, its political aspirations, autobiographical strategies, and kinship with spy novels and other novelistic genres.[4] Indeed, it performs various functions as it explores civilization and barbarism, Ranquel customs and Argentine culture, many times intentionally blurring the boundaries between the dichotomies Sarmiento and others had postulated. As Carlos Alonso and David William Foster have argued, from different perspectives, Mansilla's text serves as an exploration of how knowledge and modernity are constructed, especially with and against the models of knowledge established by earlier Argentine intellectuals.[5]

As Mansilla crafts his text, he carefully weaves various discourses of power collecting authorial prestige for what will ultimately be a political argument against the extermination of the Ranquels.[6] One of the many discourses from which he draws his rhetorical strength for his argument is that same science that endowed the Generation of 1837 with cultural authority, phrenology. In this chapter, I will examine the textual interplay between science and ideology that emerges as Mansilla fashions himself as the phrenologist/ethnographer who can speak with authority about Ranquel culture and the Argentine condition in general.

In this project, Mansilla positions himself both within and against the tradition established by the Generation of 1837.[7] Since they had already established much of their rhetorical authority through the appeal to scientific travel literature and phrenology, Mansilla's work simply follows in the proven tradition of his literary and political predecessors. He presents a text modeled, at least in part, on Humboldt's travels and descriptions and in addition includes various references to phrenology. Mansilla, however, opposes the Generation of 1837 generally and Sarmiento specifically.[8] On a personal level, we know that Mansilla felt slighted by Sarmiento when the Argentine president rebuffed his request for a ministerial position in the latter's government.⁹ The fact that the dictator Rosas, Sarmiento's enemy, was his uncle further muddied Mansilla's relationship with Sarmiento. Indeed, Mansilla challenged José Mármol to a duel because of the unflattering portrayal of Mansilla's mother in *Amalia*.¹⁰ Personal reasons aside, he used *Una excursión* to attack both implicitly and explicitly the concepts of *civilización* and *barbarie* that the anti-Indian and anti-gaucho Sarmiento had developed in *Facundo* and Mármol had imitated in his novel.¹¹ What we see in Mansilla's text, then, is both a repetition of the scientific discourse that had become an important element for the production of textual authority in nineteenth-century Argentine writing as well as an expansion, adaptation, and critique of that same discourse. Mansilla positions himself as one who can write more scientifically than his predecessors and as one whose ideas are more scientifically sound. I will examine this process in three arenas: initially Mansilla's repetition and expansion of the scientific travel model, his use of phrenology as a privileging element for his political agenda, and finally his proposed new humanitarian science that will oppose and resolve the inhumane science he sees employed in the writings of the Generation of 1837. In all three areas we see Mansilla's continual self-fashioning as an authority on science as well as one who can popularize and make understandable scientific precepts for the layperson. We also see the strategies by which Mansilla inserts himself within what Argentine society's Foucauldian "régime of truth," that is, within those cultural structures able to produce discourse that will be accepted as true. Once inserted within this régime, Mansilla is then able to manipulate the truth that the régime creates as he simultaneously questions the structures that guaranteed the truth value of the scientific discourse employed by those who were both his literary predecessors and his political contemporaries. Throughout the process, we will see Mansilla negotiate and attempt to revise the power structures that mediate both his writing as well as his own political presence.

While criticism has not analyzed the impact of scientific travel literature on *Una excursión a los indios ranqueles* as exhaustively as it has in the case of *Facundo*, there do exist a number of well-studied examinations of this phenomenon in the writings of Mansilla. One also finds several important studies on the mechanism of Mansilla's creation of textual authority. González Echevarría mentions the text repeatedly in *Myth and Archive* as part of his alternative canon of scientifically based (that is scientific-travel based) literature. However, he focuses his critical attention on *Facundo* and *Os Sertões* and uses *Una excursión* as more of a secondary example of the rhetorical situation he analyzes in his selected texts. Indeed, *Una excursión* merits a scant two pages of sustained analysis in his book. One should not perhaps consider such a brief treatment a defect, since the critic makes convincing and adequate arguments with the texts he chooses as examples. Nonetheless, Mansilla's work offers a rich interplay of scientific discourse and ideological posturing that will allow us to explore more fully the developing role of test tube envy in nineteenth-century Argentina.

Indeed, several other critics have noted in passing the influence of Humboldt and other scientific travelers on the work.[12] María Guzzo is the only one to study that relationship in depth. She compares Mansilla to Sarmiento in their use of the scientific traveler as narrative model, noting in particular their common development of a scientific and ethnographic discourse and highlighting Mansilla's text as one that would be recognized by the International Geographic Congress of Paris in 1875 (Guzzo 1997, 102). Guzzo rightly identifies the importance of these scientific elements in Mansilla's text, an importance that can only be underscored by the word *excursión* in the work's very title. Indeed, the French award that the book receives further situates it within a scientific context, the award classifying the book as a kind of geographical manual. At the same time, Mansilla employs a variety of scientific models in the relation of his excursión that extend well beyond that of naturalist traveler. Guzzo and González Echevarría's studies serve, then, as a starting point for further discussion of Mansilla's incorporation of scientific discourse in his writings.

Mansilla goes to great lengths to distinguish his use of travel literature from that of the Generation of 1837. We see this distancing initially in a number of remarks where he comments on the ethnological fieldwork he undertakes. The following paragraph appears near the beginning of the text, as Mansilla creates the persona that he will use to interpret what he will experience:

> Esta circunstancia por un lado, por otro cierta inclinación a las correrías azarosas y lejanas—el deseo de ver con mis propios ojos ese mundo que llaman Tierra Adentro, para estudiar sus usos y costumbres, sus necesidades, sus ideas, su religión, su lengua, . . . contra el torrente de algunos hombres que se decían conocedores de los indios. (Mansilla 1993, 60)

2: A DANDY NEW SCIENTIST 59

[These circumstances, on the one hand; on the other, a certain inclination to hazardous and distant forays, a desire to see with my own eyes the world they call *tierra adentro*, so as to study its customs and ways, its needs, its ideas, its religion and language . . . against the urging of certain men who claimed familiarity with the Indians.] (Mansilla 1997, 4)

From near the beginning of the text, then, Mansilla fashions himself as the new anthropologist, a careful observer of culture and nature who undertakes firsthand fieldwork with the subject of his study and then reports on his observations. Such a positioning attempts to endow his writing with scientific authority on a number of levels. Initially, Mansilla taps into the anthropological debate of the nineteenth century in which the importance of fieldwork began to be considered. We should pause at this point to review and examine the context of ethnography and anthropology that surrounds Mansilla's writings.

George Stocking has referred to the latter half of the nineteenth century as an intermediate stage in the development of anthropology. During this time, and especially toward the end of the century, anthropology as a discipline experienced a transition from the stay-at-home anthropologists/ethnologists who interpreted the ethnographic writings of others to the anthropologists who did their own fieldwork. These new anthropologists became both ethnographer and ethnologist simultaneously. Clifford describes the shift in the methodological conception of ethnology and ethnography:

The fieldworker-theorist replaced an older partition between the "man on the spot" (in James Frazer's words) and the sociologist or anthropologist in the metropole. This division of labor varied in different national traditions. In the United States for example Morgan had personal knowledge of at least some of the cultures that were raw material for his sociological syntheses; and Boas rather early on made intensive fieldwork the sine qua non of serious anthropological discourse. (Clifford 1988, 26–27)

Clifford also describes the early results of this ongoing shift with his comments on the state of anthropology at the end of the nineteenth century where we see the importance of fieldwork grow even further:

With Boas' early survey work and the emergence in the 1890's of other natural-scientist fieldworkers such as A. C. Haddon and Baldwin Spencer, the move toward professional ethnography was under way. The Torres Straits expedition of 1899 may be seen as a culmination of the work of this "intermediate generation," as Stocking calls them. The new style of research was clearly different from that of missionaries and other amateurs in the field, and part of a general trend since Tylor "to draw more closely together the empirical and theoretical components of anthropological inquiry." (1988, 72)

This movement culminates in the early twentieth century where fieldwork serves as the basis of all authoritative anthropology. Following this trajectory to the present day, we now occupy a point in which even that basis is under criticism.[13]

Mansilla anticipates this transitional phase in anthropology as a scientific discipline by about fifteen years in his *Una excursión*, and occupies a point squarely within it in the writing of his *causeries* in *Entre nos* (1889–90).[14] This predating of the final shift of anthropological attitudes notwithstanding, he illustrates the growing discomfort that was to be found in the ethnography and ethnology of the day, in which the interpretation of culture was left to those who had not experienced it firsthand. To be sure, the ethnological interpretations advanced by what Clifford calls "the anthropologists of the metropole" still carried scientific authority. Nevertheless, a space in the authoritative discourse of anthropology was beginning to open for the field-working anthropologist, one who observed, reported, and interpreted. Indeed, Mansilla is able to exploit both sides. On one side he maintains the ability to write ethnography despite a lack of training as a professional anthropologist. Alternatively he claims authority for his writing by virtue of the basis of his own fieldwork.

Returning to Mansilla's self-fashioning, then, the final part of the quotation mentioned earlier is especially important as Mansilla positions himself against the earlier ethnologists who wrote on indigenous culture without acquainting themselves with it firsthand. The remark situates Mansilla's text specifically against Sarmiento, as Sarmiento was particularly notorious for basing his works of popular ethnography on secondhand information—Sarmiento's reputation is attested to in a passage we will examine shortly where Mansilla criticizes those who claim knowledge of the Pampa without firsthand experience. In *Una excursión*, Mansilla presents Sarmiento as the traditional ethnologist isolated from his subject of study. He then positions himself as the new, more authoritative anthropologist who knows intimately that which he interprets. This identification of Sarmiento and himself as occupying different points along the line of development of anthropology allows Mansilla to gain rhetorical power as a figure who updates and revises the theories of the past. By so positioning himself, Mansilla uses this identification to produce rhetorical benefits in areas beyond the merely scientific realm.

This dynamic can be seen to insert Sarmiento's strategy toward Rosas in a more scientific context. Alonso has shown how Sarmiento positions Rosas as precursor to Unitarian power on a more political timeline by proposing the "new government as the absolute antithesis of Rosas," one that overcomes Rosas's tyranny through dialectical opposition (Alonso 1979, 123). Alonso's astute characterization of Sarmiento's political positioning finds an echo in Mansilla's use of anthropology as a mode for differentiating him from Sarmiento. If Sarmiento's new government learned from the old, Mansilla's new anthropologist wields more scientific authority because he supersedes those who have preceded him. By transferring this differentiation politics to anthropology, Mansilla is also able to state his case for access to political power in a different situation. Sarmiento's goals were revolutionary, Mansilla's goal is reform, specifically reform that allows him better access to political power. His self-presentation as new anthropologist situates him as logical successor to the power structures instituted by Sarmiento's own use of scientific discourse and as more able in the administration of scientific taxonomy that contributed to Sarmiento's own authority.

Furthermore, Mansilla attempts in various instances to place his text within the ethnographical domain. Two episodes are sufficient to show these attempts. Initially, Mansilla comments on his "recuerdos etnográficos":

> Este cerro está cerca de Achiras, y su nombre [Intiguasi] significa en quechua, si no ando desmemoriado en mis recuerdos etnográficos y filográficos, *casa del sol.* Diéronselo los Incas en una de sus famosas expediciones por la parte oriental de la Cordillera. *Inti*, quiere decir sol, y *guasi*, casa. (Mansilla 1993, 212)

> [The hill is near Achiras and its name, if my ethnographic and philographic memory serves me well, means "sun house" in Quechua. The Incas gave it its name in one of their famous expeditions to the east side of the Andes. *Inti* means "sun," *guasi* "house."] (Mansilla 1997, 93)

Mansilla places his travels within an ethnological framework with his use of the term "etnográfico," a usage that is made stronger by his carefully explained linguistic analysis of the Incan name of the hill. Not only does he drop the name ethnography, but he also bases his ethnographical prowess on his knowledge of Quechua. Here Mansilla combines name-dropping, or in this case discipline-dropping, with specific evidence of his scientific prowess. The result is a double privileging for Mansilla's self-fashioning as anthropologist.

Much later in the book he recounts an argument with Mariano Rosas that ends with the Ranquel leader speechless, unable to "refutar esta argumentación etnológica." We note the following narration of the exchange between the two:

—No es cierto—me interrumpió Mariano Rosas—; aquí había vacas, caballos y todo antes que vinieran los gringos, y todo era nuestro.
—Están equivocados—les conteste—; los *gringos*, que eran los españoles, trajeron todas esas cosas. Voy a probárselo:
Ustedes le llaman al caballo *cauallo*, a la vaca *uaca*, al toro *toro*, a la yegua *yegua*, al ternero *ternero*, a la oveja *oveja*, al poncho *poncho*, al lazo *lazao*, a la yerba *yerba*, al azúcar *achúcar* y una porción de cosas lo mismo que los cristianos.
¿Y por qué no les llaman de otro modo a esas cosas?
Porque ustedes no las conocían hasta que las trajeron los gringos. Si las hubieran conocido les habrían dado otro nombre.
¿Por qué le llaman al hermano *peñi*?
Porque antes de que vinieran los padres de los cristianos ustedes ya sabían lo que era hermano.
. . .
No pudiendo Mariano refutar esta argumentación etnológica, . . . (549–50)

["That is not true," interrupted Mariano Rosas. "There were cows and horses and everything else here before the gringos came and it was all ours."
"You are wrong," I said, "The gringos, who were the Spaniards, brought all those things. I will prove it to you. You call the horse *cauallo*, the cow *uaca*, the bull *toro*, the mare *yegua*, the calf *ternero*, the sheep *oveja*, the poncho *poncho*, the lasso *lazo*, the herb tea *yerba*, sugar *achúchar*, and many other things just as the Spaniards did. And why is it that you do not call them by some other name? Because you didn't know these things until the gringos brought them. If you had known them before, you would have given them another name. Why do you

call your brother *peñi*? Because before the fathers of the Christians you already came you already knew what a brother was. . . .
Faced with this irrefutable ethnological argument . . .] (Mansilla 1997, 299–300)

In this case, Mansilla presents himself as familiar with a type of ethnological discourse, and able to confound with his expertise. His comments on the Ranquel language suggest both a familiarity with their language as well as an understanding of the linguistic influence of one culture on another. The identification of his linguistic arguments as ethnological serves a dual function. Initially, he simply shows off what he knows about Ranquel linguistics and the patterns of colonization. Secondly, this identification places the argumentation within the realm of science, reminding the reader of Mansilla's assumed roles as ethnographer and ethnologist in the text.[15] In these ways, Mansilla gains a degree of authority as an anthropologist who has experienced the Ranquels firsthand and is therefore uniquely prepared to describe and interpret their culture in an authoritative manner.

It is also important to note that by occupying this space, Mansilla not only participates in this relatively new trend in anthropology, but also evokes more completely the textual authority of Alexander von Humboldt. Sarmiento evokes Humboldt as a rhetorical support, to be sure, but his use of Humboldt's ideas and theories is somewhat limited, as we saw in the first chapter of this study. One finds, for example, the epigraph in *Facundo*, the similar descriptions of nature, and the call for an observer who can interpret Argentine reality. What we do not see in *Facundo* is that observer out in the field physically observing the subject. Mansilla evokes Humboldt more completely as the writer and interpreter of his own travels and explorations. His emphasis on his position as eyewitness, then, looks both forward to developments in anthropology and backwards to the figure of Humboldt. Indeed, such an attitude exemplifies what Christopher Herbert, commenting on the importance of the eyewitness in anthropological theory, has called "the hegemony of a Baconian insistence on 'the direct observation of facts' in social inquiry" (Herbert 1991, 12).

Mansilla extends his authority as ethnographer to that of a natural historian, or observer of nature in the following remark:

Más de seis mil leguas he galopado en año y medio para conocerlo y estudiarlo. [the Argentine countryside where he was to travel with his army]

> No hay un arroyo, no hay un manantial, no hay una laguna, no hay un monte, no hay un médano donde no haya estado personalmente para determinar yo mismo su posición aproximada . . . (Mansilla 1993, 62)

> [More than six thousand leagues have I ridden in a year-and-a-half's time to survey and study this land. No stream, spring, lagoon, hill, or dune did I leave unobserved as I personally went about determining approximate positions and getting the lay of the land.] (Mansilla 1997, 5)

He continues his trope of author as eyewitness as he extends his field of study from the anthropological domain to that of Argentine geography. By so doing he continues his double self-privileging as he evokes the figure of Humboldt and the scientific traveler, that is, he is like Humboldt both because he is an eyewitness and because he has studied the natural world. In this sense he evokes the authority of the many scientific travel diaries produced throughout the nineteenth century.[16] He simultaneously underlines how his writing distinguishes itself from that of earlier writers who had also tried to evoke the rhetorical authority of the scientific travelers. As Mansilla struggles to distinguish himself from his antecessors even as he participates in the discursive power structures they have established, this double look to both the past and the future of ethnology seems especially appropriate.

One of the clearest criticisms Mansilla makes of Sarmiento's purportedly scientific discourse appears again towards the beginning of *Una excursión* as he once more creates a revisionist space from which he critiques earlier writers on the subject of Argentine geography and ethnology:

> Los que han hecho la pintura de la Pampa, suponiéndola en toda su inmensidad una vasta llanura, ¡en qué errores descriptivos han incurrido! Poetas y hombres de ciencia, todos se han equivocado. El paisaje ideal de la Pampa, que yo llamaría para ser más exacto, pampas, en plural, y el paisaje real, son dos perspectivas completamente distintas.
> Vivimos en la ignorancia hasta de la fisonomía de nuestra Patria. (144)

> [Those who have rendered an image of the pampa, imagining it in all its immensity one vast plain, how mistaken their descriptions have been! Poets and men of science alike have got it all wrong. Their idealized pampa, which in deference to the truth I would call pampas, in the plural, and the real pampas, offer two entirely different perspectives. We live in ignorance even of the physiognomy of our own homeland.] (Mansilla 1997, 48)

This quotation reinforces the rhetorical moves of the previously cited passages while directing his attack specifically at Sarmiento's *Facundo* and the scientific discourse Sarmiento had employed in his description of the pampa as a great, open, threatening space. Mansilla here is evoking specifically Sarmiento's description of Argentina at the beginning of chapter 1 of *Facundo*:

> Allí, la inmensidad por todas partes; inmensa la llanura, inmensos los bosques, inmensos los ríos, el horizonte siempre incierto, siempre confundiéndose con la tierra entre celajes y vapores tenues que no dejan en la lejana perspectiva señalar el punto en que el mundo acaba y principia el cielo. (Sarmiento 1845, 11)

> [There, there is immensity everywhere, the plains are immense, the forests, the rivers the horizon is always uncertain, always confusing itself with the earth between forests and tenuous vapors that do not allow one to know from a distance where the world ends and the sky begins.]

Mansilla's inclusion of the words *inmensidad* and *fisonomía*, both terms that appear extensively in *Facundo*, focuses his attack on the Argentine president's descriptions of Argentine geography. This repetition of vocabulary, coupled with the terms *poeta* and *hombre de ciencia*, relegates Sarmiento to a rhetorical and scientific space inferior to that of the firsthand observer (Mansilla) who can accurately describe both the pampas and the people who live there. It is in this quotation specifically that Mansilla positions his scientific method as observer against what he insinuates to be the spurious scientific discourse Sarmiento employed in *Facundo*. By correcting both the poets and the men of *ciencia*, Mansilla implies that his text supersedes theirs on both levels. That is, his will be both more poetic and more scientific. The specific use of the word *fisonomía* in his declamation of Argentine ignorance about the Argentine countryside serves as an important marker as well, alluding both to the Humboldtian use of the word to which I referred in the first chapter as well as to Sarmiento's continued use of the term. This positions Mansilla once again as the logical successor to the political power Sarmiento built using phrenological discourse.

Mansilla's allusion to the phrenological discourse used by Sarmiento and others effectively evokes that discursive system even as he introduces it into a different cultural and scientific context. From the time of the publication of *Facundo* (1845) and *Amalia* (1851), phrenology's standing among scientists had begun its downward descent. Roger Cooter remarks on the marked drop in status phrenology suffered during the second half of the nineteenth century: "From the perspective of the first half of the nineteenth century, nothing appears more certain than that during the second half of the century phrenology entered a precipitous decline" (Cooter 1984, 256). Nevertheless, its power as a perceived scientific discipline continued among laypersons until the end of the century, especially as one moved farther from Europe. As we observed in chapter one, José María Ramos Mejía in his *Las neurosis de los hombres célebres en la historia argentina*, makes wide use of phrenology in his psychological study of the prominent Argentine leaders of the nineteenth century. Diana Sorensen describes the many scientific discourses Ramos Mejía employs in his text: "Ramos Mejía brings to bear ideas culled from Comte, Charcot, and Claude Bernard, regarding biology, phrenology, and nervous diseases, on the study of Rosas, and of other personalities in the nineteenth-century history of the area" (Sorensen 1996, 107). Ramos Mejía's work, heavily influenced by Sarmiento's own analysis, acts as a testament to the longevity of phrenology's scientific authority in Argentina.[17] While the book was widely refuted during its time, the simple fact that Ramos Mejía would choose phrenology as an authoritative science suggests its continuing cultural power. Indeed, and as suggested in the previous chapter, the influence that political and literary discourse wielded serve to prop up phrenology's cultural authority as a valid scientific discipline.

To dismiss phrenology as a historical force in the late nineteenth century, then, would be irresponsible. Cooter concurs in his argument for a continued consideration of phrenology as an important cultural phenomenon in the late nineteenth century:

> No less than early-nineteenth-century expressions of antiphrenology, late-nineteenth-century expressions of contempt for the "humbug" of phrenology are cultural signals, the dismissal of which on that basis would be no less intellectually arrogant than the dismissal of phrenology from the earlier part of the century. (Cooter 1984, 257–58)

The European expressions of contempt signaled a perceived need to quash the cultural popularity of the discipline as science, paradoxically affirming its continuing authority. *Una excursión* and Ramos Mejía's later book provide Argentine examples of Cooter's argument for the enduring cultural importance of phrenology by showing that it could still function as a source of textual authority, one that shows clearly how literature first created the scientific authority before employing it as a rhetorical strategy.

If Sarmiento used phrenology as a key word almost in passing, Mansilla explored and explained the discipline in depth. Enrique Poplizio goes so far as to title one of the chapters in his biography of Mansilla "Examen craneoscópico." The chapter recounts a visit Mansilla made to London in 1851 where he had his head "read" by Donovan, one of the many practicing phrenologists to be found in London during that time period (Popolizio 1985, 62–63). Popolizio remarks on the phrenologist, "Donovan, que explotaba una pretendida ciencia ya del todo desacreditada entre los entendidos, se mostró, no obstante, sagacísimo psicólogo" (63). Indeed, Mansilla's biographer goes rather far in his critique of a discipline that could still wield scientific authority beyond the psychological abilities of its practitioners. While by 1851 phrenology's authority as a science was admittedly on shaky ground among many (although not all) scientists in London, it still retained legitimacy generally among the other classes.[18] Mansilla's own experience with the phrenologist confirmed for him the scientific standing of the discipline. His description of the experience in his *causerie* "Esa cabeza Toba" reveals both the authority and the utility Mansilla attributed to phrenology:

Había entonces en Londres un frenólogo célebre,—llamado Dónovan.
El niño puso su cráneo bajo la inspección de los dedos del sabio, y éste habló así:
"No puede llamarse seguro (*safe*) el tipo de cabeza, por faltarle *secretividad* y cautela, esto es discreción y circunspección, al paso que están en condiciones muy activas las facultades productivas de la afición á las mujeres y á la buena mesa.
Es malo ser tan abierto, franco y cándido como esta cabeza; pues para hacer con seguridad el viaje de la vida se necesita alguna astucia, reserva, rebozo. El que abra á todo el mundo el depósito de su corazón, se verá pronto despojado de su contenido, con grave daño de sí mismo.
Es natural, franco, ingenuo, inartificioso, valiente. Aficionado á los placeres, amistoso, generoso, confiado é inclinadísimo á obrar según los demás: comerá con los gastrónomos, beberá con los bebedores, fumará con los fumadores, besará con los besucadores y así (*and so on*).
Si bien valeroso y confiado, es, no obstante, poco dado á la esperanza, y abandonará por imposible lo que vea que no puede ejecutar en el acto."
Y seguía con las cualidades intelectuales,—que clasificaba de *claras,*

rápidas y prácticas, agregando que carecían de *profundidad* y *solidez*, y dando consejos útiles para producir con la ayuda del tiempo y de la voluntad las modificaciones necesarias para hacer el viaje de la vida menos penoso.
Desde aquel entonces,—han pasado veintisiete años,—el joven ese ha tenido muchas ocasiones de volver sobre sus pasos, recordando en el momento oportuno el análisis craneoscópico de Dónovan.
Inclinando á la confidencia, cien veces ha retrocedido, diciendo en su interior: "Es malo ser tan abierto, franco y cándido como esta cabeza." (Mansilla 1993, 207–8) [emphases in original]

[There was once in London a celebrated phrenologist named Donovan. The boy put his head beneath the inspection of the wise man who spoke like this . . .
"This type of head cannot be called safe, because it lacks secretiveness and caution, that is discretion and circumspection, they indicate in active conditions a tendency to chase women and to enjoy good food. It is bad to be so open, frank and candid like this head; for, in order to make the voyage of life safely, one needs to be astute, reserved, guarded. He that opens the depths of his heart to the world will see himself quickly robbed of those depths, with great harm to himself. It (the head) is natural, frank, trustworthy, without artifice, valiant. Lover of pleasures, friendly, generous, trusting and inclined to peer pressure: he will eat with the gluttons and drink with the drunks, smoke with the smokers and kiss with the lascivious and so on.
"If it is courageous and trustworthy, it is also little given to hope, and will abandon as impossible anything that cannot be done quickly." And he continued with the intellectual qualities that he classified as clear, quick and practical, adding that it lacked depth and solidity, and gave useful counsel that could help produce, with the help of time and willingness, the modifications needed to make the voyage of life less painful.
From that time, twenty-five years have passed, the young man has had several occasions to go over his steps, remembering in opportune moments the cranioscopic analysis of Donovan. Leaning to that confidence, he has gone back one hundred times, saying to himself, "It is bad to be so open, frank and candid like this head."]

In this story, Mansilla develops an image of phrenology that emphasizes its societal practicality. Phrenological readings provide the youth (Mansilla himself) with a mapping of his personality traits that then act as a warning and a guide to him throughout his life. The phrenologist gains the status of mentor when he uses the discipline to divine his personal characteristics and then advise him on the best course of behavior to overcome any shortcomings. Additionally, the warning against being too open also strengthens the predictive power of phrenology as the entire narrative attests to the science's success in wresting personal secrets from the youth's head. The context of the telling of the story, some thirty-five years after its occurrence, functions as a revisitation of a discipline of the past. The perspective gained from the time past rejuvenates the power of phrenology by commenting on its lasting usefulness. This action, coupled with the appearance of phrenology in such supposedly scientific texts as Ramos Mejía's aforementioned work, suggests phrenology's continued position as science in late nineteenth-century Argentine culture.

Mansilla continues to consider the theme of phrenology as a guiding philosophy with several references to his experience with Donovan and its implications throughout his writings. In *Una excursión*, he refers to his own phrenological makeup as he criticizes the musical ability of the hapless black man who bears the brunt of much of his criticism in general. Mansilla uses phrenology specifically as a knowledge that keeps him from making a fool of himself, knowledge that Mansilla depicts the black man as clearly lacking:

> El negro no tardó en irse con la música a otra parte. Bendije al cielo.
> Como poeta festivo, como payador, no podía rivalizar con *Aniceto el Gallo* ni con *Anastasio el Pollo*.
> Ni siquiera era un artista en acordeón.
> Yo tengo, por otra parte, poco desarrollado el órgano frenológico de los tonos, pudiendo decir, como Voltaire: *La musique c'est de tous les tapages le plus sopportable*.
> Es una fatalidad como cualquier otra, que me priva de un placer inocente más en la vida.
> Te contaría a este respecto algo muy curioso, un triunfo de la frenología, o en otros términos, la historia de mis padecimientos infantiles por la guitarra. Y te la contaría a pesar del natural temor de que me creyesen más malo de lo que soy; porque tengo la desgracia de ser insensible a la armonía. (Mansilla 1993, 333)

> [The black man didn't hesitate in taking his music somewhere. I thanked my stars.
> As a festival poet, as a singer, he couldn't rival Aniceto the Gallo or even Anastasio the Pollo.
> He couldn't even play the accordion.
> I have, on the other hand, a very underdeveloped phrenological tone

organ, able to say, like Voltaire : *La musique c'est de tous les tapages le plus sopportable*. It's a fate like any other, one that deprives me of an innocent pleasure of life.
I would tell you something very curious, a triumph of phrenology, or in other words, the story of my youthful struggles with the guitar. And I would tell you, despite the natural fear I have that people would believe me to be worse than I am, because I am, unfortunately, tone deaf.]

He recounts this triumph later in the text as well as in a *causerie* in his collection *Entre nos* (1889–90). In both he indicates that phrenology helped to explain his inability to learn the guitar and thus kept him from following a fruitless pursuit. He notes in *Una excursión*, for example,

Y sea que estuve inspirado, cosa que no me suele suceder—no recuerdo haberlo estado más de una vez, cuando renuncié a estudiar la guitarra, convencido de la depresión frenológica que puede notarse, observando en mi cráneo el órgano de los tonos—(Mansilla 1993, 394)

[And whether or not I was inspired, which does not generally happen to me—I only remember it happening once, when I gave up studying the guitar because of the phrenological depression on my skull where the tone-sensitive organ would ordinarily be found—](Mansilla 1997, 208)

In this instance, as well as in the others in which he discusses his apparently well-informed decision to abandon the guitar, phrenology appears as a true biological description that is directly connected to the ability (or lack of ability) that it indicates. The matter-of-fact presentation of this relationship also exhibits phrenology's authority on an empirical level. Simply put, a phrenological analysis of his head indicated an inability to play a musical instrument that proved accurate in Mansilla's failure to learn the guitar.

Mansilla refers to his phrenological makeup throughout his texts. In *Una excursión* he uses it both to indicate his lack of musical talent as well as his lack of patience: "Yo, que por mí temperamento sanguíneo-bilioso no soy muy pacienzudo que digamos, he descubierto con este motivo que el deber puede modificar fundamentalmente la naturaleza humana" (67). While such a remark does not now immediately evoke images of phrenology, his self-description makes use of adjectives that formed an important part of phrenological language. "Sanguine" and "bilious" were adjectives long-used in medicine but appropriated by phrenologists to describe the personality of certain character types, personalities that were evidenced both by traits and by their physical manifestation in the cranium.[19] Just as in his analysis of his phrenological organ of tune (located on the side of the head and whose absence would suggest a dearth of musical talent), the use of phrenological language here privileges his descriptions as true because they are couched in scientific language. Furthermore, the reference to duty overcoming nature reminds one of Combe's use of phrenological reading as a method for helping people to identify and overcome weaknesses in character.[20] What results is a series of phrenological references that are both systematic and complete in their evocation of the discipline.

In the *causerie* "¿Por qué?," Mansilla again employs phrenology in his self-description:

> No es que me falte malicia,—creo que me sobra, por mi desgracia. Es que mi conformación cerebral es así. Estoy seguro de que si Pirovano hiciera mi análisis craneoscópico encontraría que, aunque tenga deprimida la circunspección, tengo algo desarrollada la idealidad. (Mansilla 1936, 1:23)
>
> [It's not that I lack malice, I think I have it in abundance, unfortunately. It's that my cerebral makeup is that way. I am sure that if Pirovano did my cranioscopical analysis, he would find that, although I have a depressed circumspection, I have a developed ideality.]

In this passage even more than the previous remarks we have studied, we see a Mansilla who is wholly familiar with phrenological language. Not only does he present his character traits as inextricably linked to his "conformación cerebral" but when he speaks of his "depressed circumspection" and the "developed ideal," he repeats exactly the language and terminology of phrenology used most often to describe the smaller and larger phrenological organs, respectively. To use such terminology rather than simply stating that he had a large organ of circumspection, further marks Mansilla as a phrenological expert. The use of phrenological language both serves to privilege his description of self, that is, to ground personal impressions about character in scientific fact, as well as to create authorial power for Mansilla. The impression that Mansilla attempts to construct implies that if he knows how to speak the language, he must be in possession of the principles of the discipline.

While Sarmiento could use the term "frenología" as shorthand in 1845 and depend upon its automatic scientific privilege, Mansilla creates a curious loop wherein he uses his rhetoric to strengthen phrenology in the face of its waning scientific prestige and then depends on that newly regained status as science to ground his ideological position. A constellation of texts provides a glimpse into this pattern: two *causeries* from *Entre nos* that we have already mentioned, "¿Por qué?" and "¡Esa cabeza Toba!" as well as *Una excursión a los indios ranqueles*.[21] Just as Sarmiento and Mármol contributed to cultural environment in which phrenology functioned as science, Mansilla must shore up that ability in the face of growing criticism.

In the *causerie* "¿Por qué?" we see one of the best examples of Mansilla's self-fashioning as scientist in his many texts. The previously quoted excerpt where Mansilla comments on his phrenological makeup appears at the beginning of the *causerie*, casting its hue over what will follow. What does follow is a meditation on philosophy, experience, and memory, described in each instance with scientific language and metaphor. Mansilla introduces the concept of empiricism early on in the text:

> Esta filosofía, que yo profeso sobre el éxito del escándalo y sobre las creederas del lector, no se ha apoderado de mí, de improviso, así como suele dominarnos una teoría nueva, expuesta con talento, aunque sea falsa, por un espíritu atrevido. No; creo ante todo en la experiencia, y la objeción de que ella haya podido aprovecharme poco, no es un argumento. Porque, si bien la experiencia es madre de la ciencia, hay que tener en vista que el hombre es un animal persistente, gobernado por su temperamento, (Mansilla 1936, 1:24–25)

> [This philosophy, that I profess despite the scandalized reaction and the beliefs of the reader, had not overpowered me suddenly, like new theories that tend to dominate us when expressed with talent even if they are false. No, I believe in experience before everything, and the objection that she has benefited me little is no good argument. Because, if experience is the mother of knowledge, one should have in mind that man is a persistent animal, governed by his temperament.]

Mansilla weaves a variety of discourses as he situates himself as one who knows about human nature. Initially, we see his dependence on experience, a theme introduced earlier in *Una excursión*. In his declaration "la experiencia es madre de la ciencia," he leaves ambiguous the word *ciencia* as both science and knowledge. In this manner, Mansilla situates himself as both a down-to-earth philosopher and as a rigorous scientist.[22] As a kind of a country philosopher, he presents a commonsense viewpoint of knowledge based on the experiences he has had. Nevertheless, as he deploys such a comment within a text that is saturated with references to phrenology and science in general, he also casts himself as a scientist, basing his collection of knowledge on a type of scientific method. Mansilla strengthens the latter presentation by creating a concept of the human as an object of study. He refers to *el hombre* as *animal*, a reference that invokes the idea of the human being as Darwinian subject. By so doing, he situates himself with Darwin, as the biologist/ethnologist who studies the human and has the authority to make pronouncements about the nature of the subject.[23] This remark, however, acts merely as an introduction for the pronouncements that follow.

Mansilla further employs scientific language in his description of memory and analysis of "luminous vibrations." In the following passage from the causerie "¿Por qué?," Mansilla uses a strategy of accumulation in his usage of scientific terminology and imagery:

> La memoria es independiente de la conciencia,—en su elaboración no entra ningún elemento psíquico. Así, cuando un estado nuevo se implanta en el organismo se conserva y se reproduce. Sucede con la memoria, como hecho biológico, lo que con algunos fenómenos inorgánicos.
>
> Las vibraciones luminosas pueden ser encerradas en una hoja de papel y persistir en estado de vibraciones silenciosas. Hay sustancias que las revelan, por decirlo así; todo tiene su reactivo. No hay misterios sino para la ignorancia. Colocad una llave sobre una hoja de papel blanco, ponedla al sol, un rato, guardad ese papel en un cajón oscuro, y al cabo de algunos años, la imagen espectral de la llave, estará ahí visible. Los problemas de la vida y de la muerte son infinitos. Pero la observación y la ciencia penetran todas las oscuridades. El microcosmos es como la gran antorcha del macrocosmos. (Mansilla 1936, 1:56)

[Memory is independent of consciousness, in its elaboration one finds no psychic element. Therefore, when a new state implants itself in the organism it conserves itself and reproduces. What happens with memory, as a biological fact, is the same as some inorganic phenomena.

Light vibrations can be enclosed in a sheet of paper and persist in a state of silent vibrations. There are substances that reveal them, to say it that way; everything has its reactive element. There are no mysteries save for the ignorant. Put a key on a sheet of paper, put it in the sun for a while and then put the paper in a dark box, and after a few years the spectral image of the key will be visible. The problems of life and death are infinite. But observation and science penetrate all darkness. The microcosmos is the great torch of the macrocosmos.]

Mansilla here employs a variety of terms that mark his description as scientific. He speaks of the human as organism, of memory as a biological fact and of its relation to inorganic phenomena. Additionally, Mansilla separates his subject from that of psychic studies—"no entra ningún elemento psíquico"—implicitly suggesting that memory can be studied by "hard" science rather than pseudoscience. The effect of this deployment of discourse is similar to that of the previous citation. Mansilla once again becomes the scientific observer of human beings, his qualifications being created through his use of scientific language and analysis to comment upon their nature. Furthermore, his use of narrative here also works to define the parameters of science. Mansilla's writing, in this case, serves to not only evoke the cultural authority of our metaphorical test tube, but to define the test tube itself. Narrative becomes what one might call, in the spirit of the title of this book, a kind of literary laboratory in which the test tube of scientific discourse is used to both appropriate and, importantly, construct the cultural authority of science itself.

Mansilla further develops his position as scientific observer through the use of analogy. By proposing the analogous experiment of the impressions left by the key, he achieves two separate aims. Initially, he once again presents himself as an observer who carefully bases his findings on the experimental process. Both his knowledge of the photographic effect of the key experiment as well as his ability to describe the process step by step create the impression that Mansilla understands science and the scientific method. Secondly, he presents himself as one who can explain science to those in ignorance. His aside, "No hay misterios sino para la ignorancia," situates the rest of his comments as instruction for those who find themselves baffled by the mysteries of memory because of that ignorance. Mansilla becomes not only the scientific observer, qualified to speak because of his experience/experiments, but the teacher of science. He acts as the source of scientific commentary for those who would not otherwise understand. He lays full claim to that rhetorical power as he proclaims the ability of science and observation to penetrate any darkness.

2: A DANDY NEW SCIENTIST 75

Mansilla follows this analysis with additional proofs, using vision as an analogy for memory, for example. He argues that just as a color will impress a remaining complementary image on one's vision, so too do experiences impress their images on one's brain.

> La percepción de un objeto *colorado* (sub-rayo, de miedo de los *aristarcos* intransigentes), suele ser seguida frecuentemente, de una sensación consecutiva el objeto continúa siendo visto con los mismos contornos; pero con el color *complementario* del color real. Lo mismo puede suceder con la imagen,—con el recuerdo. Ella deja, aunque con menos intensidad, una imagen consecutiva. . . .
> Como se ve, científica y pintorescamente hablando, la memoria de las cosas pasadas no es más que una visión espectral en el tiempo y en el espacio. (Mansilla 1936, 56–57)[24]

> [The perception of a colored object (I underline it for fear of some intransigent aristarcos), seems to be followed frequently by a consecutive sensation of the object continuing to be seen in the same shape but with the complementary color to the true color. The same happens with the image, with memory. It [memory] leaves, though with less intensity, a consecutive image. . . . As one can see, speaking scientifically and with pictoresque imagery, the memory of things past is no more than the spectral vision in time and space.]

Throughout the analogies and conclusions he draws, Mansilla maintains his use of scientific terminology as well as his position as one with the authority to explain. He presents the analogy as a type of experiment, basing the test on what he suggests is a biological phenomenon. He then labels his descriptions and analogies as "scientific," suggesting that the reader should accept his description of memory as scientifically true, just as his description of vision is scientifically accurate. He ends his remarks on memory with the following observations:

> La memoria, como ya lo dije, es un hecho biológico de los más complejos e interesantes. Cualquiera que sea el número de las células cerebrales (se cuentan por millones), destinadas a recibir, como en depósito, nuestras impresiones, sería un error creer, que, una vez allí, quedan sepultadas per in aeternum como un secreto en una tumba, si esas impresiones las hemos recibido en un estado de inconsciencia. (Mansilla 1936, 75)

> [Memory, as I have stated already, is among the most complex and interesting biological facts. However many brain cells there are (the count

is in the millions), destined to receive, like a deposit, our impressions, it would be an error to believe that, once those impressions arrived there, they would be buried forever as if in a tomb if we received these impressions in an unconscious state.]

Once again we see Mansilla express his philosophical and personal remarks on memory in terms of scientific terminology as it relates to brain cells. By so doing, he reminds the reader that, while his subjects tend toward the social and the personal, his theories are grounded in science. This continued strengthening of the connection between his discourse and science acts as an enduring element in his writings.

The effect of his use of scientific discourse in "¿Por qué?" is manifold. We have already commented on its contribution to the creation of Mansilla's scientific persona. Mansilla in effect explains the *por qué* that his article's title proposes, implicitly indicating that he knows the *por qué* of his topic because of his scientific approach. The effect of this discourse on the phrenological principles he mentions near the beginning of the article is also important. By using phrenological descriptions within a text that also employs more up-to-date scientific theories (although these may not necessarily be viewed as correct by all scientists of the time), Mansilla implies that phrenology exists on an equal footing with the theories of brain cells and the human being as animal that enjoyed greater scientific favor.

Mansilla caps his use of phrenology in two separate instances. In these episodes, he develops phrenology as a science of the future, a discipline that holds the key to solving societal ills. Phrenology becomes, then, not just a good science developed in the past that one should not discard, but the future answer to the questions with which Argentina grappled at the end of the nineteenth century. In "Esa cabeza Toba," an article about a head being an obvious place for such a pronouncement, he remarks:

> Francisco de Paula Moreno, el intrépido explorador de las ignotas tierras australes, conserva el cráneo, ya lo sabéis. Hay en él quizá una revelación antropológica que descubrir. Algo que haga dar un paso osado más á una ciencia en pañales,—destinada á cambiar en días no lejanos los destinos de la humanidad: LA FRENOLOGÍA. (Mansilla 1936, 2:206) [emphasis in original]

> [Francisco de Paula Moreno, the intrepid explorer of the unknown southern lands, keeps the cranium, as you already know. There is, per-

haps, in it an anthropological revelation to be discovered. Something that takes one more bold step towards a science in diapers, destined to change, in a not-to-distant future, the destiny of humanity: Phrenology.]

Phrenology, rather than a pseudoscience of the past becomes the key to the future. By linking the discipline with the idea of a future anthropological revelation, Mansilla presents phrenology as an essential element of the study of human beings. He further supports phrenology in the passage that immediately follows the previous quotation:

> Esta ciencia se enseña ya en Estados Unidos hasta en las escuelas primarias. Aquel pueblo iniciador, en esto también pretende adelantarse á las soluciones.
> ¿Os reís?
> Pues yo os digo, en verdad, que la frenología puede enseñaros y serviros más que un curso completo de filosofía. (Mansilla 1936, 206)

> [This science is already taught in the United States, even in elementary schools. That forward thinking nation, in this also tries to arrive at solutions early.
> You laugh?
> Then I'll tell you truthfully, that phrenology can teach you and be of more use to you than a complete course on philosophy.]

While "¿Os reís?" suggests a slight anxiety as to phrenology's cultural authority, Mansilla quickly repositions it as an accurate representation of reality. By combining the cultural authority of the United States with the potential of phrenology as anthropological science, Mansilla builds rhetorical authority both for his pet discipline as well as for his own words. Furthermore he implicitly presents science as the hope of the future while he relegates philosophy to the past. Phrenology emerges from the passage as a "ciencia" that holds the promise of societal solutions.

To protect himself further, Mansilla distances himself from science proper as he simultaneously reinforces his position as translator of science. He continues:

> Ya conocéis mi manía, y mi defecto. Lo confieso. No soy impersonal cuando escribo. No he aprendido mi ciencia en los libros. He leído en el mundo, meditando sobre las páginas instructivas de una vida borras-

cosa, llena de vicisitudes, bebiendo á veces consuelo en las tristezas del alma y en las amarguras del pensamiento. (Mansilla 1936, 206)

[You are already familiar with my obsession and my defect. I am not impersonal when I write. I have not learned my science from books. I have read in the world, meditating the instructive pages of a tempestuous life, full of vicissitudes, at times drinking consolation from the sadness of the soul and the bitterness of thought.]

By distancing himself from the academic science presented in books, he further strengthens the connection he has forged between the science/knowledge he writes and the importance of experience in the creation of that knowledge. The quotation, while seeming to distance Mansilla from scientists, serves to increase the scientific prestige he has constructed for himself by grounding his knowledge and assumptions on what he implies is a more scientific approach. Mansilla ends his defense of phrenology with the already mentioned story of his own phrenological reading.

This trip through his later *Entre nos* allows us to understand better the references to science and phrenology that appear toward the end of *Una excursión a los indios ranqueles* and especially in the epilogue. We turn now to Mansilla's description of his gaucho guide Mora in *Una excursión*.

Mora es un hombrecito como hay muchos, de regular estatura. Un observador vulgar le creería tonto; se pierde de vista. Es gaucho como pocos, astuto, resuelto, y rumbeador. No hay ejemplo de que se haya perdido por los campos. En las noches más tenebrosas él marcha rectamente a donde quiere. Cuando vacila, se apea, arranca un puñado de pasto y sabe dónde está. Conoce los vientos por el olor. Tiene una retentiva admirable y el órgano frenológico en que reside la memoria de las localidades muy desarrollado. Cara y lugar que vio una vez no las olvida jamás. Sólo estudiando con mucha atención su fisonomía se descubre que tiene sangre de indio en las venas. (Mansilla 1993, 433–34)

[Mora is a little man like many, of a normal stature. An inexperienced observer would think him stupid; he would be mistaken. He is a gaucho like few, astute, resolved, and one who enjoys life. He has never been lost in the field. In the darkest nights he goes exactly where he wants. When he is in doubt, he stops, takes a handful of grass and knows where he is. He knows the winds by their smell. He has excellent retention and a very well developed phrenological organ of memory of places. He never forgets a face nor a place that he has seen but once. It is only with careful study and special attention to his physiognomy that one discovers the Indian blood in his veins.]

Phrenology once again appears in a supportive rhetorical role, validating the comments Mansilla makes about Mora's excellent memory. Just as Mansilla's underdeveloped tune organ explained his inability to play the guitar, Mora's well-formed memory organ confirms his ability to remember places. Mansilla also situates the phrenological observer within a privileged space, distinguishing his commentary from that of the *observador vulgar* that would not be able truly to read Mora's abilities. Yet phrenology's rhetorical function is not limited to this specific situation. To understand more fully the dynamic at work, we must look next at Mansilla's epilogue to *Una excursión*. It is here where Mansilla argues fervently against those who would exterminate the Ranquel Indians, pleading instead for a policy of absorption through racial assimilation.

In this section, he treads a fine line between the evils of and the benefits of civilization. Specifically between the fact that apparently civilized people want to exterminate the Indians, and the scientific proofs Mansilla uses that come from a "civilized" education. At one point in his impassioned plea against eliminating the Ranquels, Mansilla asks the question: "¿La frenología ha pronunciado acaso su última palabra?" [Has phrenology pronounced its last word?] (687). While this question may seem somewhat mysterious appearing as it does seemingly unannounced, when read in the context of the various references made to phrenology throughout Mansilla's work, we realize the rhetorical task it performs. Mansilla's use of phrenological discourse in his description of Mora privileges the figure of the young gaucho as the model of miscegenation, Mansilla's proposed solution to the *cuestión del indio*. If the mixture of races can produce a success like Mora whose abilities correspond to clear phrenological manifestations, then one should obviously consider such a solution before eliminating the possibility of developing other human beings like Mora.[25]

This, then, is the goal of Mansilla's argument. Mansilla wants to create a new, moral science of human beings based on his anthropological and phrenological findings. An impassioned Mansilla delivers his vision of a new science:

¿La moral será algún día una ciencia exacta?
¿A dónde iremos a parar, si la anatomía comparada, la filosofía, la fre-

nología, la biología, en fin, llegan a hacer progresos tan extraordinarios, como la física o la química los hacen todos los días, tanto que ya no va habiendo en el mundo material nada recóndito para el hombre?
¿Qué le falta descubrir?
Por medio de la electricidad, de la óptica y del vapor ha penetrado ya en las entrañas de la tierra y en los abismos del mar hasta insondables profundidades; ha descubierto en los cielos remotos e invisibles luminares y su palabra recorre millares de leguas con mágica y pasmosa rapidez. (Mansilla 1993, 667)

[Will morality be an exact science someday? Where will we stop, if comparative anatomy, philosophy, phrenology, biology, and so on make such extraordinary progress like physics and chemistry does every day, so much so that there remains nothing unknown to man?
What is left to discover?
With electricity, optics and vapor it has penetrated in the innards of the earth and the abysses of the sea to the unsoundable depths; it has discovered in the remote heavens invisible lights and its word covers thousands of leagues with magical and amazing speed.]

In this passage we see Mansilla's philosophical, moral, scientific, and rhetorical project in full view. The many references to phrenology's ability to reveal truth about the human, Mansilla's own position as scientific observer with the authority to pronounce the truth about human beings, the comparison of phrenology to the successes of the harder sciences, the coming of a new science that will reveal the nature of humans, all work together as he proposes an answer to the question of what to do with the indigenous peoples of western Argentina.

From the examples of both the Generation of 1837 as exemplified by Sarmiento and Mármol as well as in Mansilla's texts, we see a clear dependence on scientific discourse as a source of rhetorical authority in nineteenth-century Argentine literature. Certainly the importance of the scientific travel narrative cannot be understated, neither for foundational works like *Facundo* nor for Mansilla's *Una excursión a los indios ranqueles* whose very title incorporates the rhetorical power of a Humboldt. We perceive, however, after a closer analysis of the different scientific discourses at play in these texts, the emergence of another facet to the nineteenth-century drive to write narrative as if it were science-based. Phrenology served the nineteenth-century Argentines well both as a source of rhetorical prestige and as a promise of the ability to read and classify scientifically that "other," be they indigenous, gaucho, or *Federalista*, against whom they wrote their words. It also acts as an important link between genres, permeating the substructure of the political pamphlet, the novel, and the travel diary.

While phrenology links *Facundo, Amalia,* and *Una excursión,* its use in them does vary widely. As noted in the first chapter, Sarmiento's use of phrenology runs counter to the reformist tendencies of the European phrenologists in his attempts to use phrenological arguments against the possible improvement of a class or race of people. In his use of phrenology as a scientific support for his position, Mansilla shows a greater understanding of the discipline and of its use throughout the world. His plan to "better" the Indians that incorporates phrenology as proof for the possibility of a "civilized" Indian suggests those reformist tendencies seen in the Scottish, English, and North American proponents of the discipline. Just as Combe used his texts to show how phrenology could be used to improve the human condition generally, Mansilla uses it as he shows how even "barbaric" races can be "improved" and integrated into "civilized" society.

This rapprochement between *civilización* and *barbarie* also illustrates the profound ambivalence that one finds in *Una excursión.* In the text we encounter an ultracivilized dandy that admires (at times) the Ranquel culture, a rough and masculine soldier at home in a tent, a scientist/anthropologist who learns his discipline from life rather than from books all in the same person. Mansilla's writings are rife with complexities and ambiguities as he weaves his way through issues that gripped his country. Just as his aim of civilizing the "savage" combines the preference for the European with an appreciation of the uncivilized human being; Mansilla's discourse offers blurred ideological situations that reflect the complexities of the times. One constant that survives these complex and at times contradictory states is Mansilla's rhetorical use of scientific reference.

In light of Mansilla's position toward the treatment of the Ranquels, one can also better understand how to reconcile Mansilla's apparent anti-positivism with his use of an epigraph by Auguste Comte that seems to support his position. María Rosa Lojo has written extensively on Mansilla's anti-positivism generally and specifically in *Una excursion,* noting that he repeatedly spoke out against "the fatality of race" that she understands as central to the theory's tenants (Lojo 1992, 83). To be sure, Mansilla's calls for a new science based on morality support Lojo's observations. However, one perceives in this rejection of the race theories of positivism a further manifestation of Mansilla's particular use of scientific discourse. Mansilla rejects the racial determinism so often associated with positivism with his use of a phrenology that he presents as a scientific discipline, a discipline presented by popularizers like Combe as capable of producing individual self improvement and societal progress. His inclusion of the epigraph from Auguste Comte, translated into Spanish no less, reminds his readers of the more humanitarian writings of Comte, where Comte exhorts charity and the brotherhood of man.[26]

> ¿No nos ordenan la religión y la humanidad aliviar a los pacientes? ¿No son hermanos todos los hombres? ¿No deben compartirse los bienes y los males que deben a su autor común? ¿Es lícito mostrarse inexorable y sin piedad con alguno de sus semejantes? (Mansilla 1993, 681)

> [Do not religion and humanity order us to assist the infirm? Are not all men brothers? Should not the good be shared and the bad given to their author? Is it licit to be without pity to one of your neighbors?]

Indeed, by including the epigraph from Comte at the beginning of the epilogue, Mansilla partially inscribes his text, with all of its use of scientific discourse and references, within the rubric of positivism, even as he rejects some of the racial conclusions derived from its principles. The result is a further privileging as Mansilla associates his ideas rhetorically with those of Comte.

Just as Mansilla's use of the scientific travel model is opposed to that of Sarmiento's by virtue of its emphasis on first-person witnessing, so too does his use of phrenology surpass that of his predecessor in the sophistication of its use. Indeed, his repetition of the paradigm of science for writing can then oppose his forerunners as he develops a mode of writing based on "better" science. Such a strategy reveals both the importance of the scientific writing model for nineteenth-century texts as well as Mansilla's ability to use it. His power to persuade depends to a large extent on his ability to cast his interpretations and positions in a scientific light as he simultaneously rejects the similarly cast arguments of his predecessors. Mansilla is able, through the use of scientific reference and his own self-fashioning as the scientist of the people, to present a discourse that enjoys the same scientific privilege as that of his predecessors while he simultaneously erodes the scientific basis they had claimed. By so doing, he could depend on the traditional rhetorical authority of science while he worked to found his "new" science on what he felt was a more humanitarian base. As Mansilla works to achieve that goal, it becomes apparent that he does not merely attempt to appropriate Sarmiento's political discourse, or even a scientific authority that exists in a completely separate state. While both of these actions occur, Mansilla goes one step further as he uses his text to suggest a shape for Argentine anthropology, both in its practice and in its political and social application. By so doing we see a clear example of how Argentine science could be subject to the literary discourse that attempted to appropriate its own cultural authority.

Una excursión a los indios ranqueles and Mansilla's other writings exhibit strongly the tendency to scientific discourse in Argentine nineteenth-century writing even as they question its earlier existence in Argentine letters. As Mansilla creates an authorial and ideological space for himself, he employs a scientific discourse that successfully challenges that of his predecessors while privileging his own political and ideological positions.[27] Simultaneously, and just as Sarmiento and Mármol did, Mansilla reframes the practice of science itself, using his narrative to create the test tube whose authority he would then use. In so doing, he perpetuates the strategies of those against whom he positions his argument. The envy in Mansilla's work operates, then, on two separate levels in the writings of Mansilla. On one, it functions just as it did with Sarmiento and Mármol and would with the Argentine Naturalists. Mansilla simply needed to borrow the cultural authority of science to construct persuasively his vision of Argentina. The second level comes into play when one realizes that Mansilla had to appropriate the figurative test tube from others besides just the scientists. In Argentine culture, Sarmiento and the generation of 1837 had already claimed scientific authority; Mansilla had to wrest control of the test tube from them. In so doing, he created a plea to save the indigenous Argentines from slaughter, a plea based on ideas of racial mixture that have in one way or another gripped many of the Latin American cultural debates that were to appear in such works as José Martí's "Nuestra América," José Enrique Rodó's *Ariel*, Alcides Arguedas's *Pueblo enfermo* and José Vasconcelos's *Raza cósmica* to name but a few of the many works that have taken a position in that argument. Mansilla's work is rarely named with these texts, but one can appreciate his prefiguration of their themes as he designs a critical discourse based on science.

3
Argentine Naturalism's Test Tube Anxiety

NATURALISM AND ÉMILE ZOLA READILY COME TO MIND IN ANY EXamination of the interconnections between literary and scientific discourses in the nineteenth century. Indeed, one would be hard pressed to find a clearer case of test tube envy in literature than Zola's fashioning of the naturalist novelist in the likeness of the experimental scientist. The naturalism we see developed in Argentina would, at first glance, seem to fit this tendency perfectly. In the writings of such novelists as Eugenio Cambaceres (1843–88), Eduardo Wilde (1844–1913), Manuel Podestá (1853–1918) and others, there is an extensive use of references to biological (and phrenological) theories of race and heredity within a narrative matrix modeled on medical discourse. Perhaps because of this apparently clear use of science as a rhetorical support, the theme of science and Argentine naturalism figures as one of the better-studied topics related to this study. Gabriella Nouzeilles, in particular, has studied Argentine naturalism and medical discourse in her recent book and several articles.[1] Her excellent work leaves little ground to be broken in the study of scientific discourse in Argentine naturalist narrative. Even so, Argentine naturalism's narrative posture vis-à-vis scientific discourse is thornier than would first appear and therefore deserves a pause for critical attention before moving on to the twentieth century.[2]

Nouzeilles's work on the use of medical discourse among the Argentine naturalists has accurately and intelligently traced the development of a narrative system of medical-scientific reference and discursive modeling in the novels of these end-of-the-century novelists. She highlights especially their incorporation of the phrenologically influenced theories of Cesare Lombroso as well as Francis Galton's eugenics in their characterization of Argentine society as a patient in need of medical attention. Nouzeilles characterizes the role of medical discourse in Argentine naturalist narrative, what she calls "ficciones somáticas," as the "authoritative criteria" for many of the prejudices of the times (2000, 21–22). The type of narrative envy described by this practice might be better characterized as one of a "stethoscope" rather than one of a "test tube." Even so, the dynamic is the same. As Nouzeilles explains, the naturalist authors employed the ideas of an authoritative discipline outside of the literary realm as a way to ground culturally the literature they produced. To be sure, their ends differed from Mansilla's as they employed references to science as part of a xenophobic, exclusionary, anti-immigrant agenda. Nevertheless, their dependence on scientific authority generally and on that of phrenology and the new theories on heredity and race specifically find a precursor in Mansilla's work.

Nouzeilles herself argues that these points formed the basis of Argentine naturalism's rhetorical authority, noting that it provided the authors an authoritative description of the foreign body that they attempted to contain in their critique of immigration and their racist attacks. (1997, 240) What we see, essentially, is that the same dynamic between science and narrative exists in Argentine naturalist texts that we saw operate in the works of their predecessors. Nouzeilles's excellent work on the use of scientific and medical discourses in the literary generation following Mansilla would seem to make anything more than a glossing of her position of tendencies of what I term test tube envy in Argentine naturalists critically redundant.

What Nouzeilles's work does in the context of the present book is strengthen the case for a continuing tendency in Argentine narrative to look to science for textual authority. What started with Sarmiento's use of phreno-physiognomy in *Facundo* turns into the naturalists' use of Lombroso's criminal craniology in many of the novels that appeared toward the end of the century. Mansilla's proposed solution of racial and cultural assimilation is countered by a negative eugenics that warns against mixing with the immigrant races pouring into Argentina. Nouzeilles has detailed precisely the importance of these theories in late nineteenth-century Argentine narrative from Gall to Lombroso and Galton (1997, 239). Nouzeilles's point is that these theories were then worked into a conception of the Argentine social organism as the medical subject, a patient who would best be treated by the doctor/narrators who were a prevalent element of Argentine narrative from the 1880s through the

1910s. These narrators adopted the position of the clinician, diagnosing the illnesses of Argentine society.

The moralizing gaze of these xenophobic narrators is, for Nouzeilles, the authoritative doctor's prescription, with an authority that drew its cultural power from references to popular science. Nouzeilles argues that naturalism's infallible narrator evoked the objective scientist and participated in the authority that that scientist wielded as the narrators presented their cases for an Argentine society suffering from severe illness depending on the authority of French naturalism as an important literary genre and scientific discourse as a persuasive objective description of reality (1997, 242). This kind of narrative modeling would certainly seem to imitate the pattern we have already observed throughout the nineteenth century where literary and ideological projects strengthen their ability to comment on society through a textual appeal to science. Indeed, Nouzeilles, without referring specifically to a concept of test tube envy, anticipates it in much of her work.

And yet the situation with Argentine naturalism and science is murkier than one would first expect. There is a clear cultivation of scientific concept and reference as a rhetorical and cultural basis for their narrative descriptions of reality. Even so, nagging ambiguities appear in the Argentine naturalist evocations of science, specifically in two points of Nouzeilles's discussion of its attempt to create a "double legitimization" using both: French naturalism and science. A comparison of the French (especially Zola's) and Argentine varieties of naturalism highlights this rather unexpected ambivalence in the Argentine naturalists' treatment of the discursive model that their selected sciences provide.

Émile Zola's conception of the narrator as a scientific observer projected a sense of detached objectivity that helped legitimize the social criticism underpinning naturalist works.[3] Evelyn Fishburn provided the following definition of naturalism within the context of her study of nineteenth-century Argentine narrative:

> Naturalism was the logical literary expression of an ideology that eschewed subjectivism and introspection and that is distinguished by its disinterest and mistrust of metaphysical conjectures, and by its concentration instead on a scientific approach limited to the evidence of observable phenomena. (Fishburn 1981, 50)

This concentration on the scientific method as the model for the construction of narrative served as the principal element of the naturalist project. Zola, in his manifesto of naturalism, *Le roman expérimental* (1880), clarified his view of the scientific observer and, by extension, the naturalist writer by noting that the writer is never worried about the why, only in the how of the subject, in its objective description (3–4). Zola situates the power he attributes to science in its ability to avoid moralizing and maintain the objective gaze of the experimental scientist. Likewise, the rhetorical power of naturalism depended in part on its ability to make statements about humanity in a scientific, objective fashion. The reasoning seems to be that if the naturalist novelist could speak about his subjects the same way a scientist would about psychology and heredity, those statements would then carry the same weight. This focus on the investment of the narrative voice with scientific authority clearly appears earlier in Sarmiento, Mármol, and Mansilla. The difference lies more in the scientific model imitated than in the rhetorical strategies by which the project was carried out.

French naturalism borrowed from several scientific theories that were popular during that era. In addition to the scientific theories Nouzeilles has identified in Argentine naturalism, we see a deterministic attitude toward race and class that employs concepts similar to those developed in Darwinist and social Darwinist thought. Zola clarifies his position in regard to naturalism and the importance of determinism within his literary agenda, preferring it always to searching for any kind of "essence" (1927, 28). In many European naturalist texts we see not only the influence of these theories in the characters and situations presented, but direct references to figures like Charles Darwin that situate the ideas on race and society presented within a specifically scientific context. In much the same way that Mansilla and Sarmiento gathered rhetorical authority through a system of reference to scientists and scientific theories combined with a textual structure that evoked scientific writing, French naturalism constructed its own literary/scientific discourse.

Through its construction of a scientific discourse Zola's brand of naturalism privileged an ideology that overturned traditionally accepted modes of operating in society. In his essay, "De la Moralité dans la Littérature," Zola develops a connection between the novelist's use of science and revolutionary ideals as he explains that while scientists can be insulated from society, writers who use scientific truths "break the contracts of silence" that keep the public from the dangerous possibilities of scientific discovery (1927, 294). Zola's writer is dangerous for two reasons. Initially, the writer has a larger audience than the scientist and is therefore a larger threat to the society's traditionally held beliefs. But it is not just the writer's reach that makes the writing risky. It is when the writer adopts a scientific discourse that is then combined with a wide readership that the writer becomes a public enemy. The naturalist author, in Zola's view, breaks with convention in order to discover and employ science's "new" truths. Zola proposed the use of these new truths in order to expose the deplorable conditions of the lower classes. In *Le roman expérimental*, he elaborates on the social function of his conception of the scientific novelist, arguing that the use of scientific truth and sociology within the novel specifically fulfilled a moral obligation to society (1927, 28–29). Throughout much of his work, Zola employs references to scientific theories and practice in his fiction as a way to ground his ideological goals of liberating the oppressed. He presents the novelist as a social scientist who uses literature to study humans and society to uncover its problems and injustice and then show how to resolve them. The new sciences to which he refers in his novels become the basis for social and socialist reform he hoped to achieve through his *naturalisme*.[4] Even more importantly, his narrator garners authority for the text presented precisely because he speaks with the viewpoint of the experimental scientist. One recalls both Sarmiento and Mansilla who used this position as a way to wield power in a hostile political environment.

The theories on literature Zola set forth have wielded significant influence throughout the literature of the world, an influence that extended to Latin America as we have already seen in the work of Nouzeilles. In her article on the relationship of Argentine naturalism to Doris Sommers's concept of the national romance, Nouzeilles demonstrates French naturalism's extensive influence:

> Read from a Darwinist perspective, the causal circuit of these love stories confirms the status quo, including segregation largely based on race. For Argentine writers keen on French naturalism, it offered them a narrative structure with which they could conduct fictional experiments. By placing their fictional couples in a particular and verisimilar plot that developed according to an experimental plan dealing with human sexuality, these novelists demonstrated that the chain of events and its causality were predetermined by the phenomena (the Tainesian "race," "time," and "milieu") under study. (1996, 26)

Evelyn Fishburn writes of the more general impact of naturalism on the Argentine narrative of the time:

The theoretical aspect of naturalism was particularly suited to fit into the conceptual framework which prevailed in Argentina at the time, and which had found its chief inspiration in Darwinism, French Positivism, and Spencerian Evolutionism. (50)

Indeed, Eugenio Cambaceres's *En la sangre* (1887), an oft-cited example of Argentine naturalism, would seem to refer in its very title to the theories of racial determinism one finds in Zola's naturalism. At first glance, therefore, it would seem that the Argentine authors of the Generation of 1880 had found in Zola's work an excellent model for their own narrative.

But, as Nouzeilles and many others have pointed out, Zolá's theories experienced profound transformations as they made their way to and through fin-de-siecle Argentine literature. Evelyn Fishburn elaborates on this particular argument:

> To conclude, therefore, Realism and Naturalism are two labels which have been abused in their application to the novels under review [among which *En la sangre* figures] . . . naturalism is confined to the focus of interest of the novels, but its principles are severely betrayed by the rhetoric and selectivity of the authors. (52)

Fishburn here refers specifically to the tendency among the so-called naturalist Argentine authors to use the naturalist focus on the misery of the lower classes, specifically immigrants, to condemn them rather than follow Zola's plan of exposing social injustice as a condemnation of the ruling class. This phenomenon has also been noted specifically by Noé Jitrik, who remarks particularly on the paradox of Argentine naturalism, that is, the use of naturalist form made popular by Zola in opposition to French writer's political and moral agenda, especially in the case of the lower classes (Jitrik 1968, 96). The adaptation of the tools of Zola's naturalism for the Argentine writers' particular designs leaves a somewhat ambiguous space for science as a rhetorical tool. While the desire for scientific confirmation remains, the conservative, even reactionary, political ideologies of authors like Cambaceres present an uncomfortable situation when coupled with the new sciences Zola had so closely tied to revolution. Indeed, Sarmiento's own revolutionary use of scientific discourse may have added to that discomfort. While they are certainly free to employ scientific reference as a basis for their particular ideological programs, they seem to be wary of Zola's use of similar references for ends that directly contradict their xenophobic agenda. A situation that arises not infrequently in Argentine naturalism is the presentation of theories of heredity and racial determinism as fact, but in a manner that does not necessarily evoke the objective narrator prized by Zola. The Argentine naturalists write as if they sensed a need for the authority of science, but were careful to avoid the scientific socialism so firmly linked to French naturalism. What one observes, then, is an uncomfortable sense of test tube envy, what one might call "test tube anxiety," where authors evoke scientific theories and then dilute them with decidedly less-scientific language, imagery, and a subjective narrator in order to avoid unwanted ideological implications.

This test tube anxiety also serves to describe the effect literary discourse under the Argentine naturalists would exercise on the practice of science. If Sarmiento and Mansilla attempted to influence the cultural definitions of science with their texts, the medical discourse created by the naturalists defined particular boundaries of what would be considered scientific, at least as far as such definitions came to bear on the issues and themes covered in their novels. That is, the xenophobic, racist agenda proposed by these authors was not only considered true because it was presented as scientific, these authors also attempted to define science and medicine as those theories and ideas that supported their agenda. Once again the idea of a literary laboratory helps to explain a dynamic in which literature created and constructed the cultural authority that it would invest in and then appropriate from scientific discourse. With medically trained novelists like Manuel Podestá and with other writers who also ably manipulated a medical discourse, the novels could function as both literature and science, each serving to define and redefine the other.

At the same time, the adoption of a medical discourse, as opposed to one based directly on the sciences employed in naturalism, acts to attenuate the naturalist science-narrative connection even as it evokes the rhetorical support of medically based sciences. If we recall Foucault's treatment of medical discourse discussed in the introduction, we remember that while medical discourse enjoys much of the prestige of scientific discourse, Foucault also considers it a less rigorous discourse, one that permits the production of information and ideas that do not meet the standards of the hard sciences. Indeed, Zola anticipated Foucault's analysis of medical discourse, emphasizing the indeterminate quality of medicine, despite its scientific grounding (1927, 34). This combination of conjecture and science creates what is perhaps an ideal opportunity for Argentine naturalism, where it can incorporate scientific theories to buttress their xenophobic ideological claims while they sidestep the objective perspective of the experimental scientist/novelist envisioned by Zola. This is an intriguing development as we have the naturalists serving as champions of apparent advances in the sciences of their days even as they contain that science within a medical discourse that allows greater human control of the so-called truths that those sciences are used to produce. Test tube envy can still be seen to function, both in the sense that we have seen in the other chapters and in the dynamic between literary and medical discourse, but is now much more constrained. This new check on the use of scientific reference reveals a fundamental anxiety about science, or more specifically, Zola's naturalist science and its socialist corollaries.

One example of this peculiarity is in Cambaceres's aforementioned novel *En la sangre*. This cautionary tale of the dangers of the mixing of the Argentine *criollo* elite with Italian immigrants focuses on the life of Genaro, one such immigrant. Genaro dreams of improving his position in Argentine society and hopes to accomplish that dream by entering the upper class through marriage. His attempts to better himself fail at every turn, however, and he becomes (or remains) a depraved individual responsible for the misery of all who surround him. The victims most affected by the cruelty of Genaro, the *criollo* family who allowed him entrance to their social circle through his marriage to their daughter, also serve as the intended readers of the novel. It is this audience that Cambaceres attempts to warn of the dangers presented by immigrants with his presentation of the socially inept and genetically disadvantaged Genaro.

Cambaceres links Genaro's depravity and failures to his Italian blood and by so doing evokes the theories of social Darwinism and eugenics prevalent in naturalism and in the sciences of the era. However, the descriptions of these deterministic theories tend simultaneously to invite and eschew specific scientific reference as a manner of building rhetorical authority. The following passage from the novel illustrates this tendency:

> Y habría querido él no ser así, sin embargo, había intentado cambiar, modificarse, día a día no se cansaba de hacer los más sinceros, los más serios, los más solemnes propósitos de enmienda y de reforma; sí, a la par que de vergüenza, en el hondo sentimiento de desprecio que a sí

mismo se inspirara, con las ansias por vivir de quien siente que se ahoga, no había cesado de agitarse, de debatirse desesperado en esa lucha; sí, a todo el ardor de su voluntad, a todo el contingente de su esfuerzo, mil veces había apelado . . . inspirarse, retemplarse, redimirse en el ejemplo de lo bueno, de lo puro, de lo noble, que en torno suyo veía resistir, sobreponerse a esa ingénita tendencia que lo impulsaba al mal . . .
¡Vana tarea! . . . Obraba en él con la inmutable fijeza de las eternas leyes, fatal, inevitable, como la caída de un cuerpo, como el transcurso del tiempo, estaba en su sangre eso, constitucional, inveterado, le venía de casta como el color de la piel, le había sido transmitido por herencia, de padre a hijo, como de padres a hijos se transmite el virus venenoso de la sífilis . . . (Cambaceres 1984, 134–35)

[And he would have liked to not be that way, nevertheless, he had tried to change, modify himself, from day to day he never tired of making the most sincere, serious, solemn efforts to improve and reform; even in his embarrassment, in the deep feeling of disgust that he inspired in himself, with the desire to live that a drowning victim feels, he had not ceased trying desperately in this fight; he had appealed a thousand time to his burning will, all his strength to inspire him, temper him, redeem him in the example of that which is good, pure and novel, against which he saw his inborn tendency to evil work.
A vain effort, within him worked the unchangeable eternal laws, fatal, inevitable like the falling of a body, like the passage of time, it was in his blood, his constitution, it came with his caste like the color of his skin, it had been transmitted by inheritance, from father to son, just as the poisonous virus syphilis passes from father to son.]

This passage, which Fishburn singles out as the "most explicit" example of the use of science in *En la sangre* (1981, 78), creates an odd rhetorical situation. The narrator evokes ideas based on Galton's eugenics and ideas of social Darwinism that were then considered to be scientifically authoritative at the same time that he textually distances his presentation from those same sciences. We see this gesture repeated in the novel several times. As Nouzeilles has argued, medical reference occupies an important position, associating Genaro's congenital depravity with syphilis. However, in the other similes the novelist uses to describe the inevitability of Genaro's slide toward evil, we see a series of references to images that are not necessarily connected with the new sciences of the times. He describes this inevitability through references to the "leyes eternas" of falling bodies, the passage of time, the inheritance of the color of one's skin; all images that while arguably based in contemporary scientific work, do not immediately or specifically evoke the authority of the "new" sciences Zola championed. Indeed, the rhetorical power of Cambaceres's use of heredity theory lies more in the way he connects it with a vision of gravity articulated by Aristotle who claimed that bodies fail because it was in their nature to do so. These similes create a situation that downplays the cultural privilege heredity and eugenics would enjoy as the new "truths" of science, grounding instead its ability to enunciate truth about human beings through a rhetorical connection with the law of gravity. The reader is to accept these ideas as eternal truths on the same level as objects falling to the ground and the passage of time, concepts that are as much a part of everyday experience as they are a part of hard science. Cambaceres further distances his rhetoric from the purely scientific with his use of the words "eternal laws," a phrase that frames his presentation of biological inheritance in a near religious sense and further distinguishes them from science's "nouvelle vérités" championed by Zola. Indeed, Cambaceres creates a situation in which scientific ideas become dependent upon their ability to evoke these eternal patterns, where scientific ideas eschew revolution for a markedly conservative function.

We see a similar dynamic appear in a separate passage of the novel, this time at the beginning of chapter 10:

> Lastimado, agriado, exacerbado a la larga, esa broma pueril e irreflexiva, esa inocente burla de chiquillos, había concluido, sin embargo, hora por hora repetida con la cargosa insistencia de la infancia, por determinar un profundo cambio en Genaro, por remover todos los gérmenes malsanos que fermentaban en él.
> Y víctima de las sugestiones imperiosas de la sangre, de la irresistible influencia hereditaria, del patrimonio de la raza que fatalmente con la vida, al ver la luz, le fuera transmitido, las malas, las bajas pasiones de la humanidad hicieron de pronto explosión en su alma. (1984, 102–3)

> [Beaten up, bitter, exacerbated, that childish joke, that innocent teasing of little children, had concluded, nevertheless, repeated hour by hour with the insistence of infancy, by causing a profound change in Genaro, a determination to remove all the unhealthy germs that fermented in him.
> And victim of the imperious suggestions of the blood, of the irresistible hereditary influence of the patrimony of race that fatally with life, upon

seeing the light, was transmitted, the evils, the low passions of humanity, suddenly exploded in his soul.]

In this reflection on the abuse Genaro endured in his childhood, one observes an even clearer evocation of the principles of inheritance proposed by the eugenics Nouzeilles has identified as a major influence in Argentine naturalism. At the same time, however, it includes fatalistic aspects that distance it from the scientific methodology Zola proposes for naturalist authors. The theories of determinism preferred by Zola are replaced by fatalistic theories of racial predisposition that prohibit any type of social reform. Furthermore, the narrator mixes the scientific treatment of Genaro's difficulties with a religious condemnation marked by identifying Genaro's soul as the seat of the eruption of evil. If Cambaceres as novelist ever acted as an experimental scientist, the narrator's comments at this point color any scientific analysis with metaphysical implications that would seem to exist beyond the reach of the naturalist novelist, at least as far as Zola's definition of naturalism. Cambaceres's use of the image of the specter of Genaro's father as a symbol of the character's bad genes later on in the novel further distances the theories of inheritance from scientific objectivity by relating them with supernatural images (1984, 194). When compared with the name-dropping and inclusion of scientific detail seen in earlier authors, Cambaceres's strategy borders on scientific aversion.

Indeed, the novel's title that seems to allude to eugenics actually violates the distinction Zola cultivates between a naturalism based on determinism and fatalism. Zola always invested the deterministic study of society in literature with a sense of optimism (1927, 31). If one is able to understand the environmental causes of misery, one can change them. Zola emphasizes the deterministic effects of environment in his discussion of human nature in literature, thereby providing for the possibility of societal reform and individual rehabilitation. Oppositely, Cambaceres elaborates a fatalistic theory of inheritance that dooms Genaro absolutely, leaving him with no hope of escaping the blood that damns him.[5]

Instead, then, of using science to prove the validity of its ideology, the novel itself serves tautologically as its own proof for the validity of Cambaceres's condemnation of immigrants. The description of Genaro gains rhetorical validity not necessarily because it is couched in scientific language or because it invokes the authority of well-known scientists, but because Genaro commits a series of horrible crimes despite his continual attempts at self-improvement. Fishburn describes the narrative techniques employed by Cambaceres to achieve the desired effect:

> The condemnation of Genaro is achieved by means of a skillfully woven narrative strategy that combines the rhetorical techniques described by Wayne C. Booth as "telling" and "showing." The first consists of an explicit rhetorical nature, such as are found in the descriptions of the protagonist quoted earlier. The second relies on the selectivity of events in the plot which illustrate a point with apparent independence. This device is used mainly in the later stages of the work, when the distance between the narrator and his character has seemingly widened, and the latter appears to move independently. Yet a close analysis of the text reveals that everything in it is always subject to the most careful monitoring on the part of the author. (1981, 79)

As Fishburn's arguments suggest, Cambaceres depends on a series of descriptions and developments of the plot for the rhetorical authority he needs to convince the Argentine elite of the danger of immigrants. As he does so, and as we see in the passages from the novel referred to above, Cambaceres eschews Zola's idealized conception of the novelist as an objective experimental scientist devoted to social reform for a subjective accusing narrator whose aim is to attack, oppress, and control the class Genaro represents. Indeed, this type of subjectivity has led Fishburn to argue: "according to strict Zolian tenets, it is possible to assert that there are no naturalist novels in Argentine literature" (51). While Nouzeilles claims the opposite, this critical disagreement serves to highlight the ambivalence in Argentine naturalism's use of the discourse of science.

Many of the other Argentine novels in what has usually been labeled as naturalist similarly accept and avoid the scientific model of the novel. Cambaceres's *Sin rumbo* (1885), Roberto Payró's *Las divertidas aventuras del nieto de Juan Moreira* (1910) also incorporate aspects of French naturalism, especially in their narrative focus on vice and the depraved and their use of medicine to portray a sick Argentina. Nevertheless, they generally avoid the objective, scientific narrator proposed by Zola, as they (or many of them) are eager to avoid the corollary social commitments. The result is a group of authors whose test tube envy is tempered by a test tube anxiety in which they depend on the authority of naturalist science while they reject certain social implications Zola invested in the use of the scientific model in naturalist literature. Indeed, the medical model becomes the most appropriate choice, one that allows them access to the authority of science even as it provides them a greater degree of control over the science they evoke. As we follow the construction of an Argentine "régime of truth" based on science, we see in the naturalist effort an attempt to expand this societal structure, grafting on new discourses that will enhance their ability to tell convincing truths in the changing context of Argentine culture as they attempt to limit the truths that the new sciences will also tell about Argentine reality. In that sense, naturalism does not just repeat the attitudes toward science that we saw earlier and that we would expect them to support. Instead, they point out new directions in narrative while grappling with the by then institutional structures that associated contemporary science with the exercise of cultural authority.

The work by Fishburn, Jitrik, and Nouzeilles on Argentine naturalism, then, provides a segue into the twentieth century that we can follow in the next chapter, even as we recognize an important ambivalence and even anxiety in the deployment of scientific discourse in turn of the century Argentine narrative. To be sure, the evocation of science continues, but *En la sangre*, the canonical work of the period, betrays simultaneously an intriguing linguistic anxiety that does and does not fit the unreserved embraces of science by Sarmiento and Mansilla. Indeed, what serves as the most concrete link between the naturalists and the earlier writers in this study is not so much the envy, but the literary attempt to define and the limit a cultural space in which science can function as a discourse that generates knowledge about Argentina and its peoples. The moment in Argentine literary history that would seem to present most clearly a case of test tube envy turns out to add an intriguing wrinkle in a tapestry of canonical Argentine texts that navigate the power structures of scientific discourse.

4
Test Tube Terror: Science and Society in Roberto Arlt

WHILE THE WRITINGS OF THE NATURALISTS BRIDGED THE NINEteenth and twentieth centuries even as they opened fissures in the development of the relationship between literary and scientific discourse, the coincidence of Roberto Arlt's birth with that of the twentieth century serves as a portent of even larger changes in the dynamic at the center of this study. Even so, we do not leave naturalism completely behind. The narrative of Roberto Arlt (1900–1942), with themes that focus on the city and the lower classes along with their destructive base behavior, has been described as naturalistic if not part of naturalism's itself. Even so, as Arlt's birth year would symbolically suggest, his literary production is clearly post-naturalist both in the French and the Argentine senses on a number of levels, including, significantly, its treatment and use of scientific discourse. Arlt's contribution to this study is important both in the continuities and the discontinuities that his writing represents. We will also examine Ernesto Sabato's depiction of science in the light of Arlt's example.

Arlt's work has been the focus of scores of critical articles and several books that have focused on a variety of themes and narrative structures employed in his fiction. Arlt is known for his dystopias, his exploration of guilt and expressionist angst, his various antiheroes, and his peculiar use of narrative technique.[1] Another aspect that has been widely recognized is his use of scientific images, inventor characters, scientific language, and theorems in his writings. Most critics note Arlt's experience as an inventor himself, remembering especially the patent Arlt received for run-resistant lady's stockings.[2] While the intersection of science and literature in Arlt's work has not been studied as completely as other areas of his work, it has been the focus of a number of scholarly articles and books we will discuss shortly.

Academic literary criticism is not the only field to recognize Arlt's penchant for things scientific. A reflective Julio Cortázar comments on the manner in which the theme of science in Arlt's writings impressed him as he revisited Arlt's work:

> Hoy, claro, lo releo con un poco más de distanciamiento intelectual, de embriones de análisis, de territorios descuidados en la primera lectura y que ahora adquieren un relieve diferente. La obsesión científica en Arlt, por ejemplo, que entonces me había dejado indiferente. ¿Influencias familiares, primeros oficios, atavismos germánicos en una época en que la química, la balística y la farmacopea parecían tener su amenazante capital en Berlín? Se sabe que Arlt murió mientras trabajaba en su improvisado laboratorio, a punto de lograr un procedimiento que hubiera evitado un drama de la época que hoy resulta increíble: el corrimiento de las mallas en las medias de las mujeres. (Cortázar 1981, viii).

> [Today, of course, I read with a little more intellectual distance, with embryos of analysis, uncared-for-areas in the first reading that now have a different importance. Scientific obsession in Arlt, for example, to which I had been indifferent back then. Family influences, first jobs, Germanic descent in a time where chemistry, ballistics, and pharmacopoeia seemed to have their threatening capital in Berlin. It is known that Arlt died while working in his improvised laboratory, at the point of developing a procedure that would have avoided a drama of the time that seems incredible today: runs in pantyhose.]

Cortázar's own literary obsession with science will form the subject of a subsequent chapter, where his specific interest in Arlt's *obsesión científica* should become clearer. The former's narrative idiosyncrasies aside, Arlt's treatment of science and technology as a theme as well as his incorporation of scientific reference and discourse are phenomena in his work that are often noted but rarely analyzed in greater depth.

The sociohistorical context of the 1920s makes Arlt's focus on science seem a natural decision. During these years Buenos Aires was a city caught up in the discoveries of the new physics as well as the exciting possibilities of new inventions and technologies. Beatriz Sarlo, in her excellent study of technology in Quiroga, Arlt, and early twentieth-century Argentine society notes that Crítica, one of the most popular newspapers of the time devoted nine articles to Einstein's 1925 visit that led to an interview with the physicist. She also observes that the interest in the theory of relativity did not abate after his visit, with *Crítica* and the new *El Mundo* continuing to report on Einstein's discoveries and publishing series providing explanations (1992, 65). *Crítica* and *El mundo* clearly reflect the public's increasing interest in the discoveries of physics, an interest that also was expressed in the growing fascination with inventions and technologies. Ortiz notes the importance of the Argentine literary scene in this visit as well, highlighting Leopoldo Lugones's acquaintance with Einstein and his work facilitating that visit.[3] We see this phenomenon evidenced in a variety of other newspapers and magazines of the same time period (Sarlo 1992, 65–66). Just as we saw in the nineteenth century, journalism continued to participate in the discursive formation of scientific practice and perception. While the science that had the power to describe the world had changed, the authority wielded by things perceived as scientific remained much the same. Sarlo specifically ties the use of scientific discourse in the description of scientific experiments and the inclusion of chemical formulae in the work of Arlt and Horacio Quiroga to the "symbolic weight" that science wielded in the popular imagination of the time (1992, 33). Arlt in particular tapped into the "symbolic weight" of science with a complex pattern of scientific reference that combines unabashed evocation of modern science with a scathing critique of the societal implications of that same science. And yet, in the midst of the technological horrors Arlt predicts with his narrative use of scientific elements, we find a familiar rhetorical use of scientific authority that continues the tendency we have already seen in Sarmiento and Mansilla. What results is an ambivalent attitude toward science as a sociocultural force that recognizes both its rhetorical authority and its future menace to humanity. This ambivalence toward science, where the excitement of new discoveries was tempered by some of the horrors of new technology, was another aspect of the era. In the wake of World War I, where chemistry was used to produce poison gas and engineers were able to design weapons that could kill the enemy in mass, intellectuals began to develop critiques of the positivists' unquestioning faith in science that had already arisen in the nineteenth century. Indeed, much of the science fiction written in Argentina during this period by Quiroga, Lugones, and Arlt emphasized the theme of science out of control. Even so, while positivism and its concomitant faith in science underwent a serious questioning by the intellectuals of the time period, the narrative mechanism of using scientific discourse as an agent for rhetorical privilege remains the same.[4]

The example of Darwinism in the early twentieth century provides an important example of a continued dependence on scientific theories for textual authority. The use of Charles Darwin and his theories as a source of rhetorical authority is certainly not a new strategy in Argentine letters, naturalism being the most recent example of a series of such cases. Still, in the 1920s, we see an increased emphasis on Darwinism in Argentine and Latin American intellectual culture. Nancy Leys Stepan characterizes the intellectual interest in Darwinism as an ideological alternative:

> They [Latin American intellectuals] embraced science as a form of progressive knowledge, as an alternative to the religious view of reality, and as a means of establishing a new form of cultural power. Evolution was adopted especially enthusiastically as a secular, materialist, modern view of the world. Darwinism, which came to Latin America in the 1870s and 1880s from a variety of English, French, and German sources, and in forms that often departed considerably from Darwin's own ideas was particularly resonant. (41)

In literary texts, we have noted already Mansilla's use of Darwin's cultural authority as scientist as a model for his own self-fashioning as popular scientist at certain moments in his writings. As we noted, naturalism generally included theories adapted from Darwin in their theories on racial hygiene. A little later, we have the example of Horacio Quiroga who used Darwin and Darwinian theories in his short fiction. Sarlo highlights Darwin in particular as a model for narrative in the River Plate region, remarking on its ability to "appear as scientific" because of its discussion of the history of human beings within a geological context (1992, 38). As Sarlo maintains, narrative could act as a scientific "report" that created a narrative truth based on science (1992, 38). Sarlo's analysis of Quiroga's use of Darwin exhibits a specific case in which the popular cultural authority of Darwinism was used in order to enhance the authority of the literary text.[5] We will see a similar pattern in Arlt, a practice that indicates the continuing rhetorical importance of scientific reference in Argentine letters during the early twentieth century.

It is at this point where my examination of scientific discourse in Latin American literature diverges from the analysis of González Echevarría. With the coming of the twentieth century, he sees a shift in the discourse of power from the scientific model to an anthropological, mythical model. Aside from the problematic terminology he uses in describing this pattern of writing—as we have seen with Mansilla and Sarmiento, anthropology is not wholly distinct from scientific travel writing in terms of rhetorical scientific authority—González Echevarría identifies a pattern that exists in a select, albeit significant, group of Latin American texts among which Arlt's writings fail to figure. While what González Echevarría argues may be accurate when one focuses on the work of Carpentier and García Márquez, if we follow a path that includes authors like Roberto Arlt, we see a continued pattern of scientific reference and a narrative modeling on scientific language as discursive strategies. While the use of scientific discourse as a narrative and rhetorical device becomes much more complicated and ambiguous, at times being used to question science's own authority, we still see clear cases where literature borrows from scientific authority as it creates its own discourse of power. The case of Roberto Arlt is especially pertinent as the system of scientific reference on a level of imagery evokes and critiques scientific authority on one plane while its inclusion affects his creation of a narrative reality in quite another.

And yet science's dual function in Arlt's work has been mostly ignored, with critics usually studying science and technology as theme and image in the Argentine inventor's narrative. Rita Gnutzman mentions its appearance both in his work generally as well as specifically in *El juguete rabioso*. In her book *Roberto Arlt o el arte de calidoscopio* she dedicates a brief section to discussion of his use of science, focusing more on its appearance than its narrative function. She notes specifically his interest in chemistry and physics manifested in the inclusion of various chemical formulas in *Los siete locos/Los lanzallamas*. Gnutzman's analysis is that this inclusion had the effect of bestowing an air of scientificity on the text in general, she argues that while his descriptions might not impress a chemist, they certainly mystify a "normal reader" (197). Gnutzman's observation reveals Arlt's development of scientific authority in his narrative. The references to chemistry and mathematics create an image of the novel as scientifically sophisticated. The reader admires his knowledge whether they understand it or not, and in either case, Arlt gains prestige as an author who can wield scientific terminology convincingly. Gnutzman goes further to describe Arlt's use of scientific language in his metaphors, such as his description of a star in *El amor brujo*: "Una estrella fúlgida taladra el cielo duro, más azul que un cristal de sulfato de cobre" [A shining star drills the hard sky, bluer than a copper sulfate crystal] (197). While Gnutzman identifies several other such instances in which Arlt employs scientific or mathematical language or metaphors, her examination of science in Arlt's work is more descriptive than analytical, arguing that it mainly contributes to a characterization of human existence as a hellish experience. Beatriz Sarlo, whose work I have cited above, provides the most complete study to date of the function of science and technology in Arlt's narrative. After describing this use rather completely, she follows Gnutzman in arguing that it functions mostly as an anti-utopian theme in Arlt's work, where science and technology are presented as the new basis for authoritarian power in society. What she does not do is examine the way Arlt's incorporation of scientific imagery and reference acts to privilege his own warnings in a way the moves well beyond the science fiction genre.

The work of both Sarlo and Gnutzman serves, then, as an ideal starting point for a discussion of Arlt's use of scientific discourse in the two novels that form a single narrative. *Los siete locos/Los lanzallamas*, perhaps Arlt's most studied work, examines the failed inventor Remo Erdosain. This antihero decides to recreate himself through murder and becomes involved in a revolutionary group headed by a man referred to as El Astrólogo. The novels follow Erdosain through a series of failures, and end with his building of a factory that makes poison gas, his senseless murder of an innocent girl, and his subsequent suicide. Arlt's condemnation of a cultural fascination with the advances of science forms a theme often noted in passing in criticism of the novel.[6] In particular, El Astrólogo's long soliloquy linking science and technology with capitalism and repressive power combined with Erdosain's use of chemistry to produce poison gas has attracted several comments by critics studying other aspects of the novel(s) as well as Sarlo's specific attention. What criticism has not examined thus far is the rhetorical relationship between Arlt's detailed description of scientific practices and his condemnation of technology. Paradoxically, Arlt gains rhetorical power for his depiction of a nightmarish scientific-authoritarian world precisely because he is able to employ scientific rhetoric in a convincing fashion.

While the accumulation of chemical formulas and scientific descriptions in his novels contributes to the narrative creation of a cold, mechanical world on a level of imagery, it grants textual authority on a rhetorical level owing to descriptions that appear to come directly from textbooks on chemistry. The sections in *Los lanzallamas* that describe in careful detail the chemical reactions responsible for the effectiveness of Erdosain's poison gas augment the sense of horror Arlt connects with advances in technology. These precise descriptions are what create a terrible reality based on what appear to be real characterizations of science. Erdosain's mysterious visitor provides just such an example as he describes his history with poison gas:

> Nosotros usamos al principio del fosgeno. Después lo dejamos por el sulfuro de etilo biclorado. A pocos días de transcurrido el combate las carnes de los gaseados se rajaban como las de los leprosos. También empleábamos el clorosulfonato de etilo, más cáustico que el fuego. Los hombres tocados por el gas parecían haber bebido ácido nítrico. La lengua se les ponía gruesa como la de un elefante, las entrañas se les consumían como si estuvieran disecándose en bicloruto de mercurio. Para variar el juego, los otros introdujeron la cloroacetona. Me acuerdo de un hombre nuestro a quien se le rompieron los cristales de la careta. A las veinticuatro horas tenía los ojos más rojos que hígados. Era, en verdad, un espectáculo triste y extraño el semblante amarillo de aquel hombre con dos hígados rojos fuera de sus órbitas, que manaban interminables torrentes de lágrimas. (1981, 443)

> [We used phosgene at first. Later we abandoned it, using sulphur of ethyl bichloride instead. After a few days of battle the flesh of the gassed soldiers fell off them as if they were lepers. We also used chlorosulfate of ethyl, more caustic than fire. The men touched by the gas looked like they had drunk nitric acid. Their tongues became thick as an elephant's, their innards were consumed as if they were dessicating in bichlorate of mercury. To vary the game, others introduced chloroacetate. I remember one of our men who broke a test tube. After twenty-four hours his eyes were redder than livers. It was, in truth, a sad and strange spectacle, the yellow face of that man with two red livers out of their sockets that poured unending torrents of tears.]

To extend the metaphor, just as a chemist with a solution, Arlt saturates the passage with references to chemicals that only such a chemist would recognize. The list of chemicals, the simile in which the affected person's skin is described as subject to a dehydrating agent, all combine to heighten the threat of poison gas of which Arlt warns with his entire novel. The technical words in this case specifically connect the science of chemistry with the terrors of poison gas. Instead of occupying the role of mere weapon, poison gas becomes a metonymic representation of chemistry as a scientific discipline because it is described with the chemistry's language. Arlt, then, envies the test tube, using scientific language to make his presentation more authoritative. Paradoxically, he does this as a way to break the test tube, symbolically attacking optimistic interpretations of science.

The image of the broken test tube in the above passage is, then, even more intriguing. On one level, the imagery is entirely consistent with the antitechnology theme of the novel. Science, like the test tube, has been shattered, and its breaking causes the tears of humanity just as it caustically destroys the eyes of one of the scientists. A discipline thought by the positivists to bring light to humanity brings only blindness. At the same time, the imagery is a delightful contradiction. The broken test tube's impact as an image of science is strengthened by Arlt's use of the language of that same broken science. Arlt may be envying a broken test tube or, in other words, depending on what he seems to claim is a defective science, but the text he creates continues to depend on the authority it draws from its able deployment of the language of chemistry.

Paradoxically, the novel gains textual authority for its philosophical and social warnings against science because it knows how to frame narrative reality scientifically. Sarlo concludes that Arlt's characters use present scientific knowledge to "imagine future organizations" that are mediated by current political situations, moments that Sarlo calls "delirios técnicos" or technical delirations (1992, 61). Those *delirios* turned scientific hypotheses can be presented as true because their basis is perceived as scientifically accurate. In *Los siete locos/Los lanzallamas*, science defeats itself. Arlt exploits science's authority as a discourse that can produce truth to create the truth of science's own present and future menace. One should note that this use of science against science is very different from the anxiety apparent in Argentine Naturalism. Arlt embraces scientific discourse as the method for his narrative attack. Cambaceres uneasily approaches and retreats from science as he presents his ideology, apparently worried more about the ideological connotations of his usage of new sciences than the societal impact of the advancement of those sciences.

El juguete rabioso, Arlt's picaresque treatment of one Silvio Astier, marks a turning point in Argentine literary history. Its publication in 1926, together with his good friend Ricardo Guiraldes's *Don Segundo Sombra*, imprints a Janus face on the year. As Guiraldes's gaucho rides off into the sunset along with the *novela de la tierra* in Argentine literature, Arlt's city dweller struggles to find meaning in a narrative that for many marks the beginning of the urban novel in Argentina and in Latin America.[7] In the novel we see the beginnings of Arlt's conception of science as a threat and the quest for scientific knowledge as self-defeating. At the same time, however, we see a use of scientific discourse that ties him more clearly to the tradition we have commented in the earlier chapters. Through a series of references to scientists and narrative situations, Arlt develops a narrative reality based on Charles Darwin's theory of natural selection. While Arlt's themes and narrative techniques differentiate his work from Mansilla and Sarmiento's, one can still perceive a link in many of his deployments of scientific discourse. We will now turn to an analysis of these considerations.

Silvio Astier is the first protagonist inventor in a series of such characters in Arlt's fiction. As the narrator of his own story, and specifically as a picaresque narrator, he employs a series of strategies designed to improve his textual status.[8] Among these strategies figures a use of scientific imagery and reference employed specifically by Silvio the fictional character in his attempts to frame himself as an important figure in Buenos Aires society. While this situation is certainly distinct from the rhetorical effect of science on the creation of the narrative reality Astier inhabits, it produces an intriguing counterpoint worthy of consideration. As a part of this narrative self-fashioning, Silvio presents himself as someone familiar with science, a man to whom people look for scientific information. Silvio reflects on his adolescent status as neighborhood scientist:

> Hipólito quería ser aviador, «pero debía resolver antes el problema de la estabilidad espontánea». En otros tiempos le preocupó la solución del movimiento continuo y solía consultarme acerca del resultado posible de sus cavilaciones. (1981, 13–14)

> [Hipólito wanted to be a pilot, but first, he said, he needed to solve the problem of "spontaneous stability." Sometimes he would be wrestling with the thorny question of perpetual motion, and we would mull over possible solutions together.] (2002, 24)

Silvio as narrator uses the offhand remark to strengthen his self-presentation as possessor of scientific knowledge, in this case, the physics of motion. We see a further development of Silvio as possessor of scientific knowledge in the episode where he is interviewed for an engineering job. He impresses his superiors in a series of questions and answers in which he is able to manage both scientific theory and vocabulary:

> —Señores oficiales: ustedes sabrán que el selenio conduce la corriente eléctrica cuando está iluminado; en la oscuridad se comporta como un aislador. El señalador no consistiría nada más que en una célula de selenio, conectada con un electroimán. El paso de una estrella por el retículo del selenio, sería señalada por un signo, ya que la claridad del meteoro, concentrada por un lente cóncavo, pondría en condiciones de conductor al selenio.
> —Está bien. ¿Y la máquina de escribir?
> —La teoría es la siguiente. En el teléfono el sonido se convierte en una onda electromagnética.
> Si medimos con un galvanómetro de tangente la intensidad eléctrica producida por cada vocal y consonante, podemos calcular el número de amperios vueltas, necesarios para fabricar un teclado magnético que responderá a la intensidad de corriente de cada vocal. (1981, 68)

> [Gentlemen—you are of course aware that selenium is a conductor of electricity when light hits it; in the dark it acts as an insulator. "The signaling device would consist simply of a selenium cell connected to an electromagnet. A star passing across the selenium would trigger a signal, since the light of the meteor, concentrated by a concave lens, would turn the selenium into a conductor."
> "Okay, fine. Now what about the typewriter?"
> "The idea is this. In a telephone, sound is converted into an electromagnetic wave."
> "If we use a galvanometer to measure the electrical intensity produced by each vowel and consonant, we can calculate the number of ampere turns necessary to create a magnetic keyboard corresponding to the electrical intensity of each sound.] (2002, 91–92)

As Silvio describes his inventions, he simultaneously presents himself as an engineer conversant in the language of the scientist/inventor. His discussion of electricity, selenium and amperes function in the scene as an attempt to impress the officials while it simultaneously presents to the narratee a character whose authority rests on his ability to manipulate the language of science. In this sense we see a self-fashioning that imitates on a fictional plane what we saw in real-life with Sarmiento and Mansilla. Astier hopes to be able to frame his discourse as rhetorically authoritative because he, as an inventor, can understand science and employ its language. Just as the nineteenth-century statesmen and writers provide historical examples of Foucault's argument that the cultural position of the speaker guarantees the truthfulness of the statement, Arlt's character gives a supporting fictional example.

The cultural authority of science also serves as Astier's major aspiration through a major portion of the novel. He continually comments on his study of scientific texts, for example. The importance of these scientific texts is underlined when the group of friends at the beginning of the novel robs a bookstore precisely because, (according to Enrique's proposal): "El club debe contar con una biblioteca de obras científicas para que sus cofrades puedan robar y matar de acuerdo a los más modernos procedimientos industriales" [The club should have a library of scientific works so that its members can steal and kill according to the most modern industrial procedures] (1981, 21). The escapade in which they actually steal the books is both humorous in its several misadventures and serious as it displays Silvio and friends' desire to obtain the books that contain the promise of scientific knowledge. The subsequent description of the club's activities also evokes a sense of the scientific, suggesting Silvio's desire to gain scientific status:

> Esto sucedía así;
> Después de almorzar, a la hora en que las calles eran desiertas, discretamente trajeados salíamos a recorrer las calles de Flores o Caballito.
> Nuestras herramientas de trabajo eran:
> Una pequeña llave inglesa, un destornillador y algunos periódicos para empaquetar lo hurtado. (1981, 18)
>
> [It happened like this:
> During the afternoon siesta, when the streets were deserted, we would venture out, discreetly dressed, to roam the neighborhoods of Flores or Caballito. Our working tools consisted of a monkey wrench, a screwdriver, and some newspapers to wrap up the loot.] (2002, 29)

The careful, objective, distanced description of their activities imitates the scientific paper that describes a given experiment objectively in order to make the process reproducible, with the listing of tools reinforcing that impression. Silvio as narrator again tries to use a scientific way of writing to privilege his position as one who knows science and knows how to speak its language. By so doing he becomes the fictional version of Mansilla and Sarmiento and attempts to access the same power for which they strove.

Yet the purpose for which the boys want the scientific texts reminds us of the sinister side of science in the narrative reality of *El juguete rabioso*. The modernization that scientific and technological discovery brings is associated with crime, specifically with murder, tainting the image of science from the beginning of the novel. We are also reminded that the scientific self-fashioning occurs, after all, at the level of a fictional narrator similar to the case of Mármol's characters. It is Silvio, not Arlt, who tries to present himself as scientifically authoritative, and when one analyzes the thematic function of Silvio's attempts to portray himself as scientific, one sees the profoundly negative connotations of science in the novel. The character's scientific aspirations only emphasize the fact that many critics have noted; Silvio's science does him no good.[9] The superiors he impresses with his scientific knowledge end up rejecting him and his knowledge. He is reminded repeatedly that only the practical counts and that his impractical inventions are worthless. Arlt's examination of the theme of science, especially as it is associated with the character of Silvio, suggests a science that is powerless to aid humanity, and serves, in fact, as a threat to it.

Arlt's treatment of the power of scientific discourse would seem to remain, then, on an ironic level, anticipating a more sophisticated critique that would come in his subsequent novels. Silvio as a character appears to mock a society that depends on the empty cultural power it has bestowed on science. Just as Silvio's attempts to embrace science result in utter failure, so too will a society obsessed with science fail miserably. This position is developed further as Arlt carefully links everyday life with science, suggesting places where life supersedes science's ability to describe it. The older Silvio, now a paper salesman, shares his new perspective on life and science:

> No parecerá entonces exagerado decir que entre un individuo y el comerciante se han establecido vínculos materiales y espirituales, relación inconsciente o simulada de ideas económicas, políticas, religiosas y hasta sociales, y que una operación de venta, aunque sea la de un paquete de agujas, salvo perentoria necesidad, eslabona en sí más dificultades que la solución del binomio de Newton. (1981, 96)

> [It's not exaggerating to say that between the buyer and the seller ties of both a material and a spiritual character have been forged, an uncon-

scious or feigned relationship based on shared ideas—economic, political, religious, and even social. Except in cases of overwhelming need, the selling of anything, be it only a packet of needles, entails more complexity than Newton's binomial theorem.] (2002, 126)

The struggles and challenges of the paper salesman now supplant the intellectual challenge of the West's greatest scientist. Silvio's use of Newton in his description of selling paper positions him above science, not because he knows how to speak the language of science, but because he has found something that is more difficult. Test tube envy, in the case of Silvio, has begun to turn to test tube disillusion.

This marks an important shift in the way in which Argentine literature shapes scientific discourse. If earlier writers attempted (and succeeded), in using narrative to shape the definition and practice of certain sciences in the nineteenth century, Arlt seems to recognize a separation between literature and science that impedes a direct influence. Arlt's novel employs a system of reference and allusion controls the image and presence of science in culture without the same pretensions of influencing the actual practice of science. While such a strategy stands at odds with the earlier texts we have discussed, it also helps us appreciate an added facet in the dynamics that occur between literary and scientific discourse. Arlt employs his attack as a method by which he limits the cultural space within which science operates. That is, if the newspapers that announced Einstein's visit helped to build the discursive authority science exercised in Argentina, Arlt's novel attempts to deconstruct that same space, effectively removing that authority. To follow imagery used in another chapter, Arlt fills his literary laboratory with a series of broken test tubes.

However, if one examines the use of scientific reference as an element of narrative construction rather than its function in the plot of the novel, one begins to notice a system that uses science as a rhetorical support not for Silvio's self-creation as narrator, but for the fictional world in which Silvio resides. It is at this point that Darwin begins to figure as a rhetorical force in the novel. In the last section of *El juguete rabioso*, Silvio encounters Lucio, a friend from the "Club de los Caballeros de la Media Noche," now an *agente de investigaciones*. In their discussion, Lucio makes a comment that he then repeats four times throughout the conversation:

> Ranún... pero mirá, che, Silvio, hay que regenerarse; así es la vida, la *struggle for life* de Darwin...
> ¡Que te has vuelto erudito! ¿Con qué se come eso?
> Yo me entiendo, che; ésa es la terminología ácrata; así que vos también te regeneraste, trabajás, y te va bien. (1981, 90)

> [But look, Silvio, a guy's got to go straight; that's life, Darwin's 'struggle for life'"...
> "A scholar now! And does that pay your rent?"
> "It's anarchist lingo—I know what I'm talking about. So you've decided to go straight, too, you're working and doing fine.] (2002, 119)

Lucio frames the reality in which the characters find themselves in Darwinian terms. Humans, just as the evolving animals in Darwin, must struggle for life, regenerate and ensure their survival. Darwin's descriptions of this process provide the background for our discussion.

> In looking at Nature, it is most necessary to keep the foregoing considerations always in mind—never to forget that every single organic being around us may be said to be striving to the utmost to increase in numbers; that each lives by a struggle at some period of its life... we forget that each species, even where it most abounds, is constantly suffering enormous destruction at some period of its life, from enemies or from competitors for the same place and food... (1993, 151, 153)

Arlt's argument that human beings struggle for life according to the same rules of natural selection as any other animal is, then, merely a repetition of Darwin's argument that the theories he presented in *On the Origin of Species* are applicable to all living organisms. Lucio and Silvio's behavior becomes the logical extension of Darwinist thought.

Lucio uses the phrase, "struggle for life," to invoke Darwin's scientific authority and therefore justify his new role, antithetical to the ideals of the youthful club. Lucio's final repetitions of the phrase include an important addendum, "La struggle for life, che ... unos se regeneran, otros caen... ¡así es la vida!" (1981, 91): [Some regenerate or "go straight" others fall, that's life.] With the inclusion of "otros caen" the struggle extends from a personal challenge to regenerate oneself to the sense of Darwinian natural selection in which species that are able to pass on their genetic makeup survive while those that cannot fall from the struggle. The phrase "así es la vida" resonates in Silvio, we see him recall the phrase in several subsequent situations, each time commenting on his own life while simultaneously reminding the reader of Lucio's words. This repetition, as well as the evocation of Darwin near the beginning of the novel by Enrique, the third member of the club (1981, 23), invites an examination of the way in which Darwin's theories of natural selection and the struggle for life shape and inform the text as a whole.

Initially, we see various references to human beings as animals, an important aspect in Darwinian theory and an obvious characteristic in a novel whose original title was *La vida puerca*. Again, Darwin's equation of human being and animal provide the necessary referent:

> Thus we can understand how it has come to pass that man and all other vertebrate animals have been constructed on the same general model, why they pass through the same early stages of development and why they retain certain rudiments in common. Consequently we ought frankly to admit their community of descent: to take any other view, is to admit that our own structure and that of all the animals around us is a mere snare laid to entrap our judgment. (1993, 326)

We should also note at this point that the identification of humans as animals also reminds us of Arlt's questioning of Sarmiento's famous civilización/barbarie dichotomy, a questioning made more effective by its adoption of scientific discourse. A number of critics have remarked on Arlt's attempts to describe the savage nature of city life, a position that consciously attacks Sarmiento's description of a privileged urban existence. They do not, however, note the similar use of scientific discourse in that attack. Indeed, the extension of the rules of natural selection to human beings effectively eliminates any dichotomy based on the identification of certain groups as animalistic and others as human. The deployment of animal imagery within the Darwinian system Arlt insinuates serves as a most effective tool in his deconstruction of the Sarmentine dichotomy.

The relationship between don Gaetano and doña María serves as the source for much of Arlt's imitation of the ideas Darwin advances in the previous passage. The description of their most prominent fight is exemplary of this situation:

> Don Gaetano pareció ahogarse de furor. De pronto arrancóse el cuello, la corbata negra y arrojóla al rostro de su mujer; luego se detuvo un

momento como si hubiera recibido un golpe en las sienes y después echó a correr, salió hasta la calle, los ojos saltándole de las órbitas, y parándose en medio de la vereda, moviendo la rapada cabeza desnuda, señalándola como un loco a los transeúntes, los brazos extendidos, le gritó con voz desnaturalizada por el coraje:—¡Bestia . . . bestia . . . bestión . . . !
Satisfecha, ella se allegó a mí. (1981, 50)

[Don Gaetono seemed to be drowning in fury. Suddenly he took off his black tie and hurled it in his wife's face; then he stopped as if he had been hit on the head and ran outside, his eyes popping from their sockets. He planted himself in the middle of the sidewalk of passersby, jerking his bare head, and pointing with outstretched arms as he shouted in a voice transformed by rage: "Bitch [Beast]! . . . Bitch! . . . Perfect bitch! Satisfied, she came over to me.] (2002, 69)

The wild description of the infuriated Gaetano presents a man more animal than human with flailing arms, unnatural voice and uncovered head. His cry of "Bestia" defines his mate as animal, an action that confirms his own description as beast. María's response further evokes the Darwinian situation. As she brings out the animal in her husband, she turns to Silvio and treats him as a victorious rival to her previous mate.[10] While the episode also exhibits Oedipal overtones, one need not stretch the imagery to see a competition between males for the right to reproduce with the female.[11]

Arlt further evokes Darwin's theories with references to the importance of reproduction in this same episode. Silvio escapes to the kitchen and begins a conversation with Miguel:

—¿Qué te parece esto, Miguel . . . ?
—El infierno, don Silvio, ¡Qué vida!
. . .
—¿Pero a que vienen esos burdeles?
—Yo no sé . . . no tienen hijos . . . él no sirve . . . (1981, 51)

["What do you think of all this?"
"It's hell, don Silvio, what a life!"
. . .
"What do these fights come from?"
"I don't know. They don't have children. He can't."]

Gaetano and María's marital problems become linked with the inability to reproduce. While such blame does not necessarily evoke

Darwinism, the blame combined with the phrase "él no sirve" in a text that evokes Darwin with the mantra-like "struggle for life" helps create a narrative reality in which success is measured by one's ability to pass genetic material on to subsequent generations. The couple becomes, then, a microcosm for the narrative reality constructed in *El juguete rabioso*. They are trapped in a sterile relationship that means death in Darwinian terms. Silvio and the rest of the characters also must function within that same reality in which one must regenerate oneself continually or cease to exist.

Such a reality allows us to interpret other remarks within an evolutionary framework as well. Silvio, in his conversation with Souza, presents the drive to evolve on a professional level:

> —Hablando de otras cosas. Según me comunicó el amigo aquí presente, usted necesita un empleo.
> —Sí, señor, un empleo donde pueda progresar, porque donde estoy . . . (1981, 53)

> ["Talking about other things. According to what my friend tells me, you need a job."
> "Yes sir, a job where I can advance, because where I'm at . . ."]

The ability to advance becomes the ultimate goal in a society ruled by the Darwinian rules of natural selection and survival of the fittest. While Silvio seems to appear as a sexual competitor with Gaetano, he ultimately is unable to win the affections of María and is left in the same sterile state as her husband. Silvio, if he is to survive, must find a situation where he can progress, as the lack of progression in *El juguete rabioso* is equated with a sterile death in life.[12]

But this is the story of one who falls rather than one who succeeds. Silvio desires immortality, a desire that has its repetition in the Darwinian continuation of beneficial traits. Silvio laments

> Pero esta vida mediocre . . . Ser olvidado cuando muera, esto sí que es horrible. ¡Ah, si mis inventos dieran resultado! Sin embargo, algún día me moriré, y los trenes seguirán caminando, y la gente irá al teatro como siempre, y yo estaré muerto, bien muerto . . . muerto para toda la vida. (1981, 71)

> [this mediocre life . . . to be forgotten when I die, that's is what's horrible. If only my inventions would turn out. Nevertheless, someday I'll

die, and the trains will keep running, people will go to the theatre like always, and I'll be dead, really dead, dead forever.]

Silvio's subsequent betrayal of Rengo stems from his attempt to find some way to keep from the death in life he describes here. In a sense, it serves as his attempt to immortalize himself, or, in a Darwinian sense, to continue his genetic line rather than die without any kind of progeny. Nevertheless, as with Silvio's failures in science, one senses that Silvio will be one of those that fall rather than regenerate themselves. The final image of the novel supports such an interpretation:

> —Perfectamente: yo le ayudaré y le conseguiré un puesto en Comodoro; pero ahora váyase porque tengo que trabajar. Le escribiré pronto . . . ¡Ah!, y no pierda su alegría; su alegría es muy linda . . .
> Y su mano estrechó fuertemente la mía. Tropecé con una silla . . . y salí. (1981, 116)
>
> [Fine, I'll help you find a job in Comodoro; but leave me now because I have to work. I'll write to you soon . . . Ah! And don't lose your joy; your joy is very refreshing"—and his hand shook mine vigorously. I tripped over a chair . . . and kept on going.] (2002, 151)

The happiness Silvio claims to have found through his betrayal of Rengo is made ironic as he trips on his way out of the room. More importantly, however, through direct reference to Darwin as well as the inclusion of scenes and episodes that evoke Darwinian theories, Arlt has created a world in which some "se regeneran," or are selected while some "caen." Silvio's trip and literal fall over the chair suggest his inclusion among the latter.

The effect of this Darwinian discourse is very different from the inclusion of other types of science in the novel. While Arlt certainly questions science's power and value, not only in *El juguete rabioso*, but in other works as well, he continues to use science as a rhetorical support in his creation of narrative reality. Indeed, Arlt uses Darwin as a password that allows him entrance to the same cultural and narrative space as his predecessors, that Foucauldian "régime of truth" from which his novel could produce true statements about the world. Even so, and as just as his predecessors did, Arlt manipulates the cultural and literary structures of scientific discourse as he pronounces different truths from those that came before. If Mansilla based his version of Argentine reality on phrenology and anthropology, Arlt bases his depiction of human reality in part on the scientific authority of Charles Darwin through a similar system of direct reference to scientific authority and inclusion of situations and episodes that draw on the explanations Darwin's theories provided.

On a separate, more metaphysical, level, one can interpret his inclusion of Darwin as consistent with his other uses of science. The critique of science that we see through Silvio's use and misuse of scientific models can be seen to stem from larger metaphysical concerns that plagued Arlt, a sense of existential anguish that runs throughout Arlt's work.[13] The failure of science in the case of Silvio signals larger failures in the institutions and beliefs of society as a whole. Silvio's disillusionment with science evident in the last section of the novel becomes a disillusionment with all those things in which society has exhibited faith. The use of references to Darwin in order to construct a narrative reality based on natural selection further strengthens that conception of a world without an overarching meaning, one reduced to an existential struggle between its members that ultimately results in their literal fall.

These attitudes come to fruition in Arlt's later works, where both the menace of science and Arlt's existential anguish become much more pronounced. Science does not merely fail to justify society's faith in it, in the form of chemistry (metonymically represented by gas warfare) it actively works for the destruction of human beings. The human being's search for meaning similarly turns more violent. If Silvio's attempt to find meaning leads him to treason, Erdosain's leads him to senseless murder. In both we see Arlt's elaboration of a theory of exaltation based on self-abasement, but in *Los lanzallamas* we see the theory taken to an extreme. In the same way, science as a literary image used in narrative has become a more extreme manifestation of the breakdown of societal institutions. The use of scientific discourse serves, then, Arlt's metaphysical concerns as it also aids in the construction of a narrative reality.

In his 1980 novel *Respiración artificial*, Ricardo Piglia's alter ego Emilio Renzi proclaims the following in a discussion about Argentine letters in the nineteenth and twentieth centuries, "El que abre, el que inaugura [the twentieth century], es Roberto Arlt. Arlt empieza de nuevo: es el único escritor verdaderamente moderno que produjo la literatura argentina del siglo XX" (Piglia 2001, 133). [He that opens, that inaugurates is Roberto Arlt. Arlt starts afresh: he is the only truly modern writer that produced twentieth-century Argentine literature.] Renzi, and presumably his author, judging from Piglia's other work on Arlt, use Arlt's innovative literary technique as the basis for their claim.[14] Nevertheless, the inventor's blend of "test tube terror" with rhetorical strategies that exploit the cultural authority of scientific discourse set the stage for many of the Argentine writer that would follow. Arlt's amalgamation of scientific background, literary goals, and disdain for positivistic ideals finds an able successor in Ernesto Sabato, the one Argentine writer included in this study who completed academic training in a scientific discipline. Sabato's subsequent break with science has become legendary, owing especially to Sabato's tendency to repeat the story in his novels and essays. He took his doctorate in physics studying under luminaries like Bernardo Houssay (Argentina's Nobel prize winner) and then graduating to a prestigious position at the Curie institute in Paris. While in Paris, he came into contact with the surrealists who were active at the time and began to doubt the value of his scientific training. He decided to abandon his profession and move back to Argentina where he lived in a hut without running water outside of Córdoba while he dedicated himself to his writing. Sabato's link to science has always been his biography; he has famously rejected any connection between science and literature, always dismissing science as irrelevant to literary objectives.[15] Indeed, his most widely read novel, *El túnel* gives no indication of its author's scientific training.

It is precisely the example of Arlt that lets us appreciate better Sabato's place within the ongoing relationship between Argentine narrative and scientific discourse. Sabato's coupling of a philosophical rejection of science with his own extensive scientific background follows the pattern we have seen in Arlt, a fellow disaffected practitioner of science. We can appreciate the echoes of Arlt especially in the manner in which Sabato exploits the authority of his scientific training to challenge what he views as a misinformed cultural enthusiasm for science and scientific progress. We will turn briefly to a consideration of Sabato's work as an appreciation of Arlt's ongoing influence in Argentine narrative.

The connection between Sabato and Arlt need not be invented here. In one of the several literary discussions in Sabato's second novel *Sobre Héroes y Tumbas*, the character Bruno makes the following observation about the nature of Argentine literature:

> Aparte de que Güiraldes es argentino por su preocupación metafísica. Eso es característico: ya sea Hernández, ya sea Quiroga, ya sea Roberto Arlt.

—¿Roberto Arlt?—
—No le quepa ninguna duda. Muchos tontos creen que es importante por su pintoresquismo. No, Martín, casi todo lo que en él es pintoresco es un defecto. Es grande a pesar de eso. Es grande por la formidable tensión metafísica y religiosa de los monólogos de Erdosain. (1968, 189)

["Güiraldes is Argentine due to his metaphysical concerns. This is typical, whether it be Hernández, Quiroga or Roberto Arlt."
"Roberto Arlt?"
"Don't doubt it. Most fools think he's important because of his picturesque qualities. No, Martin, that aspect of his work is almost completely defective. He's great in spite of that. He is great because of the immense metaphysical and religious tension of his monologues."]

Sabato creates a kind of literary genealogy for himself in this passage. He makes metaphysics the criteria for truly Argentine literature and then situates Arlt in a prominent position in that genealogy. He is especially concerned with the interpretation of Arlt as he makes a point of describing misunderstandings of Arlt's importance and then presenting his criteria as the accurate reading of the Argentine writer. Sabato's emphasis on Arlt also converts the latter in a literary forebear of sorts as Sabato is clearly describing a vein in Argentine literature that culminates in his own metaphysically obsessed novels. The association Sabato claims becomes more profound when we consider that application of that "preocupación metafísica" to the place of science and positivism in Argentine culture and literature.

Arlt's presence in *Sobre Héroes y Tumbas* extends beyond an allusion in one of Bruno's soliloquies. In "Informe sobre ciegos," the third section of the novel that describes the character Fernando's insane attempt to write a treatise on blindness, we find an image that ties Sabato's novel back into *Los lanzallamas*. As Fernando watches Celestino Iglesias, the ironically named scientist and subject of his report, he remembers:

Y quién sabe si esa idea, cada día más obsesionante no fue apoderándose de mi subconciencia hasta actuar por fin, como dije, en forma de invisible pero poderoso campo magnético, determinando en alguno de los seres que entran en él lo que yo más deseaba en ese momento de mi vida: el accidente de la ceguera. Examinando las circunstancias en que Iglesias manipulaba aquellos ácidos, recuerdo que la explosión fue precedida por mi entrada en el laboratorio y por la repentina, casi por la violenta idea de que si Iglesias se acercaba al mechero de Bunsen ocurriría una explosión. (1968, 277–78)

[And who knows if that idea, increasingly obsessive didn't end up overpowering my subconscious until it acted like, as I said, an invisible but powerful magnetic field, causing in one of the people that entered in it that which I most desired at that point of my life: blindness. Examining now the circumstances in which Iglesias was handling those acids, I remember that the explosion was preceded by my entrance in the laboratory and by the sudden, almost by the violent idea that if Iglesias approached the Bunsen burner there would be an explosion.]

Fernando's musings on his own metaphysical responsibility deflect the effect somewhat, but the passage is still striking in that it describes a chemist blinded by the science that he practices. This laboratory accident that causes blindness is the same as the trauma suffered by the hapless beggar in Arlt's work that wanders about with his "Blinded by Science" sign testifying of the mishap that came as a result of his scientific aspirations. Iglesias suffers a similar fate, condemned to blindness because of his inability to recognize science's inherent dangers. Sabato's location of blindness as a result of chemical accidents further links his work into the tradition he had described earlier in the novel. The rest of "Informe sobre ciegos" fortifies this central image of science as threatening with Fernando's "scientific" report turning equally more ludicrous and menacing as the section progresses.[16]

This critique of science becomes, for Arlt and Sabato, an identifying characteristic of Argentine literature, the loss of faith in scientific promise concomitant with a more generalized metaphysical crisis. It would also seem to presage an end of test tube envy in their works if not in all of Argentine narrative. Indeed, were it not for what we saw in Arlt's use of Darwin and chemistry, we would assume that this condemnation of science as a positive force in Argentine narrative signaled the end of a discursive practice along with the demise of positivistic faith in science. While Sabato does not simply repeat Arlt in his use of scientific discourse, he does follow that example in his own use of scientific language.[17] In that practice specifically, we can still observe similar echoes of test tube envy in his critique of science, especially in his autobiographical and semiautobiographical work.

Throughout his essays and certainly in the semiautobiographical

Abaddón el Exterminador, Sabato carefully crafts a persona based on the image of the writer as a reformed scientist.[18] The novel is itself a loosely organized string of discussions that deal with Bruno (a character held over from *Sobre héroes y tumbas*) and Sabato's search for meaning (or recognition of the lack of meaning) as they deal with horrific stories of human cruelty. *Abaddón*'s early 1970s Argentine context provides a particularly grim view of the human situation. As they discuss the reality of their existential searches, the characters make several references to Sabato's experiences as a scientist in their discussions, culminating in Sabato (the character) relating his decision to leave science:

> Trabajaba en el Laboratorio Curie como uno de esos curas que están dejando de creer pero que siguen celebrando misa mecánicamente, a veces angustiados por la inautenticidad.
> —Te noto distraído—Me observaba Goldstein, con la escrutadora y temerosa expresión con que un buen amigo del cura, teológicamente ortodoxo, lo hubiese estudiado durante la celebración de la misa.
> —No ando bien—le explicaba—. Nada bien.
> Lo que en cierto modo era verdad. Y así un día llegué hasta el extremo de manipular con descuido el actinium, del que durante varios años llevé luego el pequeño pero peligroso estigma en un dedo. (1975, 277)

> [I worked in the Curie Laboratory like one of those priests that is losing his faith but keeps celebrating the mass mechanically, at times tortured by inauthenticity.
> "You look distracted," Goldstein would say, with that searching and fearful expression of the priest's good friend who is theologically orthodox and would have been watching him during those masses.
> "I'm not doing very well," I would explain, "not very well at all."
> Which was true. And one day I went so far as to handle actinium carelessly, causing a small but dangerous stigmata on my finger that would accompany me for years.]

Sabato continues, narrating his slide into alcoholism and his eventual abandonment of science despite the economic uncertainty that such a decision caused him and his family. The passage itself is a mixture of scientific criticism built on the authority of one who has personally experienced science from the inside. Just as with the nineteenth-century writers that we have studied, Sabato builds a character who can speak with authority because of the scientific knowledge that he possesses. Just as with Arlt, Sabato creates a situation in which the criticism of science gains power because it comes from someone who knows it firsthand. In this passage, Sabato uses his authority as practitioner of science to empower his conversion of science as objective, truth finding and telling practice into that of a doubt-ridden religion. Sabato presents us with a scientist at work in one of the discipline's most prestigious laboratories, handling material whose name he knows because of his scientific experience. He then subverts science as a rigorous discipline by couching its description in religious metaphors that upend science's claim to objectivity. The authenticity of the situation is what makes the comparison of scientific study and religious practice all the more damning for science as a discourse of power, repeating the paradox we saw in Arlt where scientific reference privileges a narrative whose rhetorical goal is the destruction of science as a discourse of power. The play between the fictional character Sabato and the extratextual fact that Sabato is relating a story based on personal experience only strengthens the authenticity that sanctions his critique.

In fact, Sabato's nonfictional description of the experience in his memoir, *Antes del fin*, is remarkable precisely because of how little it differs from its relation in his "novel" Abaddón. Rather than provide any details that would distinguish between the fictional and nonfictional relations of the event, Sabato merely retells the experience in much the same manner as he did in his novel, merely adding some details:

> En el Laboratorio Curie, en una de las más altas metas a las que podía aspirar un físico, me encontré vacío de sentido. . . .
> La beca me fue trasladada al Massachussets Institute of Technology, . . . donde publiqué un trabajo sobre rayos cósmicos. . . . [Pero cuando] tomé la decisión de abandonar la ciencia, recibí durísimas críticas de los científicos más destacados del país. El doctor Houssay me retiró el saludo para siempre . . . Y Guido Beck, emigrado austriaco, discípulo de Einstein en una carta se lamenta diciendo: «En su caso, perdemos en usted un físico muy capaz en el cual tuvimos muchas esperanzas.
> El mundo de los teoremas y un trabajo sobre rayos cósmicos que acababa de publicar en la *Physical Review* apenas se divisaban en la inmensa polvareda. (2002a, 73–74)

> [In the Curie Laboratory, one of a physicist's highest aspirations, I found myself empty. . . .
> My grant was transferred to MIT, . . . where I published an article about

cosmic rays.... When I decided to abandoned science, I was the brunt of severe criticism from my country's most important scientists. Doctor Houssay cut me off completely.... Guido Beck, Austrian immigrant, disciple of Einstein, wrote in a letter "In this case we lost a very capable physicist in whom we had a great deal of hope."]

Sabato loads the narration with a series of references that give the impression of his status as a leading scientist in Argentina. He notes that his position at the Curie Laboratory is one of the "más altas metas" to which a physicist could aspire and then notes that he transferred to MIT, casually dropping the names of two of the most prestigious scientific institutions in the world. He mentions his scientific publication twice, emphasizing the title of the journal in the second instance in a gesture further emphasizes the importance of a contribution to science that, in the end, consists of a single paper. His description of the reaction of his colleagues further underscores his position as an important scientist. Not only do physicists connected with Einstein lament his loss but, as Sabato repeats several times in *Abaddón*, Argentina's most prestigious scientist, Bernardo Houssay, is personally offended by his decision. The rather obvious self-aggrandizement that occurs in this passage casts light on the textual dynamics at work in *Abaddón* where Sabato (the character and the author, it would seem) presents a biting criticism of the scientific worldview that garners its authority from the speaker's scientific formation.

Sabato complements this autobiographical strategy with a similar use of scientific reference in his essays. His description of the history of science and scientific thought in *Hombres y engranajes* is probably the best example of Sabato's Arlt-like attack on science. In the essay, he compares scientific positivism with capitalism and condemns both as responsible for much of the evil he sees in the world and specifically for the "deshumanización" against which he warns in the entire text. The essay can actually be interpreted as an attack on nineteenth-century test tube envy in its most blatant form, an attack that includes the ideas held by all of the nineteenth-century writers discussed in this book.[19] In this direct attack on a long-standing tendency in Argentine letters, we find a series of moments in which Sabato employs textual strategies similar to those we saw in *Abaddón* that we will pause to explore briefly.

Sabato is particularly vehement about science enthusiasts who do not understand the science that they champion. Note his condemnation of positivistic thinkers:

Lo que se quiere destacar aquí es cómo llegó a dominar la mentalidad de la ciencia y cómo cayó en los extremos más grotescos cuando se aplicó en las regiones alejadas de la materia bruta. Y la curiosa pero explicable paradoja de que sus más fanáticos defensores sean los hombres que menos la conocen. Al fin y al cabo, los primeros que en el siglo XX comenzaron a dudar de la ciencia fueron los matemáticos y físicos de modo que cuando todo el mundo empezaba a tener ciega fe en el conocimiento científico sus más avanzados *pioneers* empezaban a dudar de él. Compárese la cautela de físicos como Eddington con la certeza de un medico, que usa toda clase de ondas y rayos con la impávida tranquilidad que da su total desconocimiento. (2002b, 43)

[What should be emphasized here is how the scientific mentality came to dominate and how it went to the most grotesque extremes when it was applied to areas far from brute material. And the curious but explicable paradox that its most fanatical defenders are those that least understand it. After all, the very first to begin to doubt science in the twentieth century were the mathematicians and physicists so that just when the world began to have blind faith in scientific knowledge, its most advanced pioneers began to doubt it. Compare the caution of physicists like Eddington with the certainty of a medical doctor that uses all kinds of waves and rays with the unflappable calm that comes from complete ignorance.]

The attack Sabato unleashes focuses precisely, then, on the nineteenth century figures we have studied thus far, people that understand science a little, but have more in common with those doctors that do not understand their instruments. Sabato bases his criticism on an important distinction between the people who believe in the cultural authority of science and those who actually understand that science, a distinction we saw Mansilla attempt to make in the previous century albeit with much less training than Sabato. The invocation of the authority of the scientist, a strategy used by the people he criticizes, is immediately apparent as well. Not only does Sabato call upon the generic "pioneers" of science for proof, he does so specifically with a reference to Sir Arthur Eddington, one of the leading astrophysicists of the early twentieth century. Sabato's argument is further strengthened by the autobiography that not only stands behind his voice as essayist but also permeates his fiction. That is, not only is Sabato right because of the scientists that agree with him, Sabato is right because, according to his autobiography, he should be considered as among those "pioneers" of early twentieth-century science. In the end, Sabato may have abandoned his scientific career, but he does not leave behind a dependence on the cultural authority of science. In that sense, Sabato forms part of the Argentine literary tradition in much more than just a preoccupation with the metaphysical.

Carlos Dubner, in his article on science and Sabato, muses on the former physicist's outright rejection of any relationship between science and literature, noting that Sabato always rejects science while embracing literature (1983, 684). Indeed, Sabato does precisely that in several instances in his essays and in his novels. His attack on scientific enthusiasts is an element of a wider attack on any who would embrace science as an answer to metaphysical questions. Therein lies the paradox that we saw in Arlt. For all of Sabato's work against science, he ends up confirming its authority on a number of fronts. On one level, his argument merely confirms the existence of the larger trend, that is, Sabato voice shouts at the wind of scientific enthusiasm as he implies throughout *Hombres y engranajes* where he laments positivism as a gross misunderstanding of scientific principle. At the same time, his argument does not end test tube envy as a narrative reality in Argentine literature. Not only will it continue, but Sabato himself depends on it in a manner similar to Arlt. While Sabato escapes more nineteenth century expressions of test tube envy that we see endure in Arlt (like his use of Darwin's theory of natural selection) he does not escape the tendency to use his status as scientist as the basis his critique of science. Even as he produces one of the most scathing critiques of the cultural authority of science seen in Argentine literature, the dynamics of test tube envy continue to operate. Sabato becomes, then, an excellent example of the way in which Arlt guided Argentine narrative, not only in his predilection for metaphysics, but in a critique of scientific positivism that does not escape the cultural power of science. Piglia's observation that Arlt marked a beginning in twentieth-century Argentine narrative finds support in the example of Sabato even as that example also shows the important lines of power that link the authors into the nineteenth century.

While Piglia is right to argue that Arlt acts as a trailblazer on many levels of Argentine literary history, his use of science links him to a chain of authors who looked to the authoritative sciences of their times as they attempted to build textual authority for their conceptions of reality and their ideological projects. To be sure, his innovative use of science against itself in *Los siete locos/Los lan-*

zallamas not only reflects the new ambiguities of the twentieth century but also underscores his many narrative and thematic advances as well. Additionally, Arlt's profound sense of existential anguish marks an important difference not only in his narrative, but also in his construction of a scientific discourse that reflects that anguish. Here is a clear development in the use of scientific discourse as narrative model. Where the nineteenth-century authors used scientific discourse for mainly political goals, Arlt sees in science a reflection of his own tortured soul. But where Arlt's metaphysics reveal a rupture in the ideological function of scientific discourse in Argentine narrative, his use of Darwin to attack the ideal of civilized urban life suggests an important continuity. The debate on civilization and barbarism seen in Sarmiento, Mármol, Mansilla, and throughout the nineteenth century appears again in Arlt. Even so, while Arlt presents his own idiosyncratic views on civilization, he follows the same rules of engagement used by his predecessors: the development of a system of scientific discourse that qualified literary statements as culturally "true." Perhaps this narrative presentation of a science that is both authoritative and destructive best reveals Arlt's devastating vision of society. While science as a discipline is fundamentally flawed, resulting in the destruction and debasement of human beings, its place in Argentine society's "régime of truth" is unchanged. Both Arlt and Sabato seem to argue that science will inexorably destroy the society and culture whose "truths" it continues to construct and uphold. For that reason, the effect we see literature exercise on science has also changed from one that focused on shaping the practice of science to one that took science as it was practiced in society and concentrated on containing its ability to exercise authority within Argentine society.

5
Borges's Scientific Discipline

ANY DISCUSSION OF ARGENTINE LITERATURE AND SCIENCE, OR EVEN Latin American literature and science in general, inevitably arrives at the work of Jorge Luis Borges. Indeed, one finds more critical work devoted to the relationship of science and literature in Borges's writing than to all the authors considered in this study combined. N. Katherine Hayles's early work on Borges and field theory in her classic *The Cosmic Web* (1984) and Floyd Merrell's book on Borges and the new physics have been joined by dozens of articles highlighting the apparent similarities between ideas described in his stories and various theories in twentieth-century science. In much of this work, Borges is held up as an almost prophetic genius whose anticipation of developments in quantum mechanics and chaos theory borders on the uncanny. In that, Borges seems to many to be a prime example of Michel Serres's contention that literature can describe a scientific theory well before scientists make the corresponding "discovery."[1] Others focus on the presence of scientific influence in Borges, enumerating and describing the possible scientific sources for Borges's ideas with some critics extending their analysis to the interacting social discourses that both exercise and receive influence as a function of the scientific ideas apparently at work in Borges's texts. In fact, when scientists themselves write about Borges, especially those from Argentina, they never fail to mention that excerpts from his work appear as epigraphs and examples throughout their physics textbooks and even in several scientific articles.[2] In the field of literature and science, both within Hispanism and in international literary studies, Borges can be considered as one of the foundational authors whose work has offered unique and essential grist for the critical mill.

At the same time, his tendency to draw into question human attempts to describe the universe and his radical destabilization of literary attempts to construct authority not only make his inclusion in this study difficult, they would appear to problematize the entire precept of "test tube envy" as an important element in Argentine narrative.[3] How do we connect Sarmiento's use of popular science in a textual construction of authority with an author who self-consciously dismantles any such attempt, not only in the philosophies he considers but also in his own writing? For that matter, how do we understand the contribution science might make to Borges's textual development of cultural authority when even the most fervent Borges/Science enthusiasts admit that many of the similarities between physics and Borges's stories are either intellectual coincidence or separate results of a shared cultural and philosophical heritage? Can we call the appearance of ideas similar to Hugh Everett's many worlds theory of quantum mechanics, chaos theory, and fractals in a story like "El jardín de senderos que se bifurcan" test tube envy if the story precedes the scientific theories by several years? Obviously not. But neither can we leave Borges aside in a consideration of the evolving and continuing power dynamic between popular science and Argentine narrative. In fact, upon closer investigation, we discover several different veins in the relationship between the Argentine author's work and science. While he certainly calls into question science's ability to construct workable descriptions of the universe, he also, paradoxically, used those descriptions to bolster his own arguments in a number of cases in his earlier work.

In this chapter, then, I propose three distinct goals. One is the appreciation of a nineteenth-century test tube envy that would lend credence to the argument in *Respiración artificial*'s discussion of Argentine literary history that Borges was the nation's best nineteenth-century author (130).[4] While Borges would move quickly from this practice later on, we see him deploy science and scientific discourse in a variety of texts from his early books *Discusión* (1932) and *Historia de la eternidad* (1936) in a way that emphasizes the disciplinary nature of power that Foucault describes and from which the idea of test tube envy springs, applied within a philosophical setting. My second aim is to chart and understand better the development of an antiscientific stance in his work, one that appears both to continue and develop the antiscientific stance we saw articulated in Roberto Arlt's work and would see in Borges's contemporary writer Sabato. Finally, I will turn to a phenomenon in the science and literature criticism dedicated to Borges's work where the clearest case of test tube envy related to Borges appears as critics garner prestige for the author by associating his work with science. In all three objectives, I will focus on a series of texts from all periods of Borges's work. By so doing, I hope to show how Borges not only suggests new directions in which Argentine narrative develops, especially in its relationship to science, but how he also provides examples of unexpected continuity with the nineteenth century.

The title I have chosen for this chapter emphasizes this tripartite structure and will encompass different meanings at different points. The initial meaning is one related to the concept of test tube envy. If, as Foucault argues, "Discipline organizes an analytical space" (1977, 143), literature can use scientific discourse to discipline textual spaces in which analysis occurs, setting up régimes that control the philosophical production of "truth." Understood in that light, scientific discipline is the discipline that scientific thought exercises on the literary and philosophical mind rather than Foucault's analysis of the discipline of the social and physical body. Nevertheless, his theoretical model is useful for understanding the power dynamics in Borges's work and it is within this definition that we see Borges's early test tube envy operate. As he explores the history of ideas in his early essays, we see a marked use of science, and particularly mathematics, to check ideas opposed to his own. Science, for this younger Borges, keeps certain philosophies in line, principally in the case of Nietzsche. As the Argentine author then proceeds in his later writings to criticize science's ability to determine what is true, his scientific discipline changes its nature. Borges takes science and scientific discourse to the woodshed, so to speak, and uses a literary discourse that sets severe limits on science's ability to guarantee truth about reality. Scientific discipline in this vein now places scientific discourse in the role of the offender in need of correction. Finally, in recent literary criticism about (rather than by) Borges, we see his writing brought into line with science. The critical interpretation of his work as proto-scientific functions as a gesture that could be said to discipline the critical and popular reception of his work. Borges, in a sense, is "rescued" by these critics who attempt to invest his work with more cultural authority by associating it with privileged modes of societal discourse, a kind of reinsertion of Borges within the power structure that scientific discourse provides in Argentina.

Borges's own intellectual interest in science has been assumed, dismissed, and documented (sometimes simultaneously) in Borges criticism. As Leo Corry shows, specific references to contemporary physics appear sporadically in his work, suggesting a familiarity with the popular literature of science if not a profound understanding of the principles the literature discusses.[5] Eduardo Ortiz argues that Albert Einstein's visit to Buenos Aires in 1925 likely fed into an early interest, if not enthusiasm, for the advances in physics that Einstein represented.[6] His 1938 review of Einstein's theories in *El Hogar* indicates as much, even if it does little to show any real understanding of the physicist's work.[7] We will return to Borges's work on Einstein later in the chapter, but we can safely state that Borges was not only aware of contemporary science but also writing about it on occasion. Importantly for the goals of this study, he also incorporated contemporary science in a number of his early articles in such a way as to forward his own peculiar philosophical interests.

In *Discusión*, one of the few early collections of essays that survived Borges subsequent suppression of that period of his writing, we find two essays dedicated to an evaluation of Zeno's famous paradoxes and their various refutations. In "La perpetua carrera de Aquiles y la tortuga," Borges evaluates the series of objections to the Greek philosopher's argument that the fastest runner will never catch the slowest turtle if the turtle has a head start. Zeno explains the paradox by pointing out that the runner, Achilles, would have to transverse an infinite number of points in order to catch the tortoise. In "Avatares de la tortuga," Borges considers the related paradox that all movement is impossible as one would have to cross that same infinite space to get anywhere. In both essays, Borges considers the objections by thinkers from Aristotle to Bertrand Russell, sometimes admiringly but always returning to the idea that Zeno's paradoxes are ultimately irresolvable.[8] We also see a use of mathematical discourse that exhibits what could be considered a peculiar case of test tube envy, in this case more an envy of the apparently objective ability of mathematics and numbers to enunciate truth where language evidently cannot. As both essays offer similar examples of this strategy, I will concentrate my analysis on "La perpetua carrera de Aquiles y la tortuga."

Throughout "La perpetua carrera" Borges shifts between three registers of language, one that functions on a literary level, a second that employs more precise mathematical and philosophical terminology, and a third that employs numbers and variables in mathe-

5: BORGES'S SCIENTIFIC DISCIPLINE 129

matical expression. His discussion of John Stuart Mill's refutation of the paradox displays all three at once:

> No anteveo el parecer del lector, pero estoy sintiendo que la proyectada refutación de Stuart Mill no es otra cosa que una exposición de la paradoja. Basta fijar la velocidad de Aquiles a un segundo por metro, para establecer el tiempo que necesita.
> $$10 + 1 + 1/10 + 1/100 + 1/1000 + 1/10.000 \ldots$$
> El límite de la suma de esta infinita progresión geométrica es doce (más exactamente, once y un quinto: más exactamente, once con tres veinticincoavos), pero no es alcanzado nunca. Es decir, el trayecto del héroe será infinito y éste correrá para siempre, pero su derrotero se extenuará antes de doce metros, y su eternidad no verá la terminación de doce segundos. (1996, vol. 1, 245)

> [I cannot predict the reader's opinion, but my feeling is that mill's projected refutation is nothing more than an exposition of the paradox. Achilles' speed need only be set as a second per meter to determine the time needed:
> $$10 + 1 + 1/10 + 1/100 + 1/1000 + 1/10.000 \ldots$$
> The limit of the sum of this infinite geometric progression is twelve (plus, exactly eleven and one-fifth; plus, exactly eleven times three twenty-fifths), but it is never reached. That is, the hero's course will be infinite and he will run forever, but he will give up before twelve meters, and his eternity will not see the end of twelve seconds.] (1999, 44)

Borges introduces the section with a strong authorial presence that emphasizes personal reaction and feeling to what has been presented as a mathematical and philosophical problem. However, instead of continuing in that register, he shifts to a mathematical illustration of the heart of Zeno's paradox. The shift creates a sense of failure in the first mode of expression, an inability to explain fully what had initially been described as a feeling. Borges then follows the mathematical expression with a more precise linguistic explanation of the phenomenon, one that eschews the very personal views expressed at the beginning for a discourse that complements the objectivity of the numbers he previously used. He continues this strategy throughout the essay, most clearly in his presentation of Bertrand Russell's discussion where he lists two corresponding series of numbers as an illustration of the infinite mathematical operations that exist within an otherwise finite set (I, 247).

Borges's discussion of Russell also includes a situation in which the Argentine writer invests the English thinker with the authority of a scientist. Borges introduces the mathematical discussion of Russell's ideas mentioned earlier with a passage that emphasizes Russell's qualifications as mathematician and scientific spokesperson:

> Arribo, por eliminación, a la única refutación que conozco, a la única de inspiración condigna del original, virtud que la estética de la inteligencia está reclamando. Es la formulada por Russell. La encontré en la obra nobilísima de William James, *Some Problems of Philosophy*, y la concepción total que postula puede estudiarse en los libros ulteriores de su inventor—*Introduction to Mathematical Philosophy*, 1919; *Our Knowledge of the External World*, 1926—, libros de una lucidez inhumana, insatisfactorios e intensos. (vol. 1, 246)

> [Here I reach, by elimination, the only refutation I know, the only inspiration worthy of the original, a virtue indispensable for the aesthetics of intelligence: the one formulated by Bertrand Russell. I found it in the noble work of William James (Some Problems of Philosophy) and the total conception it postulates can be studied in the previous books of its inventor—*Introduction to Mathematical Philosophy*, 1919; *Our Knowledge of the External World*, 1926—unsatisfactory, intense books, inhumanly lucid.] (1999, 45–46)

Borges presents Russell not only as an intellectual who has thoughtfully challenged Zeno, but as the author of important mathematical and scientific treatises. The incorporation of bibliography, in this case bibliography that actually exists, functions in a way not dissimilar to the method of scientific citation seen in earlier Argentine writers. Borges's description of his discovery of Russell's work also contributes to this similarity. Just as Mansilla recounted the personal effort that qualified him as one who knew about the Ranquel tribe, Borges emphasizes the actions that allow him to incorporate scientific ideas in his philosophical discussions. Borges's analysis of Zeno and Russell gains influence because of the personal research that backs up that analysis.

The use of numbers and mathematical expression highlights a complementary use of mathematics in the building of rhetorical influence. The shift to formulae as an explanatory strategy contributes to the construction of an authorial persona that is, in part, a mathematician who best explains himself through numbers. Borges as that author is, then, uniquely qualified to speak about the matter as his use of mathematics elevates him to the ranks of the thinkers that he discusses. The use of numbers also highlights a second element in the essay: the failure of language to explain adequately a particular concept. As we saw in the first passage from the essay, Borges shifts from a literary tone to mathematics when the language seems unable to express the idea that he attempts to express. It is only after he resorts to the series of fractions that he can then speak about the concept. It is perhaps in this aspect that we can see most clearly a kind of literary envy for the assumedly objective ability of mathematical discourse.

The critique he proffers of the books, the ambivalent and almost joking tones that he uses as he introduces the ideas also create a situation that is both unique and, paradoxically, a continuation of the literary practice under examination. Borges creates a textual persona familiar with mathematics and the literature of mathematics who also possesses an intelligence that surpasses the concepts described therein. In that sense, the persona Borges creates goes beyond the nineteenth century scientific persona so important to *Facundo* and *Una excursión a los indios ranqueles*. Borges combines the scientific familiarity that granted privilege to Sarmiento's writings with a critical perspective of science that hints at the pessimistic view of science that Arlt had developed in his work. Furthermore, the literary judgment Borges passes on Russell's writing serves a final function. Not only has science strengthened a textual position, Borges has enveped Russell's scientific writing within his much more stylized textual world. Such an inclusion, with its concomitant reduction in cultural authority, presages the critique Borges would later make of any special truth-producing ability that science might enjoy.

"Avatares de la tortuga" presents many of the same arguments with the same textual strategies discussed. In fact, Borges uses entire sections of prose in both essays, not surprising when we remember that the articles were prepared individually rather than as parts of an intended whole. The repetition of these strategies, and specifically the heavy use of mathematical expression in his explanation of Zeno and his detractors merely reemphasizes their importance within Borges's early textual practice.

The conclusion of both "La perpetua carrera de Aquiles y la tortuga" and "Avatares de la tortuga" is that Zeno's paradoxes are only resolvable if we accept a world based on idealism. While Borges has used mathematics in a way that privileges his ability to draw that conclusion, his distribution of mathematic explanation has served a second, complementary function. By couching both Zeno's paradoxes and the refutations in mathematical expression, Borges creates a textual environment in which the competing theories are equally true (or perhaps equally false). In part, Zeno's paradoxes endure because they can be expressed in the same objective language as their refutations. Again we see a kind of textual leveling that I discussed in the previous paragraph. Zeno's ability to construct truth is strengthened by the sharing of a mathematical discourse whose style links the ancient paradox with the more modern, apparently scientific, objections to that paradox. At the same time, the absurdity of a paradox that so clearly contradicts an empirical observation of movement contaminates the mathematics that endowed it with persuasive power. If mathematical language can describe absurdity as objective fact in the same way that it describes observable reality, it loses part of its cultural ability to enunciate usable truth.

In that complicated flow of cultural authority, we see the fissures in mathematics and scientific thought that would break them apart in Borges's later works. The weakening of science's power to produce objective truth that occurs as a function of Borges's use of mathematical expression will lead, eventually, to texts like "El idioma analítico de John Wilkins" where Borges will explode any ability to quantify or describe objectively the universe. Even so, we cannot categorically state that Borges leaves behind the simpler use of mathematics as a preferred mode for expressing particular ideas. The function of mathematics as an explanatory presence demanded by the periodic failure of language will endure in Borges's work, appearing in texts like "Examen de la obra de Herbert Quain" where he will again resort to numbers and graphs to describe the structure of the fictional author's novels. While the Argentine author will continue to maintain a playful attitude toward the implications of mathematical concepts, especially in stories like "La biblioteca de Babel," he never completely loses an apparent respect for the explanatory power of mathematical expression.[9]

A more complete example of Borges's fleeting test tube envy appears in his essay "La doctrina de los ciclos," appearing in the 1936 collection of essays *Historia de la eternidad*. The essay contains one of Borges's most clearly and carefully planned attacks on Frederich Nietzsche, a philosopher whose work Borges was known to despise.[10] The *doctrina*, as Borges describes it, states, "El número de todos los átomos que componen el mundo es, aunque desmesurado, finito, y sólo capaz como tal de un número finito (aunque desmesurado también) de permutaciones. En un tiempo infinito, el número de las permutaciones posibles debe ser alcanzado, y el universo tiene que repetirse" (1996, vol. 1, 385.) [The number of all the atoms that compose the world is immense but finite, and as such only capable of a finite (though also immense) number of permutations. In an infinite stretch of time, the number of possible permutations must be run through, and the universe has to repeat itself (1999, 115).] Borges then remarks that the idea moves from an "insipid" beginning to a terrifying conclusion and that it is common to attribute the idea to Nietzsche although Nietzsche was certainly not the first to propose the concept. The rest of the essay presents a series of philosophical and scientific challenges to the theory, moving from explanations of the size of an atom to a consideration of Georg Cantor's theories to the implications that the laws of thermodynamics hold for Eternal Return. The essay also considers the positions of Christian, Jewish, and Greek philosophy in relation to Nietzsche. The text concludes with a bibliography that includes both Nietzsche's *Die Unschuld des Werdens* and *Also sprach Zarathustra* as well as Borges's favorite works in popular science by Bertrand Russell and others like *Introduction to Mathematical Philosophy*, *The ABC of Atoms* and *The Nature of the Physical World*.

Most critics have read the essay as one of many that explores the nature of infinity, a concept that would occupy a great deal of the Argentine writer's attention throughout his life and that would serve as the central theme for many of his best known stories, including "Las ruinas circulares" and "El jardín de senderos que se bifurcan" among countless others. In the face of those who have taken the essay as an important articulation of Borges's views on infinity, René DeCosta argues that it is a mistake to take the text seriously, especially when attempting to understand Borges's take on eternity (1999, 35). DeCosta is right in identifying the importance of humor in the essay, but such a stance does not preclude the equal importance of understanding the rhetorical operations of Borges's critique of Nietzsche. If Borges playfully scolds the idea of Eternal Return, the structure of that scolding is tied into a tradition that includes a similar textual disciplining of Juan Manuel Rosas and Facundo Quiroga undertaken by Sarmiento. While we may not have access to Borges's "true" opinions on eternity or entropy, we can appreciate a carefully planned attack on Nietzsche that incorporates elements of a nineteenth-century test tube envy.

One strategy that echoes those elements is the positioning of Borges's caricature of Nietzsche against a series of physicists and mathematicians that the Argentine will invoke in his discussion of the concept. Near the beginning of the essay, Borges immediately turns to Rutherford as a source for his description of the characteristics of atoms:

> Antes de refutarlo—empresa de que ignoro si soy capaz—conviene concebir, siquiera de lejos, las sobrehumanas cifras que invoca. Empiezo por el átomo, El diámetro de un átomo de hidrógeno ha sido calculado, salvo error, en un cienmillonésimo de centímetro. Esa vertiginosa pequeñez no quiere decir que sea indivisible: al contrario, Rutherford lo define según la imagen de un sistema solar, hecho por un núcleo central y por un electrón giratorio, cien mil veces menor que el átomo entero. (1996, vol. 1, 385)

> [Before refuting it—an undertaking of which I do not know if I am capable—it may be advisable to conceive, even from afar, of the superhuman numbers it invokes. I shall begin with the atom. The diameter of a hydrogen atom has been calculated, with some margin of error, to be one hundred millionth of a centimeter. This dizzying tininess does not mean the atom is indivisible; on the contrary Rutherford describes it with the image of a solar system, made up of a central nucleus and a spinning electron, one hundred times smaller than the whole atom.] (1999, 115)

Borges makes a series of textual gestures that incorporate the cultural authority of science within a playful web of authorial presence and absence. His first declaration not only gently mocks his efforts to discredit Nietzsche's ideas, it also separates the authorial "yo" from the declarations of truth that science will then provide. The descriptions of the atoms are then couched in a scientific mode of expression that appears to operate in much the same way as we saw in authors from Sarmiento to Arlt and Sabato, the specificity of the language conferring the authority of science on the statements Borges includes. He further strengthens the authority of his statements with invocation of Rutherford's definition of atomic structure, again a move that echoes Sarmiento's use of Humboldt. Borges adds a wrinkle to the process by stepping out of the way of the language he introduces, situating the scientific description of atoms as anterior to his own, more philosophical, refutation of Nietzsche by doubting his personal ability to refute the German philosopher. Still, the deployment of science in the service of Borges's proverbial axe strengthens the case for the writer's participation in our ongoing story of test tube envy.

Borges' use of scientific authority in this section extends beyond the simple use of language and citation. The weight that he creates for his discussion of atoms is one that simultaneously constructs Nietzsche as a thinker who has not thought through the implications of his theory. Rutherford and the scientific description of atoms inscribe a textual space that excludes Nietzsche by virtue of his ignorance of atomic theory, indeed, by his implicit rejection of it as Borges will later note. In an essay devoted to discrediting a circular notion of time, Nietzsche is characterized as occupying a point in a linear history of ideas previous to the science that makes his theories obsolete. While the discussion of the immense number of atoms in the universe does not necessarily disprove Nietzsche's theory, as Borges will later admit, it does suggest that the person who supports it is not considering the immense variety possible in the universe. Borges remarks after discussing the millions of possible combinations of ten atoms, "Si una partícula casi infinitesimal de universo es capaz de esa variedad, poca o ninguna fe debemos prestar a una monotonía del cosmos" (Vol. 1, 385) [If an almost infinitesimal particle of the universe is capable of such variety, we should lend little or no faith to any monotony in the cosmos] (1999, 116). The use of the exact terminology that endows his statements with the air of scientific authenticity ends up serving double time as a contrast to a perceived sloppiness in Nietzsche's postulation. This position will then strengthen Borges's later criticism that Nietzsche fails to acknowledge the long history of Eternal Return in Western philosophy, suggesting that Nietzsche's intellectual "laziness" combines an ignorance of science with an inability to acknowledge his philosophical debts.

Borges invests his use of scientific terminology with a playful tone that we see in his statement of false modesty concerning his ability to refute Nietzsche and in a subsequent declaration of a lack of the requisite patience involved in computing possible atomic configurations. This play between personal modesty and biting scientific critique absents Borges once again as author from the scientific terminology that appears in his essay. It is in that strategy that we see a key difference between Borges's use of scientific reference, at least in this essay, and the use we have observed in previously considered writers. Instead of suggesting that his authorial persona has the ability to function as a scientist, Borges excludes himself from the scientific scene. While this approach sets him at odds to the other writers we have studied so far, it frees him to combine a deployment of the cultural authority of science with the self-reflexive play and ironic commentary for which the Argentine author is so well known. If Borges will use this textual playfulness to criticize scientific thought severely in subsequent writings, here it enhances science's truth-telling power. In its somewhat isolated sphere, the scientific discourse at work can continue to operate along side Borges's corrosive humor as a complementary line of attack.

The rest of the essay continues in the same vein described above. Borges's first refutation of Nietzsche appears in a consideration of Georg Cantor's mathematical descriptions of infinity.[11] While the atomic theory Borges introduces reveals the somewhat dated quality to Nietzsche's thought, it does not, as noted before, disprove the concept under consideration. Borges turns to Cantor for the "proof" needed to discredit Nietzsche's theory completely. In his presentation of the mathematician's set theory Borges returns to a series of linguistic structures and name-dropping that continue the strategy already seen in his use of Rutherford. He incorporates a series of mathematical formulae as examples of the infinite qualities that Cantor predicted in finite sets, a strategy that endows his philosophical essay with the form of a mathematical treatise in an even more developed strategy than the one we saw in his discussion of Zeno. Borges then continues to incorporate mathematical expression with scientific reference as he strengthens his attack on the German philosopher. Borges's final description of Cantor's theory displays all the aspects of the textual strategy we have discussed:

> La serie de los puntos del espacio (o de los instantes del tiempo) no es ordenable así; ningún número tiene un sucesor o un predecesor inmediato. Es como la serie de los quebrados según la magnitud. ¿Qué fracción enumeraremos después de 1/2? No 51/100 porque 101/200 está más cerca; no 101/200 porque más cerca esta 201/400; no 201/400 porque más cerca . . . Igual sucede con los puntos, según Georg Cantor. Podemos siempre intercalar otros más, un número infinito. Sin embargo, debemos procurar no concebir tamaños decrecientes. Cada punto "ya" es el final de una infinita subdivisión. (1996, vol. 1, 387)

[The series of points in space (or in instants in time) cannot be ordered in the same way: no number has a successor or an immediate predecessor. It is like a series of fractions arranged in order of magnitude. What number will we count after 1/2? Not 51/1000 because 101/200 is closer; not 101/200 because 201/400 is closer; not 201/400, because . . . According to Cantor, the same thing happens with points. We can always interpose more of them, in infinite number. Therefore we must not try to conceive of decreasing sizes. Each point is "already" the final degree of an infinite subdivision.] (1999, 117)

Borges use of fractions here continues his previous use of mathematical forms earlier in his discussion of Cantor that in turn weds Cantor's authority as mathematician with the theories that Borges advances against Nietzsche. In that sense we have a double privileging of Borges's critique. Cantor's mathematical prestige is enhanced by the mathematical expressions used to illustrate his theories. Nietzsche, however, enjoys neither the scientific status nor the explanatory power of the equations. The essay uses this reinforcing gesture to inscribe a rhetorical space where Cantor (and earlier Rutherford) are "right" because they are recognized as mathematicians and scientists. Borges, then, is also "right" because he uses their ideas and, just as importantly, their language. Borges ends the section on Cantor stating: "Si el universo consta de un número infinito de términos, es rigurosamente capaz de un número infinito de combinaciones—y la necesidad de un Regreso queda vencida. Queda su mera posibilidad, computable en cero" (vol. 1, 387). [If the universe consists of an infinite number of terms, it is rigorously capable of an infinite number of combinations—and the need for a Recurrence is done away with. There remains its mere possibility, which can be calculated as zero (1999, 117).] Borges presents his declaration of victory in a combination of Cantor's authority, mathematical calculation, and disciplinary language. The textual battlefield suggested by the phrase "queda vencida" is one configured by mathematics and computation with Nietzsche's failure a direct result of his inability to participate in that discourse.

The rather scientific introduction and refutation of the Nietzsche's thought gives way in the following section of the essay to a more philosophical and personal evaluation of Nietzsche, one replete with references to the Bible and quotations from John Stuart Mill, Saint Augustine, and Miguel de Unamuno. The initial presentation of Nietzsche's ideas seems to serve, then, as a kind of heavy rhetorical artillery that breaches Nietzsche's philosophical defenses and opens him up to the more personal and less scientific analysis that Borges will perform in the essay's second act. Subsequently, the tone of the essay changes substantially, a tone probably best appreciated in Borges's description of the moment Nietzsche proposes Eternal Return:

> Nietzsche quería ser Walt Whitman, quería minuciosamente enamorarse de su destino. Siguió un método heroico: desenterró la intolerable hipótesis griega de la eterna repetición y procuró educir de esa pesadilla mental una ocasión de júbilo. Buscó la idea más horrible del universo y la propuso a la delectación de los hombres. El optimista flojo suele imaginar que es nietzscheano; Nietzsche lo enfrenta con los círculos del eterno regreso y lo escupe así de su boca. (vol. 1, 389)

> [Nietzsche wanted to be Walt Whitman; he wanted to fall minutely in love with his destiny. He adopted a heroic method: he disinterred the intolerable Greek hypothesis of eternal repetition, and he contrived to make this mental nightmare an occasion for jubilation. He sought out the most horrible idea in the universe and offered it up to mankind's delectation. The languid optimist often imagines himself to be a Nietzschean; Nietzsche confronts him with the circles of the eternal recurrence and spits him out of his mouth.] (1999, 120)

Borges's personal characterization of Nietzsche's motives contrasts starkly with the more detached style evident in the mathematical and scientific discussions we saw earlier. At the same time, this change in tone complements his previous strategies. Nietzsche continues to occupy a position anterior to contemporary to scientific discovery in the history of ideas constructed in the essay. Borges associates Nietzsche first with the Greeks, then with the Christian God who similarly expels lukewarm believers from his mouth, but not with the scientists of the nineteenth and twentieth century who, according to the essay, disprove his ideas. The references to scientific theory and specific scientists and mathematicians serve a preparatory role, then, outlining a textual field divided between science haves and have-nots. One recalls Sarmiento's statement following his pseudoscientific discourse on the gauchos, "He necesitado andar todo el camino que dejo recorrido para llegar al punto en que nuestro drama comienza" (1845, 35)[I have found it necessary to traverse this path to arrive at the point where our story begins]. In a

5: BORGES'S SCIENTIFIC DISCIPLINE   139

similar fashion, Borges uses scientific discourse to set up his much more subjective discussion of Nietzsche.

Borges finishes his refutation of the circular doctrine with a similarly circular spiral in the structure of his essay. In the third part, he returns to another scientific basis for his rejection of Nietzsche's theories. Initially he reaffirms Nietzsche's intellectual position as anterior to scientific discovery by remarking "Tampoco habló—y eso merece destacarse también—de la finitud de los átomos" (1996, vol. 1, 385) [Nor did he mention—and this is noteworthy as well—of the finite nature of atoms]. He then alludes to yet another scientific principle that defeats Nietzsche's personal philosophy. Borges concludes his discussion in the third section of the essay:

> Nietzsche recurre a la energía; la segunda ley de la termodinámica declara que hay procesos energéticos que son irreversibles. El calor y la luz no son más que formas de la energía. Basta proyectar una luz sobre una superficie negra para que se convierta en calor. El calor, en cambio, ya no volverá a la forma de luz. Esa comprobación, de aspecto inofensivo o insípido, anula el "laberinto circular" del Eterno Retorno.
> La primera ley de la termodinámica declara que la energía del universo es constante: la segunda, que esa energía propende a la incomunicación, al desorden, aunque la cantidad total no decrece. Esa gradual desintegración de las fuerzas que componen el universo, es la entropía. Una vez igualadas las diversas temperaturas, una vez excluida (o compensada) toda acción de un cuerpo sobre otro, el mundo será un fortuito concurso de átomos. (vol. 1, 391)
>
> [Nietzsche appeals to energy; the second law of thermodynamics declares that some energetic processes are irreversible. Heat and light are no more than forms of energy. It suffices to project a light onto a black surface to convert it into heat. Heat, however, will never return to the form of light. This inoffensive or insipid-seeming proof annuls the "circular labyrinth" of the Eternal Return.
> The first law of thermodynamics declares that the energy of the universe is constant; the second, that this energy tends toward isolation and disorder, though its total quantity does not decrease. This gradual disintegration of the forces that make up the universe is entropy. Once maximum entropy is reached, once different temperatures have been equalized, once any action of one body on another has been neutralized (or compensated for), the world will be a random assemblage of atoms.] (1999, 121–22)

The passage reactivates many of the strategies already in evidence in Borges's use of Rutherford and Cantor. Nietzsche is again shown as incorrect in his reasoning because he does not have access to scientific fact. In this case, even his arguments about energy are contradicted by the scientific laws of thermodynamics that control the energy Nietzsche had used as evidence for his own argument. It is in this instance especially where we see the disciplinary effect of science in Borges's rhetoric. Nietzsche's thought is shown to be unlawful, that is, in violation of the laws of nature that invalidate his proposal. Science, in this case thermodynamics, appears as an accurate description of the universe whose accuracy endows Borges's critique of Nietzsche with a similar claim to truth. The other textual aspects of this use of science remain constant. Borges as authorial presence is absent, his use of personal pronouns and ironic asides have waned to nothing after appearing throughout the second section. Additionally, scientific theory continues to occupy an objective space within the text that authorizes Borges's critique of Nietzsche's ideas. Finally, the specific use of thermodynamics as a concluding argument incorporates the discussion of atoms and their structure that appears at the beginning of the essay, bending the structure of the text into a thematic circle.

The bibliography at the end of the essay, with its inclusion of several contemporary popularizations of science displays yet another gesture of test tube envy in which Borges authorizes the scientific discussion that appears in the pages of "La doctrina de los ciclos." It simultaneously expands the play of authorial absence and presence that we have noted earlier. The bibliography creates the impression that the author/scientists of the books quoted are the speakers of the science used in the essay rather than Borges. This abandons the nineteenth-century construct of the author as man of science and letters or even the narrative persona created by a twentieth century Arlt whose voice combined scientific knowledge with literary expression. In a method that reaffirms his obsession with citation and literary allusion, Borges attempts to disappear behind the texts that provide the science for his discussion. At the same time, however, he uses a bibliography of real books in a discussion of a real philosopher. The apparent gravity of the discussion and its citation of science works, then, to suggest a point in which Borges took quite seriously the rhetorical power of science and used it to privilege his own positions in a way similar to his nineteenth-century forebears regardless of the humor with which he presents his argument.

Lest we take Piglia's comment too much to heart and place

Borges firmly in the nineteenth century, we must also recognize that "La doctrina de los ciclos" is more than an argumentative essay against a particular aspect of Nietzsche's philosophy. As noted earlier, Borges structures his consideration of Nietzsche's cycles in a circular manner, a form that gently ironizes the scientific arguments that he deploys against Nietzsche. For example, the mocking adjective "insípido" appears only twice in the essay, in the first paragraph of the first section and then in the last paragraph of the third. It first modifies the description of Nietzsche's opening arguments, emphasizing the insipid nature of the initial assumptions of the doctrine. It appears at the end once again, this time qualifying the inevitable implications of the second law of thermodynamics: the final heat death of the universe. The circular structure of the essay, emphasized by the linguistic parallels that Borges introduces through careful word choice produces a situation in which the two theories that are meant to disprove one another end up as mirror images. That is, the hopelessness of an eternity of Platonic years is, by and large, the hopelessness of the eventual heat death of the universe as predicted by entropy and the laws of thermodynamics; the immobility implicit in an eternal return to the exact configuration of a finite number of atoms is replaced by the immobility of those atoms that have reached the disorder of absolute entropy as Borges understands it.

It is in that final view of science that we see a Borges much more in line with the developments in twentieth-century Argentine thought already observed in Arlt. If Borges exhibits a clearer sense of test tube envy than even Arlt with his particular use of scientific discourse in "La doctrina de los ciclos," he does not champion science as any kind of philosophical answer. The temporal sequencing of the history of ideas Borges employs as a part of his attack on Nietzsche, placing the German philosopher before modern science, also reflects on the position of science in Borges's thought. The circular structure of the essay is really more of a downward spiral with the rhetorical victory of science occurring with the descent into the static, dead world that its theories apparently predict. The third section ends in the following manner: "La luz se va perdiendo en calor; el universo minuto por minuto se hace invisible. Se hace más liviano, también. Alguna vez ya no será más que calor: calor equilibrado, inmóvil, igual. Entonces habrá muerto" (vol. 1, 391). [Light is gradually lost in the form of heat; the universe, minute by minute is becoming invisible. It grows more inconstant, as well. At some point, it will no longer be anything but heat an equilibrium of immobile, evenly distributed heat. Then it will have died (1999, 122).] Borges claimed that Nietzsche meant to expel the silly optimist from his camp with the concept of Eternal Return. Even so, science's defeat of Nietzsche offers no safe haven for the now beleaguered positivist. In "La doctrina de los ciclos" the lack of an eternal return merely means the eventual paralysis of the universe. Borges's final note, an observation that even if Nietzsche is right, it means absolutely "Nada" for either practice or the thinker, further strengthens this view. Reality, as science describes it, ends up in the same existential absence of hope implied in an unending repetition of events.

Even in this pessimistic evaluation of science, we continue to see an echo of the practice of the nineteenth century that reverberates in a post-Schopenhauerian world. In a manner similar to Arlt's use of Darwin in *El juguete rabioso*, we see modern science used as proof of a negative vision of the world. Science's loss of power to offer hopeful solutions to problems may have disappeared with the decline of positivism, but its inability to do so merely confirms the pessimistic vision that Arlt and others shared during the beginning of the twentieth century. Science need not offer the constructive answers of the previous century to wield cultural influence or create socially valid truth. Borges's use of scientific reference in "La doctrina de los ciclos" would appear to fit within that practice, where his pessimism is only more profound as a result of its grounding in scientific theory. While the hopeful appreciation of science that was prevalent in the nineteenth-century literature has clearly changed profoundly, science's power as a discursive mechanism endures. Science continues as a kind of disciplining mechanism in this case, one that allows and disallows certain modes of thought. In the case of this essay, Nietzsche's thought, and then Nietzsche himself, become unruly bodies subject to the intellectual discipline that science affords. In that sense, the spiral structure of the essay offers a competing interpretation with that afforded by its circularity. The move from objective descriptions of science and mathematics, to a personal description of Nietzsche, back to the impassive language of science creates a situation in which science frames the unlawful subject and where Nietzsche's threatening body is subjected to the discipline of the scientific ideas that quite literally surround it in the essay. From that perspective, parts one and three can be seen as a textual vice around Nietzsche that results in capital punishment, present both in the death of his idea as well as the heat death of the universe. In such a tortured setting, Borges's characterization of Nietzsche's proposal as an attempt to describe the "crucifixion" of immortality is completely appropriate if somewhat chilling. The interplay between Nietzsche and discipline trace the circular structure of the essay, the philosopher first appearing as the offending body, then as one that disciplines others (in this case the *optimista flojo*), and finally returning to the role of the punished body as his ideas fall under the controlling eye of science once again. Foucault's description of the literal control of imprisoned bodies becomes an excellent metaphor for the textual discipline that Borges applies to his philosophical subject.

Still, as we saw in the gentle irony of an essay that uses a circular structure to associate science with the doctrine that it is to have disproved, Borges does not view science as an all-powerful panopticon and would not maintain even a tempered appreciation of science's cultural authority in his later writing. Eventually, the slightly ironic gaze toward science that we begin to appreciate in "La doctrina de los ciclos" would undermine any more pronounced expression of test tube envy in the work of Borges. His subsequent essays and especially his stories would, at times, use mathematics or scientific ideas but never in a way that attempted to tap any kind of cultural authority. Indeed, after "La doctrina de los ciclos," science appears as a theme in Borges only when it is shown to function as one of many systems of thought as fraught with error as their human creators. Among several, three texts illustrate science's fall from discursive power in Borges's thought, "El idioma analítico de John Wilkins," the essay from *Otras inquisiciones* that Foucault credits with inspiring his *The Order of Things*, the very well known "Tlön, Uqbar, Orbis Tertius" from *Ficciones*, and "El etnógrafo" a very short story from the later collection of poetry, *El elogio de la sombra*. In all cases we see science relegated to a thematic role that merely supports Borges's more generalized critique of human systems of thought.

If we take into account the impact of Foucault's work on contemporary literary studies, "El idioma analítico de John Wilkins" could be said to be one of Borges's most influential works.[12] At first glance, the essay appears to be a discussion of the artificial language that Wilkins proposed in the seventeenth century as well as a somewhat mocking evaluation of Wilkins's negligible impact in Western thought. Foucault praises the essay, characterizing his response to it as something akin to Kuhnsian paradigm shift. The French historian explains that he had arrived at the section describing a "cierta enciclopedia china" [a particular Chinese encyclopedia] that presents an absurd taxonomy of animals divided by characteristics like "pertenecientes al emperador," "perros sueltos," and "que de lejos parecen moscas" [belonging to the emperor, loose dogs and that at a distance look like flies] among several other equally humorous categories when he experienced a kind of intellectual epiphany (1996, vol. 2, 86). Foucault remarks on the unsettling effect of his reading experience in the first sentence of *The Order of Things*:

> This book first arose out of a passage in Borges, out of the laughter that shattered, as I read the passage, all the familiar landmarks of my thought—*our* thought, the thought that bears the stamp of our age and our geography—breaking up all the ordered surfaces and all the planes with which we are accustomed to tame the wild profusion of existing things, and continuing long afterwards to disturb and threaten with collapse our age-old distinction between the Same and the Other. (1970, xv)

Foucault's reaction is, as usual, somewhat hyperbolic. Nevertheless, as he proceeds to present his own taxonomy of history's taxonomies, his point about the revolutionary implications of Borges's gentle mockery of a seventeenth-century intellectual is well taken. By introducing what is an incredibly absurd classification system to Western eyes along side more accepted taxonomies, he invites the reader to question the objectivity of any attempt to classify the universe. Borges says as much later in the essay: "He registrado las arbitrariedades de Wilkins, del desconocido (o apócrifo) enciclopedista chino y del Instituto Bibliográfico de Bruselas; notoriamente no hay clasificación del universo que no sea arbitraria y conjetural. La razón es muy simple: no sabemos qué cosa es el universo" (1996, vol. 2, 86). [I have examined the arbitrary collection of Wilkins, of the unknown (or apocryphal) Chinese encyclopedia and of the Bibliographic Institute of Brussels; there is, plainly no classification of the universe that is not arbitrary and conjectural. The reason is very simple, we do not know what the universe is.] John Wilkins's attempt at a linguistic taxonomy is merely one more among the many that Borges deems impossible. Borges's enunciation of that impossibility is what opens up the new path of inquiry that Foucault would follow so fruitfully in his published works.

In Borges's presentation of Wilkins and his creation of an analytical language as one in a series of similar attempts throughout history, we see a textual process similar to that seen in "La doctrina de los ciclos." In that essay, we saw a kind of historical containment that firmly situated Nietzsche along a timeline moving toward the scientific discoveries that would disprove his ideas. Nietzsche's intellectual body falls subject to the control of the history that Borges constructs. In "Wilkins," we see a similar kind of intellectual discipline applied to a historical body. Just as he did with his very personal analysis of Nietzsche's motives, Borges creates a human Wilkins with a biography and a historical context whose ideas occupied their own limited space in a much grander history of ideas. Borges's subsequent dismantling of those ideas, particularly of the desire to classify, can be seen as a breed of the discipline that controls an unruly body (or in this case, mind). This is an apt image for an author who titles his collection of essays "inquisiciones." Ironically, of course, the disciplined body subjected to Borges's control is castigated precisely because it is too "ruly," or rather, too organized to be an accurate representation of the universe. Behind Borges's playfulness and laughter-provoking descriptions lies a will to control, or in this case, a will to dismantle intellectual and philosophical error. Just as Nietzsche's Eternal Return ends up in "Nada," Wilkins arrives at the same place; Borges begins the essay noting that Wilkins's entry in the *Encyclopedia Britannica* has been eliminated. Both thinkers, in one form or another, are placed under erasure.

While a similar disciplinary operation occurs in the two articles, the mechanisms for that operation are quite different. The test tube envy implicit in Borges's use of Cantor and entropy against Nietzsche disappears in the latter essay as the scientific thought inherent to Cantor's work and the laws of thermodynamics falls subject to the same criticism that disciplines Wilkins's language. If Borges opposed modern scientific thought to Nietzsche in a temporal succession of ideas, the series that he employs with Wilkins suggests a kind of intellectual eternal present. In this present, human beings from all time periods attempt the same fruitless taxonomies made absurd by an inherent inability to understand the universe. Along those lines, the essay from *Otras inquisiciones* exhibits a much more revolutionary quality in Borges's writing, especially in the context of a tendency in Argentine literature to favor scientific discourse. "El idioma analítico de John Wilkins" can be seen to represent a moment in which not only does science's ability to function as a positive force come under attack as it did in Arlt, but its very ability to tell truth about the universe comes under inquisition. At that point, one could say that any test tube envy that Borges might have suffered early on in his writing has been left on the couch. Such is certainly the case in the two stories where we see a similar depiction of science's inability to escape the provisional and the subjective. Both "Tlön, Uqbar, Orbis Tertius" and "El etnógrafo" employ images of science as an institution that is at best arbitrary in its attempts to classify the universe and at worst, menacing.

If Wilkins's attempt to create a taxonomy of language is characterized as not "el menos admirable" of humankind's several efforts to classify, the work of the group of scientists in "Tlön" is downright sinister. Just as in the essay, the well-known story begins with the absence of an encyclopedia article, with Wilkins it is his missing entry, in "Tlön" it is an article about a mysterious place called Uqbar that may or may not exist (the uncertain existence applies equally to the place and the encyclopedia article). The story follows the narrator's encounters with this country that appears as three related spaces named Tlön, Uqbar, and Orbis Tertius. This world obeys physical laws absurdly based on the tenets of idealist philosophy where objects only exist when observed and where languages consist only of verbs. While such a place is relatively harmless as an abstraction, the narrator observes that Tlön has begun to contaminate the "real" world in a manner that he compares to Nazism. "Tlön" ends with a hopeless narrator who is witnessing the resulting destruction of his world. Many consider the story to be one of Borges's finest, owing to its humorous mix of philosophical play, science fiction, and implicit political critique.

The story has been the focus of scores of critical works and has been well interpreted in countless articles.[13] What interests me most in this study is the manner in which Borges uses the story to articulate his growing antiscience stance. While it certainly offers many enlightening interpretative possibilities, it also serves as an important point in Borges's trajectory from test tube envy to Arlt's test tube terror to what one might term "test tube disdain." Indeed, as many have argued, "Tlön, Uqbar, Orbis Tertius" can certainly be seen as the depiction of a science fiction dystopia similar to the literary warnings by Quiroga, Lugones, and Arlt mentioned earlier.[14] Borges describes Tlön as the creation of a secret group of individuals who had proposed the intellectual creation of a planet. The description contributes to the sense of foreboding that culminates in Tlön's invasion of the narrator's world:

> ¿Quiénes inventaron a Tlön? El plural es inevitable, porque la hipótesis de un solo inventor—de un infinito Leibniz obrando en la tiniebla y en la modestia—ha sido descartada unánimemente. Se conjetura que este *brave new world* es obra de una sociedad secreta de astrónomos, de biólogos, de ingenieros, de metafísicos, de poetas, de químicos, de algebristas, de moralistas, de pintores, de geómetras . . . dirigidos por un oscuro hombre de genio. Abundan individuos que dominan esas disciplinas diversas, pero no los capaces de invención y menos los capaces subordinar la invención a un riguroso plan sistemático. (Vol. 1, 434–35)

> [Who, singular or plural, invented Tlön? The plural is, I suppose, inevitable, since the hypothesis of a single inventor—some infinite Leibniz working in obscurity and self-effacement—has been unanimously discarded. It is conjectured that this "brave new world" is the work of a secret society of astronomers, biologists, engineers, metaphysicians, poets, chemists, algebrists, moralists, painters, geometers . . . guided and directed by some shadowy man of genius. There are many men adept in those diverse disciplines, but few capable of imagination— fewer still capable of subordinating imagination to a rigorous and systematic plan.] (1998, 72)

The description of the secret society emphasizes the role of the sciences in the construction of worldviews. Alongside the artists and philosophers, the scientists contribute to the systematic creation of a world whose reality is described as absurd. The combination of the various groups of thinkers also has the effect of relegating science to one among many that contribute to the artificial creation of reality. In Tlön, the artist's depiction of reality is equal to the astronomer's description of the cosmos and the chemist's manipulation of the elements. Once again, we see the kind of leveling effect that we observed in Borges's defense of Zeno, where mathematics became contaminated by the systems that employed its tools. Borges then extends his characterization of the group by emphasizing their servile role, commenting on their subjugated status to the "dark man of genius" who directs their efforts. Again, the removal of the scientists from a position of power emphasizes a reality in which science serves at the pleasure of power instead of endowing a subject with some kind of cultural authority.

The foreboding implicit in his description of these scientists is made explicit in a later comment in the story. The narrator, now hopeless at the appearance of objects from what was supposed to be a mad, invented world, remarks in a postscript:

> Casi inmediatamente, la realidad cedió en más de un punto. Lo cierto es que anhelaba ceder. Hace diez años bastaba cualquier simetría con apariencia de orden—el materialismo dialéctico, el antisemitismo, el nazismo—para embelesar a los hombres. ¿Cómo no someterse a Tlön, a la minuciosa y vasta evidencia de un planeta ordenado? Inútil responder que la realidad también está ordenada. Quizá lo esté, pero de acuerdo a leyes divinas—traduzco: a leyes inhumanas—que no acabamos nunca de percibir. (1996, vol. 1, 442)

> [Almost immediately, reality "caved in" at more than one point. The truth is, it wanted to cave in. Ten years ago, any symmetry, any system with an appearance of order—dialectical materialism, anti-Semitism, Nazism—could spellbind and hypnotize mankind. How could the world not fall under the sway of Tlön, how could it not yield to the vast and minutely detailed evidence of an ordered planet? It would be futile to reply that reality is also orderly. Perhaps it is, but orderly in accordance with divine laws (read: "inhuman laws") that we can never quite manage to penetrate.] (1998, 81)

Once again, we see the ideas that presage Borges's critique of Wilkins in the outright rejection of humankind's ability to understand, much less describe, the universe. But where Borges includes Wilkins in a rather harmless list of attempts to provide order for the universe, the scientific efforts of the Tlön group are compared to communism, anti-Semitism, and Nazism. The scientists are described merely as servants of the political power wielded by the ideologues of the mid twentieth century. While Arlt certainly anticipates this view of science with the Astrologer and his subversive group who plot scientifically inspired mayhem in *Los siete locos/ Los lanzallamas*, the marked difference is the lack of a dependence on scientific reference or use of scientific discourse in the creation of the critique. In that sense it fulfills the general tendency of Argentine science fiction to eschew specific scientific detail in a more thematically based focus. Still, as we saw in the subsequent "Wilkins," it strengthens a vein in Borges that runs counter to much of what we observed in "La doctrina de los ciclos."

The much later "El etnógrafo" provides a final example of the antiscience posture that predominates in Borges's writing. The story first appeared in *Elogio de la sombra* (1969), one of Borges's several collections of poetry that he wrote later in his career. In it Borges recounts the story of a North American student named Fred Murdock who goes to live with a Native American tribe as a part of an academic thesis focused on the tribe's secret rituals. After two years with the indigenous peoples, he returns to his adviser to report that he has learned the tribe's ritual secret but that he has decided not to publish his findings as the secret has taught him that "la ciencia, nuestra ciencia, me parece una frivolidad" (vol. 2, 368). [Science, our science, seems mere frivolity to me (1998, 335).] The final sentence of the story informs us that Murdock proceeded to use his secret knowledge to live his life, marrying and divorcing and ending up as a librarian at Yale.

The story is, in many ways, a repetition of the themes and structures that appear in most of Borges's work, a confirmation of Borges's statement that his work was a series of rewritings of the same two or three stories.[15] While Borges was referring specifically to the gauchos, labyrinths, and reflections on memory that populate his writings, the critique of science is another theme he revisits. The final criticism Murdock makes of science and knowledge generated in an academic setting reminds one of the faulty system builders of John Wilkins, the bewildered adviser appearing as yet another in the series of hapless intellectuals who fail to understand the hopelessness of their project. To this now standard critique in his work, Borges adds a wrinkle that turns a scientific discipline, in this case anthropology, into a proof of Gödel's theorem that all mathematical sets inevitably contain an element that disproves their validity.[16] In "El etnógrafo," Borges describes a system that generates its own collapse as Murdock's thesis work is what leads him to a knowledge of the falsity of his academic context. The anthropological fieldwork, so essential to the construction of anthropology as a scientific discipline in the late nineteenth and twentieth century as we saw with Mansilla's *Una excursión a los indios ranqueles*, brings about the downfall of the discipline's ability to produce usable knowledge. Borges underscores this self-destructive tendency with the title. The term ethnographer emphasizes writing as a characteristic of anthropology in a story about an anthropologist who decides not to write having destroyed all of his field notes. On that level, "El etnógrafo" functions as a kind of morality tale in which science is depicted not only as useless, but also as ultimately subject to self-destruction. Borges's scientific discipline, just as in "John Wilkins" and "Tlön," becomes a severe discipline of science and scientific thought.

The idea of discipline as we have discussed so far is especially appropriate for an interpretation of "el etnógrafo," where Fred Murdock is described several times as a kind of disciplined body attempting to negotiate the discursive systems that mediate his sense of identity. Borges first describes him as "Naturalmente respetuoso, no descreía de los libros ni de quienes escriben los libros. Era suya esa edad en que el hombre no sabe aún quién es y está listo a entregarse a lo que le propone el azar" (Vol. 2, 367). [He was naturally respectful, and he distrusted neither books nor the men and women that write them. He was at that age when a man doesn't yet know who he is, and so is ready to throw himself into whatever chance puts in his way (1998, 334).] The description reinforces the idea of a docile body, one that accepts the strictures and definitions imposed on it from outside, in this case, the discipline imposed by an academic context of books and professors. The use of "entregarse" to define a key characteristic in Murdock's personality emphasizes the submissive nature that leads him to accept the suggestions of his adviser to study indigenous languages and then to do fieldwork with a tribe to learn the secret revealed to initiates. The concept of scientific discipline as applied to Murdock functions thematically, then, in a way similar to its rhetorical operation in "La doctrina de los ciclos." Science checks Murdock's behavior, determining to a degree what he can think and how he can act. Borges describes a situation in which scientific thinking works principally as a Foucauldian disciplinary system that keeps potentially threatening bodies in line with culturally accepted modes of knowledge production. Ironically, it is not unlike the discipline that he applied to Nietzsche.

However, while Borges subjects Nietzsche to that discipline permanently in a presumably nonfiction situation, the fictional Murdock will eventually escape. The passage describing Murdock's assimilation in the tribe outlines the adoption of a new disciplinary system:

> Más de dos años habitó en la pradera, entre muros de adobe o a la intemperie. Se levantaba antes del alba, se acostaba al anochecer, llegó a soñar en un idioma que no era el de sus padres. Acostumbró su paladar a sabores ásperos, se cubrió con ropas extrañas, olvidó los amigos y la ciudad, llegó a pensar de una manera que su lógica rechazaba. (1996, vol. 2, 367)

[He lived for more than two years on the prairie, sometimes sheltered by adobe walls and sometimes in the open. He rose before dawn, went to bed at sundown, and came to dream in a language that was not that of his fathers. He conditioned his palate to harsh flavors, he covered himself with strange clothing, he forgot his friends and the city, he came to think in a fashion that the logic of his mind rejected.] (1998, 334–35)

Borges takes Murdock through a careful process of rebirth, a rebirth characterized by the subjection of his body to a new disciplinary regime. The privations implied in his living conditions and his adaptation to new sleeping patterns dictated by nature produce changes in both his interior, as represented by his sense of taste, and his exterior, evident in the clothes he wears. This regime transforms Murdock, exchanging his previously submissive body into an entirely new being. His final conversion from Western European to Native American thought acts as the culminating point for his transformation and serves as foreshadowing of the rejection of science that is to follow. The change of the discursive structures that constitute his identity do indeed produce an important change in Murdock's self. At the same time, his transformation attacks the process by which science constructs knowledge. If Murdock's sense of self can change so radically as a result of his cultural assimilation, science as a guarantor of truth becomes context specific, a quality that defeats the popular conception of science as a discipline of absolutes.

At the same time, we should not imagine that "El etnógrafo" is the tale of an escape from regressive science to a liberated state in contact with some kind of universal truth. Indeed, Borges maintains in "John Wilkins" that taxonomies and system building are inescapable despite their several flaws. The emphasis on the physical discipline that transforms Murdock suggests that the indigenous mode of thinking is merely another human attempt to order nature. In that sense, the story's three act structure—Murdock before the experience with the indigenous culture, the experience, and the rest of Murdock's life—reveals the three systems in which Murdock lives and functions. He begins subject to the scientific academy, exchanges it for the indigenous systems of the tribe, and then to the arbitrary taxonomies of a university library. Borges's rejection of science, then, is not merely an outright antiscience attack, but a part of the well-documented, antisystems philosophy that runs throughout his thought. At this point, Borges's test tube disdain is such that science does not even merit its own specialized attack, it is simply one in a long list of failed human attempts to make sense of the universe.

It is in light of this "test tube disdain" that Rafael Catalá's summation of Borges's position in science and literature studies borders on startling. In *The Encyclopedia of Literature and Science*, Catalá concludes: "Borges is one of the masters of the synthesis of literature and science, because in the few pages of a short story science and literature become one" (2002, 51). This is a position iterated by countless articles and books, many of which center on Catalá's earlier comment in the same entry, "the concept of space-time in physics [is] very useful to the understanding of the story 'Garden of the Forking Paths'" (2002, 51). Certainly physics and "El jardín" are not the only combinations that appear, a perusal of the critical literature reveals investigations of Borges's use of, anticipation of, and/or similarity to chaos dynamics, field theory, neurology, mathematics, artificial intelligence, and quantum mechanics.[17] Without necessarily refuting the connections and the relationships that have been highlighted in a score of books and articles, I would invite a consideration of the implications of this critical gesture. That is, especially in the case of those critics who have commented on Borges's anticipation of ideas in contemporary science, we see created with their remarks a vision of Borges who owes his position as a leading writer to a near-miraculous anticipation of scientific discovery.

The following expressions of wonder and/or appreciation at the perceived similarities between Borges's short stories and contemporary physics help characterize the state of science and literature criticism as it pertains to the Argentine author:

> La complementariedad e incertidumbre que analizamos en "El jardín de senderos que se bifurcan" de Borges ejemplifican cómo los conceptos de la física, que forman parte de la episteme del siglo veinte, reverberan en la literatura hispanoamericana moderna. (Rivero-Potter 1997, 469)

> [The complementarity and uncertainty that we analyze in Borges's "The Garden of the Forking Paths" exemplify how the concepts of physics, that form a part of the episteme of the twentieth century, reverberate in modern Spanish-American literature.]

> Desde ese día me encontré con varias citas borgeanas en textos científicos y de divulgación científica: alusiones a "La Biblioteca de Babel"

5: BORGES'S SCIENTIFIC DISCIPLINE 153

para ilustrar las paradojas de los conjuntos infinitos y la geometría fractal, referencias a la taxonomía fantástica del Dr. Franz Kuhn, en "El idioma analítico de John Wilkins" (un favorito de neurocientíficos y lingüistas), invocaciones a "Funes el memorioso" para presentar sistemas de numeración, y hace poco me sorprendió una cita a "El Libro de Arena" en un artículo sobre la segregación de mezclas granulares. (Rojo 1999, 188–89)

[Since that day, I have encountered various quotations from Borges in scientific texts and among scientists: Allusions to "The Library of Babel" to illustrate the paradoxes of infinite pairs and fractal geometry, references to the fantastic taxonomy of Dr. Franz Kuhn in "The Analytical Language of John Wilkins" (a favorite of neuroscientists and linguists), invocations of "Funes, His Memory" as a way to present number systems, and a little while ago I was surprised to find a quotation from "The Book of Sand" in an article about the segregation of granular mixes.]

In the end we have seen that some of the most "fantastic" of Borges' fantastic stories have a clear relation to proposed models of physical reality. Concepts like the Aleph, the one as the many, relative time, and alternate realities have everything to do with the ever-expanding worldview that theorists in the field of physics have contributed to. With so much common ground between scientific theory and Borges' stories, it is difficult to deny that such a connection exists. (Gomez 1999, 19)

Scaling features, self-similarities, and fractal topologies are the backbones of Borges writing, particularly in "The Garden of the Forking Paths." (Schreiber and Umansky 2001, 77)

Regardless of what significance we may attach to this, there is no question that Borges has given us in this story and ingenious labyrinth with a labyrinth within a labyrinth which expresses what are regarded as valid scientific viewpoints by many modern physicists. (Capobianco 1989, 37).

While the tone of these passages moves from slightly defensive to boldly declarative, the common theme is one that presents Borges's work as inseparable from contemporary scientific thought. If some, like Rivero-Potter and Gomez, argue that Borges is willfully manipulating the physics that he understood and others merely commenting on the clear similarities, all set a high value on the fact that Borges's work incorporates that which is scientifically "valid" or accurate models of "physical reality" to the extent that it even appears within scientific discourse itself. I have no desire to dispute the connections suggested here, what intrigues me is the way in which critics effectively reinsert their construction of Borges within a system that not only recognizes but depends on scientific authority. Borges's status as leading twentieth-century writer seems to hinge on his ability to tap into scientific advances, his relative worth as subject of critical attention connected with texts that either prophesy future advances in physics or accurately incorporate previous and coetaneous scientific theories.

What makes the critical focus all the more remarkable is the previously explained rejection of scientific practice that we see develop in Borges's thought. The paradox appears to be that Borges's renown as a writer depends, in this particular critical evaluation, on his association with a discipline that he spent a good bit of ink mocking. "El jardín de senderos que se bifurcan" is an excellent example of the tension that this paradox produces. The story has been interpreted both as a meditation on Einsteinian relativity and as an anticipation of chaos theory, fractal geometry, and quantum mechanics. I would argue that it simultaneously includes yet another trapped scientist in Borges's long line of scientific failures. Let us now turn to the story at the epicenter of much of the Borges science/literature criticism.

The standard argument in the criticism that explores the relationship between contemporary science and "El jardín" tends to describe quantum theory as it relates to Everett's many worlds theory and then compare it to the nature of the temporal and physical labyrinths that Borges presents in the story. The many worlds theory is the 1960 attempt by Hugh Everett to resolve a key issue of quantum mechanics dealing with the undecidability of quantum particles between two equally probable states. Everett argued that in such instances, reality actually splits in two, with the particle occupying one state in one reality and the other state in the second.[18] Especially in its popularized form, the theory does bear a resemblance to the theory of time that appears in the story. As many may recall, "El jardín de senderos que se bifurcan" narrates the encounter of a Chinese spy, Yu Tsun, with a sinologist, Stephen Albert, who has discovered the meaning of a cryptic statement by Tsui Pen, Yu Tsun's illustrious ancestor. Tsui Pen had retired, indicating that he would either write a book or build a labyrinth, and then died, leaving only a nonsensical book that lacked any kind of logical continuity and no sign of a labyrinth. Albert had discovered that this missing labyrinth was the nonsensical book, and that the book was, in turn, a definition of time in which all possible outcomes occur in a constantly bifurcating temporal system with all possibilities occupying their own reality. The obvious similarity between the bifurcating nature of time as described by Borges and the bifurcations inherent to Everett's theory or those common to fractal theory and chaos dynamics form the basis of these critical explorations. The criticism ranges from an appreciation of Borges's genius, to an evaluation of the similarities, to an argument for the interrelationship of science and literature as similar modes of knowledge. Ultimately all the criticism finds justification in the perceived connections between science and the story even if the dynamics that generate these connections are generally understudied. Alberto Rojo, for example, ends his very able discussion of the similarities concluding that Borges just happened to anticipate the idea, a curious coincidence that is, after all, right at home in the Borgesian universe that we as his readers all inhabit (1999, 197).

There are notable exceptions to the tendency to study the similarities in isolation from the cultural and philosophical dynamics that provide the underpinning of their genesis. N. Katherine Hayles argues ably that Borges's work provides evidence of the cultural extension of field theory through both science and literature. Thomas Weissert's study of the story's use of chaos dynamics is another example in which the critic is as interested in what Borges tells us about the cultural relationship between science and literature generally as he is in the specific, chaotic, operations at the heart of the story. The key to understanding Borges's relationship with science, for Weissert, is the previously mentioned Michel Serres remark that many times literary texts discover scientific laws well in advance of the scientists. While such a philosophy would seem to allow Weissert to sidestep thorny questions of intentionality, he simultaneously argues for an interpretation of the story in which Borges knowingly includes direct references to modern physics, specifically Albert Einstein. While the sinologist's surname is, for him, an obvious allusion, he reinforces his point commenting on the varying instances of relativity that appear throughout the story. Weissert argues that Stephen Albert's death, when paired with literary structures that anticipate bifurcation theory in chaos dynamics, acts as a harbinger of scientific advances to come in which Einstein's theories give way to the work on chaos that would revise the physicist's views.[19] The argument is attractive, if somewhat oddly presented. Weissert tries to combine Serres's vision of a literary prophecy of scientific discovery with the argument that Borges was indeed attempting to say something about Einstein, noting at one point,

> The scientific verification that there is no absolute frame of reference with which one may orient oneself in relation to other reference frames had a direct influence on Borges' work. Relativity theory was generally available to the scientific reader well before "Garden," and considering Borges' propensity for scientific thought, we may safely assume that he was familiar with it. (1991, 230–31)

Weissert's attempt to play Borges both ways is intriguing if slightly misdirected. While Borges may certainly have constructed a web of references to Einstein and relativity theory, the story functions within Borges's view of science in a very different way.

Weissert was not wrong in assuming Borges's familiarity with popularized versions of Einstein's work. As we noted earlier, Borges's would have been well aware of Einstein's visit and the review he did of *Relativity and Robinson* shows clear familiarity with the physicist's work. With the references to relative frames of reality and the significant function of the name Albert in the story (not only the surname of a main character, but the name of the site that Germany is to bomb), one could probably grant Weissert's assertion safely. However, the idea that Borges might be at the edge of scientific discovery with his text may be going a little too far. Many years after the publication of "El jardín," Borges reacted to the enthusiasm of admirers who were commenting on the links between his work, especially "Jardín," and the new physics in the following manner: "La idea de que no hay un tiempo. Creo que esa idea ha sido en cierto modo cobijada por la física actual, que no comprendo y que no conozco. La ideas de varios tiempos. ¿Por qué suponer la idea de un solo tiempo, un tiempo absoluto como lo suponía Newton?" (vol. 4, 204)[The idea that there is no one time. I think that this idea has been adopted by modern physics, something I don't understand and with which I am not familiar. The idea of multiple times. Why assume the idea of just one time, of an absolute time like the one proposed by Newton]. We should certainly not take the comment at face value, especially considering Borges's tendency to make contradictory evaluations of his work.[20] Still, the comment does suggest a more likely reading of the ideas on time that appear in "Jardín." Borges uses his profession of ignorance to divert attention from modern physics to the history of ideas, grounding his own ideas about relativity not on Einstein, but on a tradition of relativistic thought. In the class where this reaction was recorded, titled "El tiempo," Borges comments on the nature of his subject, suggesting that scientists and philosophers like Leibniz, Bradley, and, of course, Zeno, already refute Newtonian ideas of absolute time and space. Curiously, a reading of Werner Heisenberg's popularizations of quantum theory show a German physicist interested in claiming a similar intellectual genealogy, locating the discoveries in quantum physics within a philosophical tradition that includes Leibniz as well as Hume and Berkeley, two more of Borges's favorite philosophers.[21] One might argue that if there are similarities between Borges's work and modern physics, it is due to a similar philosophical heritage rather than some kind of prophetic ability on the part of Borges.

So what is Einstein doing in "El jardín de senderos que se bifurcan"? In a sense, the story is not dissimilar from another story in *Ficciones* that ends with a death in an intellectual labyrinth, "La muerte y la brújula." Both stories describe apparently deep thinkers who use their extensive readings to create labyrinths, Albert builds his based on Tsui Pen's chaotic book, Erik Lonnrot of "La muerte y la brújula" uses his readings of Kabalistic philosophy to map out a labyrinthine criminal plot. Both thinkers are murdered at the end by a second character whose violent nature quickly lays to ruin the intellectual machinations of the labyrinth. Stephen Albert's interpretation of Tsui Pen's ideas not only creates a labyrinthine incarnation of time, it also traps him inside (like all good Borgesian labyrinths). The images that run throughout the story emphasizing the relative nature of time and the variety of temporal frames are, ultimately, only ever the one in which Yu Tsun seeks out a victim named Albert in order to pass a message to his superiors. The bifurcating paths of time are only part of the labyrinth Albert himself has constructed and, like all inhabitants of labyrinths, the one in which he will die. If Stephen Albert is a double for Einstein, he is an Einstein who operates much as the other scientists in most of Borges's work. He, like them, are unable to avoid the faulty system building to which their discipline aspires. Albert merely joins those that end dead or lost or both in their labyrinths. In that sense, Einstein and Albert are the hapless Asterion, cheerfully awaiting the visitors that will kill them, random chance will once again triumphing over the most carefully prepared definitions of reality that, according to Borges, inevitably fail. The emphasis on the history of science in Borges is not only about the failure of past systems of thought, as Weissert argues in this particular case and as we have seen in texts previously discussed. If Newton gives way to Einstein in a series of Kuhnsian revolutions, Borges does not argue that this series culminates in ideas that are closer to the "truth." The existence of these revolutions casts current ideas on the nature of the universe in the same vein as previous attempts to understand the universe.

Borges's work marks a path, then, that simultaneously points out continuities in Argentine test tube envy even as it directs frontal attacks on the authority of science and its ability to construct truth within society. Especially in his early works, we see a system of discipline that relies on scientific authority and the perceived objectivity of mathematic explanations to maintain control over the ideas Borges considers. Indeed, Borges will never completely abandon the tendency to invest his texts with the explanatory power of mathematics, as critics like Capobianco and Merrell have noted. Even in the same lecture on time where he denied any knowledge of physics, he uses mathematical notation to explain an idea.[22] At the same time, he extends the critique of science we saw in Arlt in new directions. If Arlt (and later Sabato) garnered prestige for their rejection of positivistic science with their able use of scientific terminology, Borges converted science into just one more artificial philosophical system bereft of true explanatory power without resorting to systems of scientific reference to prove that point. The apparent connection with Einstein in "El jardín" does nothing to build any kind of rhetorical power for Borges's description of bifurcating time, indeed, the story seems to close down the idea of bifurcating time as it collapses back into a spy story narrated with many of the trappings of a typical noir film.[23]

What does bifurcate in Borges's work is a mode of discursive practice. While Argentine narrative has never been so monolithic as to exclude all writing that did not incorporate scientific reference, Borges acts as an excellent example of the two modes of discourse that would continue to enjoy influence through the course of Argentine letters. If Arlt marked a complete break with the hope that science could solve social problems, Borges frees his literary discourse, eventually, from the envy that continued to inhabit Arlt's work. One could also argue that it marks a point in which discourse is broadened to accept other discursive strategies to an extent that they were not up until then. Even so, the space Borges creates, or at least reveals, does not place test tube envy under erasure in Argentine narrative, nor does it succeed in ending the cultural authority enjoyed by science in popular culture. As we have seen, even Borges criticism has proved to reinsert Borges within a tradition of test tube envy that his own work helps to undermine. Nor will this apparent tension resolve later, for while an important portion of Argentine narrative will follow Borges's break with scientific discourse, other principal authors will continue to observe the relationships of power between science and literature. Especially in the cases of Julio Cortázar and Mempo Giardinelli, the test tube envy that disciplined Facundo Quiroga and kept Nietzsche in line will continue to exercise influence over Argentina's textual bodies.

6
Cortázar's Quantum Values

CORTÁZAR'S SURPRISE AT REDISCOVERING ARLT'S *OBSESIÓN CIENTÍFICA* mirrored his own complex interest in the function of science in contemporary culture. Much as Arlt uses Darwinism as a scientific underpinning for the narrative world of *El juguete rabioso*, Cortázar seems to employ science playfully in a series of what-if narratives where characters and situations follow the quantum rules of uncertainty as well as imitate well-known quantum theory thought experiments. One might say that if Borges's genius was his anticipation of the discoveries of quantum physics, Cortázar's is his incorporation the discoveries already made. At the same time, Cortázar's lighthearted approach to the scientific concepts he employs masks their role in his very serious questioning of reality.[1] While we can observe Cortázar's playful marriage of narrative and quantum mechanics most clearly in his novel *62: Modelo para armar* and in several short stories, the Argentine author displays his particular brand of test tube envy in the seminal *Rayuela* (1963) with a deployment of the scientific authority of quantum physics in a philosophical attack on rationality.

Cortázar's interest in quantum physics as a model for fiction appears repeatedly in his writings. In the teasing essay "Julios en acción" [Julios in Action] in *La vuelta al día en ochenta mundos* [Around the Day in Eighty Worlds]—a play on the Jules Verne title that also nods to the many worlds theory described in the previous chapter—Cortázar pokes fun at a series of discoveries in the new physics of the late 1960s even as he develops a very serious vision of reality based on those discoveries:[2]

> A todo esto varios cronopios se han excitado enormemente porque acaban de enterarse de que a lo mejor el universo es asimétrico, lo que va en contra de todas las ideas recibidas. Un investigador llamado Paolo Franzini, y su mujer Juliet Franzini (¿Se ha advertido cómo a partir de

un Julio que redacta y otro Julio que diseña se van incorporando aquí dos Jules y ahora una Juliet, a base de una noticia aparecida un 7 de julio?) saben muchísimo sobre el mesón eta neutro, que salió del anonimato poco ha y que tiene la curiosa particularidad de ser su propia antipartícula. Apenas se lo descompone, el mesón produce tres pimesones de los cuales uno es neutro, pobrecito, y los otros dos son positivo y negativo respectivamente para enorme tranquilidad de todo el mundo. Hasta que (los Franzini de por medio) se descubre que la conducta de los dos pimesones no es simétrica; la armoniosa noción que la antimateria es el reflejo exacto de la materia se pincha como un globito. (1967, 18)

[Certain cronopios have been quite excited to learn that the universe itself may be asymmetrical, a fact that runs counter to one of the most illustrious of received ideas. A researcher named Paolo Franzini and his wife Juliet Lee Franzini (have you noticed how a writing Julio, working with an illustrating Julio, has already considered two more Julios and now a Juliet, in reference to an article that appeared on 7 *July*?) know a great deal about the neutral meson *eta,* which only recently emerged from anonymity and which has the curious quality of being its own antiparticle. The moment it decomposes, it produces three pi-mesons, one of which, poor thing, is neuter, while the other two are positive and negative, which is a great relief to everyone. And then we discover (this is what the Franzinis have shown) that the conduct of the two charged pi-mesons is not symmetrical; the harmonious proposition that antimatter is the mirror image of matter is deflated like a balloon.] (1986, 15)

This quotation demonstrates the various stances Cortázar assumes as he examines and incorporates quantum physics into his fiction and worldview. On a ludic level, Cortázar rejoices in the coincidental conjunction of Julios and then pities the poor neutral pi-meson, activating the dual meaning of the Spanish *neutro* as both neuter and neutral. This pun, with its implicit personification of quantum particles, becomes especially important to Cortázar's play as he will incorporate the rules of quantum physics in his stories, suggesting that visible reality operates in much the same manner as subatomic particles act on the quantum level.

The playfulness notwithstanding, Cortázar reveals in this passage a serious stance in which he activates the revolutionary potential of the discoveries of quantum physics. He initiates the paragraph commenting the excitement of the *cronopios* (among whom Cortázar figures prominently) upon discovering that reality may not be as symmetrical as once believed.[3] In fact, the excitement can more properly be identified as one of vindication rather than discovery as Cortázar and his band of *cronopios* already conceived reality to be disorderly and irrational.[4] He also cultivates a spirit of revolution as he notes the destruction of harmonious notions of reality, an element of the iconoclasm one finds generally in Cortázar's work. With this combination of vindication and revolution, quantum physics becomes a symbol of Cortázar's conception of the universe as absurd. Earlier in the piece, Cortázar admits as much, "Mis eruditas lecturas del correo científico de *Le Monde* (sale los jueves) tienen además la ventaja de que en vez de sustraerme al absurdo me incitan a aceptarlo como el modo natural en que se nos da una realidad inconcebible" (1967, 18) [My readings of the Science pages of *Le Monde* (appearing Thursdays) have a further benefit: rather than turning me away from the absurd, they encourage me to accept it as the natural mode by which we are shown an inconceivable reality (1986, 14)]. "Julios en acción" acts as a microcosm of Cortázar's use of quantum mechanics in his fiction where he plays with what he has learned about quantum physics in order to describe an absurd reality he sees as the "really" real.

If we remember the revolutionary feeling surrounding Einstein and the new physics that we observed earlier, we can interpret this response as a continuation of the enthusiasm manifested in the Argentina of the 1920s and 1930s. In fact, Cortázar's combination of musings on the philosophical implications of quantum mechanics with his continued reference to *Le Monde* help to provide cultural context of the science that will serve as literary material. The presentation of popular media as source of scientific theory also situates Cortázar's comments within the nineteenth-century tradition we saw in Rivadavia's *La abeja argentina*. The joy that the *cronopios* experience stems from the fact that a newspaper has confirmed their suspicions about an absurd reality, just as Sarmiento found in phrenology an explanation of his idiosyncratic views on civilization and barbarism. In both the nineteenth and the twentieth-century examples, the beliefs find confirmation not just in science, but in a science that enjoys popular culture's attention as evidenced in its newspapers. At the same time, one can appreciate a process in which Cortázar's writing attempts to inscribe the cultural space in which those scientific discoveries function, imposing metaphysical meaning upon what would otherwise be a physical description of particular subatomic particles. The control that literature exercises on the cultural image of science in the case of Cortázar can be seen to represent the twentieth-century extension of the manner in which nineteenth-century writers attempted to use narrative to define science within their own sociopolitical context.

In Cortázar's case, the cronopios's excitement also reflects what Foucault noticed as an important shift in the cultural presence of science and the scientist. According to Foucault, the individual gained power in society by virtue of the connection the physicist could make between society and atomic science.

> It seems to me that this figure of the "specific" intellectual has emerged since the Second World War. Perhaps it was the atomic scientist (in a word, or rather a name: Oppenheimer) who acted as the point of transition between the universal and the specific intellectual. It's because he had a direct and localized relation to scientific knowledge and institutions that the atomic scientist could make his intervention; but, since the nuclear threat affected the whole human race and the fate of the world, his discourse could at the same time be the discourse of the universal. Under the rubric of this protest, which concerned the entire world, the atomic expert brought into play his specific position in the order of knowledge. (1980, 127)

As we saw with the figure of Darwin, and as Foucault would later admit, the power of the individual scientist was not new with atomic physics. Nevertheless, both Foucault and Cortázar are responding to an important phenomenon of the twentieth century, that of the physicist as a guarantor of scientific truth. In the context of this study, the renowned physicist occupies the cultural space to which Lucio Mansilla aspired, that of the knowledgeable scientist who wields power because of the popularized explanation that he can provide. Oppenheimer, Einstein, Heisenberg, and many other physicists gained cultural stature as those who could explain the universe. With that stature, they (and their writings) served as another guarantee of societal truth and, subsequently, as a potential structure that literature could incorporate in its production of truth as it simultaneously attempts to redefine the cultural context in which those scientists and their discoveries operate. Ironically, it is that very status that may have set up Einstein as Borges's target in "El jardín de senderos que se bifurcan."

Cortázar has presented his conception of quantum physics as proof of an absurd universe on several occasions. In his long essay, *Teoría del túnel*, he introduces Heisenberg's uncertainty principle, which states the impossibility of determining both the position and velocity of an electron or any other particle because of the effect of the observer taking the measurement. Cortázar views the principle as a scientific manifestation of the surrealist philosophy, a philosophy whose vindication serves as a focal point of the essay:

> En un sentido último, quitándole a los términos toda connotación partidista e histórica, actitudes como el cubismo, futurismo, ultraísmo, la conciencia de relatividad, la indeterminación en las ciencias físicas y la crítica al concepto de legalidad, el freudismo y este niño viejo el existencialismo, *son surrealismo*. (1994c, 107) [Italics in original]

> [In a final sense, cleansing the terms of their historical and political connotations, attitudes like cubism, futurism, ultraism, relativity, uncertainty in the physical sciences, and the criticism of the concept of legality, Freudianism, and that old child existentialism, *are surrealism*.]

By situating principles of physics such as relativity and uncertainty within a definition of surrealism, Cortázar applies the truth value Western culture has invested in science in order to privilege the surrealist stance.[5] The privileging of concepts, however, is bidirectional; he simultaneously rescues quantum physics from his critique of Western science, saving it through association to the surrealist conception he holds as a more accurate depiction of reality. Quantum theory and relativity become exempt from the condemned scientific and mechanistic literary practices Cortázar attributes to realist narrative in the essay. Cortázar further associates himself and his thought with the new physics in an interview with Sara Castro Klarén, where he notes clearly his preference for the writings of Einstein, Oppenheimer, and Heisenberg.[6] Notwithstanding these remarks, Cortázar does more than pay lip service to quantum physics as he develops his philosophy. The narrative influence the new physics exercises on Cortázar's fiction is best appreciated in its manifestations in his work.

Cortázar's remarks coupled with supporting narrative possibilities have made irresistible the critical desire to see parallels between popular descriptions of quantum mechanics and the Argentine author's narrative aims.[7] Critics have presented arguments that range from the presence of "wormholes" in Cortázar's short stories to his narrative development of the Copenhagen interpretation. On the latter subject, several have argued that John Wheeler's conception of a participatory universe in which reality can be seen to depend on observation finds an echo in Cortázar's creation of a participatory narrative universe where characters participate in the construction of their narrative reality and the reader is obliged to contribute to the construction of the text. Indeed, such similarities act as an important beginning point, where we can begin to see Cortázar's aestheticization of science in novels like *62: Un modelo para armar* and in many of his short stories. At the same time, we should not stop at the identification and appreciation of that aestheticization, but continue to the power structures suggested by those narrative and aesthetic decisions.

In order to appreciate this relationship better, we should pause to describe one of the more famous experiments used to validate the Copenhagen interpretation; the double-slit light experiment with its accompanying concept known as the collapse of the wave function.[8] The experiment has its root in a centuries-old debate in the history of science concerning the nature of light and whether it moved as a wave or a particle. The double-slit experiment is used to show that the nature of light is actually dualistic, that it moves as both a wave and a particle. The idea is to shoot photons at a screen with two slits in it that will allow the light to pass through and arrive at a second screen where the photons display light patterns. If the light is allowed to pass through the two openings, it creates a wave-like interference pattern on the second screen. In fact, during the nineteenth century this experiment was used to prove that light was indeed a wave, contrary to Newton's theory of light as a corpuscle or particle. However, if one closes one of the slits, allowing the light to pass through only one opening, the photons fail to create a wave pattern on the screen, producing instead a pattern suggestive of light traveling as a particle. The only difference between the two experimental situations is the role of the observer. The light is the same, but the physicist has changed, deciding to observe the reality of light from a different perspective. This decision seems to change the very reality the scientist attempts to observe. Physicists have suggested that what happens is that the photons travel in a state of nonexistence on probability waves coming into existence only when they arrive at a point of observation and are forced to "choose" according to those probabilities how and where to appear.[9] At the point of observation the probability wave collapses into reality, in the case of light, the photon is forced to appear as either a wave or a particle when it is in fact both and/or neither.

Cortázar seems to reflect this idea in his work not only with his multiple observers who change reality through their observations and acts of attention, but also through the imagery he employs as these observers create the reality that surrounds them. The case of *62: Modelo para armar*, Cortázar's novel based on chapter 62 of *Rayuela* in which Morelli proposes a novel that avoids any kind of psychological coherence, is especially illuminating. In the first section, Cortázar creates a situation in which reality flows by Juan, the main character, until his attention freezes it and by so doing invests it with a specific meaning. As the novel opens, Juan muses on a phrase he overhears in a restaurant, the "Je voudrais un château saignant" that he immediately converts into "Quisiera un castillo sangriento" (I would like a bloody castle). He then continues to play with its meaning, ascribing significations that change the nature of the phrase. Cortázar uses a variety of images and references that seems to suggest a similarity between the spoken phrase and the photons from the light experiment. Juan's observation of the *comensal* who had pronounced the phrase develops just such a situation, "Según el espejo el comensal estaba sentado en la segunda mesa a espaldas de la que ocupaba Juan y así su imagen y su voz habían tenido que recorrer itinerarios opuestos y convergentes para incidir en una atención bruscamente solicitada" (1996, 10). [According to the mirror, the *comensal* was seated at the second table with his back to the one where Juan was sitting and so his image and his voice had to follow opposite and converging paths to come together in one brusquely solicited act of attention.] The image of words traveling through space, arriving at a point of attention directly mirrors the trajectory of the photons traveling on their probability waves toward a destination determined by observation. Cortázar strengthens this image with a play on the translation of *sangriento* as "bloody" instead of the "rare" intended by the *saignant* of the *comensal*. The narrator observes, "Juan . . . había hecho trampa sin la menor conciencia de que el desplazamiento de sentido en la frase iba a coagular de golpe otras cosas ya pasadas o presentes de esa noche" (1996, 10). [Juan . . . had played a trick without the smallest idea that the displacement of the meaning of the phrase would suddenly coagulate other things both past and present in that night.] Cortázar develops the image of coagulated blood in a manner very similar to the image of traveling words. Blood as a liquid flows (in waves) until it coagulates, imitating the flow of words that continue until solidified and consequently distorted by the attention Juan bestows upon them. Cortázar further emphasizes the connection between observation as a fixing power and coagulation by associating the word *coagular* with the events of the night that will change presently perceived reality.

Throughout the rest of the novel, Cortázar inundates the reader with flowing images that are frozen or fixed by a look or by the attention of a character. The word *coagular* appears many more times, applied to blood and moments in time, reminding the reader of the vampiresque theme that Cortázar develops in the novel as well as suggesting a world where quantum reality serves as the basis for visible reality.[10] Later in the novel, Cortázar introduces the image of a basilisk, repeating the use of this image on several occasions as well. The basilisk is especially appropriate to the present discussion as it suggests a creature that freezes (kills) the flow of life with a gaze, an act of attention. In all three cases we see images of flowing forms converted into solid, static objects by observations that impose a distinct reality on the objects perceived. Just as Cortázar personifies elements of quantum physics, he "quantizes" visible reality in *62: Modelo para armar* through the use of a consistent system of imagery and situations.[11] Continuing in the vein of "Julios en acción," Cortázar exploits the metaphorical possibilities of popularized versions of quantum mechanics as a way to explore alternate visions of reality that violate rational or commonsensical ideas of life and the universe.

Another instance that illustrates Cortázar's tendency to aestheticize quantum theory in his fiction concerns the thought experiment known as Schrödinger's Cat designed by the physicist Irwin Schrödinger. This thought experiment, designed—ironically it turns out—to reveal the absurdity of quantum physics, has turned into one of its most powerful images and tools for its popularization. The titles of John Gribbin's best-selling popular descriptions of quantum physics, *In Search of Schrödinger's Cat* and *Schrödinger's Kittens and the Search for Reality* attest to the way Schrödinger's mockery of the Copenhagen interpretation has become one of the most powerful analogies used to explain it. The experiment calls for placing a cat in a box with a vial of poison and a mechanism designed to break the vial and release the poison. The trigger for this mechanism is controlled by a radioactive particle whose probability of decay is exactly 50 percent, producing, then, an equal probability that the cat will either live or die. Under these conditions Schrödinger argued that, if the Copenhagen interpretation were true, closing the box and activating the mechanism would cause the cat to enter a state of limbo. The cat would continue in this state, neither alive nor dead (or perhaps both), until one opened the box and through observation forced the collapse of probability to find either a live or a dead feline. While the thought experiment aimed to show why it was absurd to argue that particles existed only as probabilities until the physicist observed the particles and forced them to choose the state in which they were examined, it also served as an excellent visualization of the very abstract theory.[12]

Jean Capello has argued that we as readers should approach many of Cortázar's short stories with this thought experiment in mind. That is, a Cortázar story is much like the cat in the box, encompassing several probabilities until the end of the narrative when the reader is forced to choose one of the options, opening the box and finding the cat, so to speak. Capello's reading of "La isla al mediodía" analyzes the story's various possibilities and the effect of the reader's choice upon them. The story recounts the obsession of an airline steward, Marini, with a Greek island in the Mediterranean. He fixates on the island as he passes over it on his route from Tehran to Rome, finally making plans to vacation on the island. Once arrived, he notices a plane, his plane, fly overhead and then crash into the sea. His attempt to rescue any survivors is cut short by the end of the story where we discover that he apparently died in the crash, that he never visited the island, and that he most likely had an experience similar to the hanged man in Ambrose Bierce's "The Occurrence at Owl Creek Bridge." According to Capello, the new physics model of reading suggests that both narrative possibilities (the live Marini and the dead one) are equally possible until the end when the reader is forced to choose the Marini that died in the crash. The critic's interest lies mainly in suggesting a way to read Cortázar while consciously avoiding any imputation of authorial intent. For Capello it is immaterial whether Cortázar is playing with quantum theory or not; it is only important that his fiction seems to imitate the rules of the branch of science in question. Nevertheless, Capello names Cortázar's practice of imitating the rules of the new physics in his fiction "new physics realism" (1997, 41).

A story that seems to reveal better Cortázar's interest in taking Schrödinger's proposition seriously is the lesser studied "Ahí pero dónde, cómo," first published in the collection of stories, *Octaedro* (1974).[13] In this rather brief story a first-person narrator addresses the reader directly, inviting him or her to identify with the narrator's extremely vivid dream of a deceased friend. This dead friend,

Paco, becomes a fixation with the narrator as he tries repeatedly to convince himself that Paco still lives while simultaneously trying to remind himself that Paco has been gone some thirty-one years. After exploring the situation from a variety of perspectives, he finally decides, with some uncertainty, that Paco is dead, but that the memory of Paco extends beyond the grave.

As the narrative progresses, Cortázar creates a situation in which Paco occupies an ambiguous space between life and death. At one point he lives in the narrator's dreams, thus momentarily resolving the narrator's confusion, "Entonces es obvio que Paco está vivo . . . mientras yo duermo: eso que se llama soñar" (1994b, 83) "It was obvious that Paco is alive, while I am asleep: that which is called dreaming." However, Cortázar immediately frustrates this resolution with the subsequent, "Pero con Paco es como si se despertara también conmigo, puede permitirse el lujo de disolver casi enseguida las vívidas secuencias de la novela y seguir presente fuera del sueño" (1994b, 83). [But with Paco it is as if he had awakened with me, that he can permit himself the luxury of dissolving almost immediately after the vivid sequences of the novel and continue present outside of the dream.] The story continues with the narrator repeatedly attempting to ascertain the reality of Paco's existence, with the narratee shifting to Paco, then back to the reader at the end when the narrator laments the loss of his dead friend. The constant play between life and death in the story seems reminiscent of the cat existing in limbo neither alive nor dead. The vacillating pronouncements of the narrator further strengthen this similarity. He starts the story pronouncing Paco dead, then alive, then dead, setting Paco's state momentarily, only to release it quickly to a limbo between the two states. These fluctuations create a situation suggestive of Schrödinger's thought experiment with an analogy between the narrator's decisions as close acts of attention and the observation in the experiment that produces a live or a dead cat. The final element that cements the comparison between the thought experiment and "Ahí, pero dónde, cómo." As the narrator tries to resolve finally the question of Paco's reality, he notes, "Pero Paco está a lo suyo, gato solitario asomando desde su propia zona sin mezclas" (1994b, 87). [But Paco is in his own, like a solitary cat looking out for its own unmixed zone.] As Cortázar connects this dead/alive friend with the image of a solitary cat, enclosed within its "zona," he further strengthens the reading of his story as a rewriting of Schrödinger's experiment. Cortázar creates a situation that explores

Schrödinger's proposition seriously, suggesting that perhaps the cat's limbo is a place that does exist and that can be occupied not only by quantum particles but also by all elements of reality.[14] The result is a story that, with "La isla al mediodía" and *62: Modelo para armar*, helps establish an important trend in Cortázar's work in which a popularized view of quantum physics serves as an important source of metaphors and images.

It is to this point that criticism dedicated to quantum mechanics and Cortázar has arrived, a review of the sometimes circumstantial similarities between popular physics and his work. As we noted before, such an enterprise is instructive, but if we limit ourselves to only that, we miss that which ties Cortázar's work into a tradition of test tube envy. The seriousness with which Cortázar treats elements of quantum physics in "Ahí pero dónde, cómo" can be seen on a much larger scale in *Rayuela*. It is there where we encounter the best example of Cortázar using his understanding of quantum mechanics in a very serious questioning of tradition, rationality, and reality. To appreciate Cortázar's project as it involves quantum theory, we should initially review the anti-Cartesian stance developed in the novel, then examine the incorporation of quantum theory, symbolized mainly by the figure of Heisenberg in the novel, and finally explore how Werner Heisenberg as a cultural object strengthens Cortázar's attack on Cartesian rationality in its several manifestations.

Cortázar's rejection of Descartes throughout his fiction and especially in *Rayuela* has received less critical attention than one would think, limited by and large to passing references and critical introductions.[15] Perhaps the theme suffers from its all too obvious position in *Rayuela* where comments like, "Cartesius, viejo jodido" (1991, 207) [Cartesius, screwed up old man], and Oliveira's complaint about the inapplicability of *cogito, ergo sum* (1991, 135), appear frequently. Certainly Descartes has seen better days and more friendly treatments than the time he spends in the mouths of *Rayuela*'s characters. The personal attack on Descartes mirrors the larger questioning of the rationality the French thinker and his famous line represent. As Juan Carlos Curutchet (among others) has argued, Cortázar uses *Rayuela* to destroy what he sees as an impossible world of reason through the rejection of reason and rationality (1972, 94–101). Sosnowski notes Cortázar's opposition of poetics and science in his work, a division already seen explicitly in *Teoría del tunel* where Cortázar frames science as the rational status quo and poetics as the revolutionary irrational. The specific references to Descartes provide a personal focal point to Cortázar's more generalized attack. Furthermore, Cortázar develops these references to Descartes as part of an implicit battle of historical scientific figures that mirror his rejection of the Newtonian/Cartesian paradigm of science (I am borrowing Thomas Kuhn's terminology) and his proposal of a different nonrational reality. René Descartes, one of Western culture's most well-known symbols of logic and rationality, serves, then, as the scientist/enemy against whom Cortázar will bring the weight of the philosophical project of *Rayuela*. By so doing, Cortázar participates in a by now established tradition of textual discipline that includes Borges's critique of Nietzsche, Mansilla's revision of Sarmiento, and Sarmiento's attack on Rosas.

Against Descartes, Cortázar positions the figure of Werner Heisenberg, the German physicist, founder of the uncertainty principle, and popularizer of quantum theory, as the opposing symbolic force. Cortázar includes explicit references to Heisenberg in *Rayuela* in two separate instances, situating the physicist each time within the notes of Morelli (the novelist character who serves partially as Cortázar's alter ego). The first instance describes Heisenberg and the recognized inventor of quantum theory, Max Planck, as personifications of the quanta:

> Creer que ese objeto es nada más que una tacita de café cuando el más idiota de los periodistas encargados de resumirnos los quanta, Planck y Heisenberg, se mata explicándonos a tres columnas que todo vibra y tiembla y está como un gato a la espera de dar el enorme salto de hidrógeno. (1991, 537)

> [Believing that this object is nothing but a coffee cup while even the most idiot among journalists is assigned to give us a précis of the quanta, Planck and Heisenberg, knocks himself out in three columns explaining that everything vibrates and trembles and is like a cat about to take an enormous hydrogen or cobalt leap.] (1966, 377)

Cortázar, or rather Morelli, deploys this comment within a complicated discussion of atomic bombs and origins. The initial connection appears to be negative, as the two scientists are related to a nuclear explosion. Nevertheless, Morelli quickly rescues Planck from the fray, noting his positive characteristics, and then proceeds to his conception of a paradise-like other world (1991, 537). Both in the above-mentioned quote as well as in the rest of the chapter,

Cortázar establishes a set of metonymic and metaphorical relations. Heisenberg and Planck become metaphors for their theory, being identified as the quanta or packets of light for which quantum theory is named. At the same time, Cortázar links them with his concept of the other side of reality, his "otro lado de las cosas." In this relationship the theories of Planck and Heisenberg privilege Morelli's paradise by conferring their particular scientific prestige while simultaneously gaining status as positive symbols through their connection to Cortázar's always privileged "other" reality.[16] Cortázar further evokes quantum physics with the reference to the cat that awaits the hydrogen explosion. Just as Schrödinger's feline awaits the possibly deadly gaze of the physicist, Cortázar's cat sits perched on the possibility of nuclear annihilation. This is perhaps the most concrete allusion to Schrödinger's thought experiment in Cortázar's fiction.

Heisenberg's appearance in chapter 98 further strengthens the novel's positive presentation of the physicist, "Morelli hablaba de algo así cuando escribía: «Lectura de Heisenberg hasta mediodía, anotaciones, fichas . . . Sensación de que Heisenberg y yo estamos del otro lado de un territorio . . . En fin sigamos leyendo; a lo mejor Heisenberg»" (1991, 609–10). [Morelli spoke of something like that when he wrote: "Reading Heisenberg until noon, notes, cards. . . . Feeling that Heisenberg and I are from the other side of a territory . . . Well, let us continue reading; Heisenberg probably . . ."] (1966, 438). Cortázar here further privileges Heisenberg, presenting him as a writer worthy of Morelli's dedicated study. He also reinforces the connection between Heisenberg and "the other side" explicitly as Morelli identifies with Heisenberg, sharing his space on the other side of the "territorio." This sharing of space extends beyond the philosophical level most obviously implied. The allusions to Descartes appear mainly in the so-called "novel" portion of *Rayuela*, those chapters apparently *imprescindibles* that form the suggested linear reading of the novel that appears as the first option in the "Tablero de dirección." Morelli's notes and their references to Heisenberg are limited to what some have termed the antinovel, that is, those chapters Cortázar has termed "dispensable." While Morelli himself does appear in the "novel," his notes, his development as a character, and his identification with Heisenberg come into play only when one reads *Rayuela* according to the second reading proposed in the "Tablero." Just as Morelli's and Heisenberg's theories refute Descartes and rationality on a philosophical level, textually Morelli, Heisenberg and the extra chapters they metonymically represent undermine the rational development of *Rayuela* as a traditional novel. This effect is achieved as the chapters break the physical flow of pages with their interjected commentaries.[17] They do indeed occupy a space together on the other side of the textual *territorio* that is *Rayuela*.

The rhetorical function of Heisenberg as a cultural referent in Cortázar's work grows from the intellectual and philosophical similarities between the German physicist's popular writings and the Argentine novelist's project. These similarities become immediately apparent in an examination of both Heisenberg's public lectures as well as his other written attempts to explain and make accessible the major tenets of quantum theory from the 1940s and 1950s. We will now turn our attention to these points of shared interest.

The uncertainty principle, specifically cited by Cortázar in *Teoría del túnel*, occupies a point of great importance in Heisenberg's explanations. Heisenberg identifies the principle as the determining point between science past and science future, "Uncertainty in quantum mechanics is the location of the dividing line between past and future" (1952, 16). The rhetoric Heisenberg employs here and in many other instances employs quantum mechanics in a manner anticipatory to Thomas Kuhn's theories of scientific revolutions. Indeed, in an act that smacks of self-promotion even as it attempts to describe developments in the history of science, Heisenberg positions his theories in the realm of revolution and the new. In fact, just as Cortázar implicitly distinguishes between bad science and good physics en *Teoría del túnel*, Heisenberg opposes quantum mechanics to the previous scientific attitudes toward reality based on Newton and Descartes. Cortázar's theory of revolution elaborated in *Teoría del túnel* and elsewhere, find, then, an important ally in the writings of Heisenberg. That is, in a cultural context of 1960s Europe and Latin America where revolutionary discourse held an important place in cultural imagination, Heisenberg's characterization of quantum mechanics as revolutionary could be easily interpreted to lend scientific support to other theories of revolution. In such an act, we see again the bidirectional flow of cultural authority between science and literature where literature tautologically uses science as outside proof even as it defines and shapes the cultural visions of that science.

Cortázar's apparent aestheticization of the participatory nature of reality in *62: Un modelo para armar* that we discussed earlier in the chapter confirms another aspect of the kinship between Heisenberg's and Cortázar's thought that serves as the basis for Heisenberg's privileged narrative position in *Rayuela*. The German physicist elaborates on the essential role of the observer as he describes the discoveries of quantum physics for a popular audience, "Now, this is a very strange result, since it seems to indicate that the observation plays a decisive role in the event and that reality varies, depending on whether we observe it or not" (1958, 52). The shift quantum theory brings from the previous objective, observer-independent reality to one contingent upon the attention of beings that simultaneously occupy a part of that reality finds an echo both in Cortázar's thought and specifically in the participatory nature of *Rayuela*. Indeed, Cortázar's claim that *Rayuela* is many different novels, depending on the order in which one reads the chapters, suggests just such a similarity. Just like the scientist in the double-slit light experiment can affect the nature of light with the decisions that they make, the reader can affect the nature of *Rayuela* by choosing the order in which they will read the chapters. The novel itself serves as a metaphor for quantum reality, with all the uncertainty inherent in the observation of subatomic particles repeated in the manner in which Cortázar forces the reader to affect the reality of the narrative.

The German physicist also comments repeatedly on the struggles his colleagues were experiencing with language. As physicists tried to use the terms and concepts learned from their education in classical physics they found that the words they used to describe phenomena simply could not give an accurate picture of reality. Heisenberg describes these linguistic difficulties:

> It was the increased range of technical experience which first forced us to leave the limits of classical concepts. These concepts no longer fitted nature as we had come to know it. We observed the track of an electron moving as a particle in a Wilson chamber and, on another occasion, we found it reflected on a diffraction grating like a wave. The language of classical physics was no longer capable of expressing these two observations as effects of a single entity. (1952, 46)

This attitude both points out the inadequacy of language as well as positioning quantum physics in a revolutionary role, one that resists the structures and foundations of the old science. With regard to the problems of the language of classical physics, Sir Arthur Eddington once noted that if one were to replace all the terms used in quantum physics with words from Lewis Carroll's *Jabberwocky* (a Cortázar favorite), the descriptions would be as accurate if not more so (quoted and expanded on in Gribbin, 1984, 192).

Cortázar has often struggled with a similar perception of the inadequacy of language. Andrés Amorós quotes Cortázar as commenting that "esa toma de conciencia de las limitaciones lingüísticas de un escritor; el hecho de que el lenguaje es una herencia recibida, una herencia pasiva en la que él no ha tenido ninguna intervención" (Amorós 1991, 37). [that consciousness of the linguistic limitations of a writer, the fact that language is a received inheritance, a passive inheritance in which he has not had any intervention.] While Cortázar's questioning of language occurs on a more fundamental level than that of Heisenberg, the feeling that traditional language no longer represents reality links the two thinkers. *Rayuela* evinces a similar attitude toward language. Members of the Serpent's Club, for example, refer to the dictionary as a "cementerio," activating the idea once again that representational power of traditional language is dead and fails to signify new realities.[18] While Heisenberg's attitude toward language tends toward a more optimistic plane, the struggle with antiquated terms and concepts suggests another reason why Morelli reads Heisenberg.

Finally, Heisenberg's criticism of Descartes in his popular writing qualifies him specially for his role in the debate Cortázar creates between the two icons of the history of science. Heisenberg characterizes Descartes as one whose theories have outlived their usefulness as a model for scientific thought:

> Previously, the examples of science could lead to philosophic systems which assumed a certain truth—like the "cogito, ergo sum" of Descartes—as the starting point from which all questions of "Weltanschauung" could be attacked. But now nature, through the medium of modern physics has reminded us very clearly that we should never hope for such a firm basis for the comprehension of the whole field of "things perceptible." (1952, 25)

In this quotation, we see the representatives of the new science relegate Descartes to history books, an example of the naïve views of the past. But, according to Heisenberg, Descartes's theories are not simply out-of-date. Descartes's influence exercised a detrimental effect on the acceptance of the implications of the new physics. Heisenberg explains:

> If one follows the great difficulty which even eminent scientists like Einstein had in understanding and accepting the Copenhagen interpretation of quantum theory, one can trace the roots of this difficulty to the Cartesian partition. This partition has penetrated deeply into the human mind during the three centuries following Descartes and it will take a long time for it to be replaced by a really different attitude toward the problem of reality. (1958, 81)

Heisenberg here engages a bit of scientific discipline of his own, presenting Descartes in the same manner as Cortázar. For both, Descartes becomes a scientist whose worldview was not only wrong, but has exercised a deleterious effect on the acceptance of the "real" version of reality. Cortázar's presentation of Heisenberg within *Rayuela* is therefore completely consistent with the physicist's role in the history of science and with his work as a popularizer of quantum mechanics. In fact, if we take Morelli as the embodiment of Cortázar's antirational project, Morelli's comment that he and Heisenberg occupy that same "other side" is profoundly true on the philosophical level, repeating the use of a Foucauldian analytical space that we saw in Borges.

Rayuela's antirational project does not limit itself to attacks on scientific figures of the past. Cortázar completes his attack on scientific symbols of rationality as he presents the contemporary science of cybernetics as a modern manifestation of Cartesian thinking. The Argentine author includes salvos of this attack in his essay "Del sentimiento de no estar del todo," published in his collage-book *La vuelta al día en ochenta mundos*, where he responds to the critical reception of *Rayuela*:

> Me sumo a los pocos críticos que han querido ver en *Rayuela* la denuncia imperfecta y desesperada del *establishment* de las letras, a la vez espejo y pantalla del otro *establishment* que está haciendo de Adán, cibernética y minuciosamente, lo que delata su nombre apenas se lo lee al revés: nada. (1967, 26)

> [I prefer those few critics who have seen in *Hopscotch* the imperfect and desperate denunciation of the establishment of letters, at once the mirror and the screen of the larger establishment that is making Adam,

cybernetically and minutely, into what his name signifies when it is spelled backwards in Spanish: *Adán, nada*, nothing.] (1986, 23)

Cortázar simultaneously invests the term cybernetics with a negative connotation as he invites a critical appraisal of the rhetorical and textual function of cybernetics in *Rayuela*. Indeed, while the passage employs the familiar iconoclastic position many critics have identified as central to Cortázar's novel, an understanding of the position of cybernetics in the history of science and the developments in physics in the twentieth century help complete our analysis of Cortázar's complicated reflections on science and scientific discourse.

Cybernetics as a scientific theory finds its beginnings in a series of meetings of an interdisciplinary group of electrical and communications engineers, mathematicians, physiologists, physicists, psychologists, and biophysicists that took place in the 1940s (Wiener 1961, 1).[19] The discipline this group founded attempted (and attempts) an all-inclusive theory of information exchange. It seeks to describe mechanical and biological systems, from toilets to human beings to ecosystems, in terms of the mechanical process by which these systems produce, exchange, and use pieces of information. Norbert Wiener christened the science "cybernetics," with allusions to the Greek for governor and helmsman (1961, 12). The helmsman translation was especially important to Wiener as it alluded to the steering mechanism for ships that was what he considered to be the first feedback system (1961, 12). These feedback systems and the mechanical way in which they were seen to operate came to serve as central metaphors for understanding cybernetic thought. Wiener's first book on the subject, *Cybernetics: Control and Communication in Animal and Machine* (1948, 1961), posits in its title the importance of the machine metaphor for cybernetics as well as its persuasiveness in the description of its subject. Wiener confirms the centrality of the mechanistic metaphor for life in his later work *The Human Use of Human Beings*, "It is my thesis that the operation of the living individual and the operation of some of the newer communication machines are precisely parallel" (1950, 15).

The influence of cybernetics spread quickly throughout the sciences. Donna Haraway notes the integral nature of cybernetic thought in the shifts in evolutionary biology. For example, shifts that have redefined the way in which scientists frame biological questions so as to incorporate what she calls the "technical-natural object," an idea that she has developed further in her "Cyborg Manifesto" (1991, 245). N. Katherine Hayles traces the growth of cybernetics through the second half of the twentieth century, arguing that it has led to a new definition of the human being as an "informational-material entity," a conception of the human being as similar in function to machine that she also calls posthuman (2000, 12). This growth in popularity as a description of life and reality along with the extension of cybernetic thought into many aspects of science situates it within a concept of scientific tradition that would make Cortázar's association of *cibernética* with the sinister "otro *establishment*" seem an obvious decision. Indeed, the writing of *Rayuela* in the late 1950s and early 1960s corresponds precisely to the growing fame of cybernetics as an important new scientific discipline.[20]

Just as Cortázar uses cybernetics to signal a methodical, calculating action that results in nullification of human beings in "Del sentimiento de no estar del todo," he invests a similar meaning in the concept as it appears in *Rayuela*. The first instance of the term occurs in chapter 73, a significant position, as it occupies the first page of the antinovel Cortázar suggests in his "Tablero."[21] As the novel elaborates a theory of cultural and literary rebellion, in this chapter the narrator describes the tendency toward tradition as "alegre cibernética" "happy cybernetics" (1991, 544). The entire passage further illuminates this use:

> Cuantas veces me pregunto si esto no es más que escritura, en un tiempo en que corremos al engaño entre ecuaciones infalibles y máquinas de conformismos. Pero preguntarse si sabremos encontrar el otro lado de la costumbre o si más vale dejarse llevar por su alegre cibernética, ¿no será otra vez literatura? (1991, 544)

> [How often I wonder whether this is only writing, in an age in which we run towards deception through infallible equations and conformity machines. But to ask one's self if we will know how to find the other side of habit or if it is better to let one's self be borne along by its happy cybernetics, is that not literature again?] (1966, 383)

Cortázar situates his concept of cybernetics within a textual environment ruled by the phrase "dejarse llevar" that reminds the reader immediately of the unfortunately titled "lector hembra" against whose passivity Cortázar rails in *Rayuela*. To the sinister connotation we find in the essay, we see the addition of a connection between cybernetics as concept and the conformist tradition from which Horacio Oliveira continually attempts to escape.[22] Cortázar reinforces the connection between cybernetic thought and conformity with a series of mechanical images in this first chapter. As we see in the preceding passage, he couches deceit among the cybernetic tools of "ecuaciones infalibles y máquinas de conformismos" that occupy "this" side of reality. He implicitly opposes "this" side, or commonly perceived reality, with an "other," irrational side he seems to prefer. He then attempts to integrate the irrational side of reality into the traditionally accepted perspective of the world.[23] Cortázar also mechanizes the body, earlier in the chapter, referring to the closed circuits of the blood, situating the cybernetic threat not only on the exterior, but also within human beings themselves (1991, 544). What emerges is a conception of cybernetics solely as a mechanizing system used by the establishment, with no allusion to the theories of information exchange that form the basis of the science of cybernetics itself.

This mechanization of life also serves to connect the critique of cybernetics with Cortázar's critique of Descartes. While cybernetics is the most modern manifestation of the concept of the body as machine, we see the idea throughout the history of ideas, not only in Descartes's descriptions of the body, but in Julien La Mettrie's *L'homme machine* and in Zola's *Le roman expérimental* as well as in a plethora of other scientific and literary works. Foucault's own connection of Descartes and La Mettrie's automated body with his concept of the docile body suggests a further reason for Cortázar's antipathy as the automated docile body is one that is controlled by the state and not prone to participate in revolution (1977, 136). The image of mechanized life also continues a tradition in Argentine science fiction as well, from Eduardo Holmberg's automatons to Horacio Quiroga's "Biógeno" in his early *El hombre artificial*. Cortázar's connection of cybernetics with the images of mechanized life serves, then, to ground the science within the tradition against which he positions Morelli and Heisenberg.

This careful construction of semiotic connections in Cortázar's idiosyncratic use of the term "cybernetics" makes its other appearance in *Rayuela* even more significant. In the apocalyptic chapter 71, Cortázar again associates the term with a false sense of optimism and security:

> Y por qué entonces inquietarse si probablemente el mundo es finito, la historia se acerca al punto óptimo, la raza humana sale de la edad media para ingresar en la era cibernética. *Tout va très bien, madame la Marquise, tout va très bien, tout va très bien.* (1991, 541)

> [And why then worry one's self about whether the world most likely is finite, whether history is coming to its optimum, whether the human race is emerging from the Middle Ages and entering the era of cybernetics. *Tout va très bien, madame la Marquise, tout va très bien, tout va très bien.*] (1966, 380)

Just as the *alegre cibernética* of chapter 73 evokes a sense of passivity toward traditional reality, Cortázar similarly sketches out the prospect of a cybernetic age, once again on *this* side of reality, that lulls people into complacency. The comforts of civilization and the evocation of the popular French song combine to bestow an ironic all-is-well attitude to an *era cibernética* that Cortázar will proceed to describe as dangerous. The concept of the coming of a cybernetic age is not new to Cortázar, Wiener announces and describes this "second industrial revolution" in his popular writings.[24] Indeed, Wiener, while excitedly describing the wonders of cybernetics, also warns of the dangers of giving up humanity to the machines that form an increasingly important element of modern life.[25] Cortázar works this warning into a broader attack against the threat of Cartesian thinking, exemplified now by cybernetics.

We see these strategies repeated in the initial presentation of cybernetics in *Rayuela* by surrounding the occurrence of the term with mechanical imagery. "Cada reunión de gerentes internacionales, de hombres-de-ciencia, cada nuevo satélite artificial, hormona o reactor atómico aplastan un poco más estas falaces esperanzas. El reino será de material plástico, es un hecho" (1991, 541). [Every meeting of international tycoons, or men-of-science, each new artificial satellite, hormone, or atomic reactor crushes these false hopes. The kingdom will be made out of plastic material, that is a fact (1966, 380).] The emphasis on an artificial reality made up of satellites and man-made hormones opposes the mechanistic concepts of cybernetics to the iconoclastic philosophy Cortázar tries to expound throughout *Rayuela*. The inclusion of the international business within this artificial world further expands the target of his attack, combining the forces of capitalism with a mechanistic view of society.[26] The linking of the "gerentes internacionales" with the overly mechanized society firmly associates the cause of this alienation with a cybernetic conceptualization of civilization. The novel extends this idea further, presenting a proposed escape from this too-perfect reality in mechanical terms, "Se le va a escapar, le va a agarrar el timón de la máquina electrónica, del cohete sideral, le va a hacer una zancadilla" (1991, 542). [He will escape from it, he will grasp the rudder of the electronic machine, the astral rocket, he will trip up and then they can set a dog on him (1966, 380).] The image of the *timón* is especially appropriate when we remember the translation of cybernetics as helmsman. On a metaphorical level, the Cortazarian hero must wrench control of the ship from the cybernetic mechanism that leads humanity happily toward nothingness. Throughout the chapter, Cortázar paints and then revisits the landscape of the nightmare of technology and rationalism he terms "la era cibernética."

Even when cybernetics is not mentioned explicitly, Cortázar includes images of mechanized life and reproductions of life that keep the theme at the forefront of the text. For example, in chapter 47 we find Talita recording her voice on a tape recorder. The scene is interesting for several reasons. Initially, Cortázar presents the situation in such a way as to confuse the speaker with the recording. The initial paragraph is presented in such a way as to hide whether Talita is actually speaking or indeed listening to her own voice.

> Soy yo, soy él. Somos, pero soy yo, primeramente soy yo, defenderé ser yo hasta que no pueda más. Atalía, soy yo. Ego, Yo. Diplomada, argentina, una uña encarnada, bonita de a ratos, grandes ojos oscuros, yo. Atalía Donosi, yo. Yo. Yo-yo, carretel y piolincito. Cómico.
> Manú, qué loco, irse a Casa América y solamente por divertirse alquilar este artefacto. *Rewind.* Qué voz, esta no es mi voz. Falsa y forzada: «Soy yo, soy él. Somos, pero soy yo, primeramente soy yo, defenderé . . . » STOP. Un aparato extraordinario, pero no sirve para pensar en voz alta, o a lo mejor hay que acostumbrarse, Manú habla de grabar su famosa pieza de radioteatro sobre las señoras, no va a hacer nada. (1991, 442)

[I am I, I am he. We are, but I am I, first I am I, I will defend being I until I am unable to fight any longer. I am I, Atalía. *Ego. Yo.* A professional degree, an Argentine, a scarlet fingernail, pretty sometimes, big dark eyes, I. Atalía Donosi, I. Yo. Yo-yo, windlass and hawser. Funny. What a nut, Manú, going to the Casa América and renting this thing just to have some fun. REWIND. What a voice, that's not my voice. False and forced: "I am I, I am he. We are, but I am I, first I am I, I will defend . . ." STOP. Wonderful machine, but it's no good thinking out loud, or maybe you have to get used to it. Manú talks about recording his famous radio script about fine ladies; he won't do anything.] (1966, 283)

The confusion of human and machine serves to evoke the cybernetic and Cartesian concepts of mechanized life, an image we see in the closed circuit of blood of chapter 73. Cortázar heightens the confusion between recorder and person as he includes the actions "Rewind" and "STOP" that interrupt the flow of words, confusing again the division between voice and recording. In addition to this confusion of human and machine, we find a further development in the image of the tape, "tan lisa, tan parejita" (442) "so smooth, so regular." The smoothness of the recorded object, combined with its undesirable status, noted in Talita's rejection of the sound of her recorded voice, suggests the negative nature of conformity that we have already seen connected with the cybernetic image. And the mechanization of speech and the resulting speech play we observe in this chapter hint at without necessarily invoking the status of cybernetics as a theory of communication insofar as it examines human communication as a mechanical exchange of information.

This connection of the recorded voice with cybernetics intersects with the conception brought forth by William Burroughs in his *The Soft Machine*, published in 1969, but written in Paris from 1961 to 1962. Burroughs, in his critique of cybernetic society, uses the image of the tape recorder to provide a negative description of the "bio-mechanical (or strict structuralist) view of language as the reflection of an inner mechanism arising from the organic machinery of the central nervous system" (Porush 1985, 101). The image of Talita with the recorder in *Rayuela* acts as a cultural intertext with that of Burroughs, (or vice versa) and reminds one of the prevalence of the fear of cybernetics and the similar methods for expressing that uneasiness among intellectuals in the 1960s.[27] At the same time, this discomfort with the reproduction of the human stands in counterpoint to Walter Benjamin's essay, "The Work of Art in the Age of Mechanical Reproduction." Benjamin describes the mechanization of art as a liberating force that frees art from an "aura" that can lead to fascism. Mechanical reproduction of art, film in particular, provides a way to politicize art and therefore make it functional on a Marxist level of interpretation. Cortázar, also an avowed Marxist, interprets this mechanization along more romantic lines, valuing the "aura" of individuality as an important element of life that mechanization eliminates.

As we noted in relation to the image of mechanized life, cybernetics figures in the Descartes/Heisenberg debate as a modern manifestation of Cartesian thinking. Not only is it possible to appreciate the similarity in the use of a mechanistic metaphor for life, but also in the logical and rationalistic structures Cortázar evokes in his critique of Descartes. These structures are repeated in the use of cybernetics to describe the too-perfect societies that lack the spontaneity and unpredictability of life. Such an association is consistent with the place of Wiener's theories in the history of science. Wiener himself situates cybernetics at the end of a series of philosophical and scientific attempts to describe life mechanically. David Porush notes as well that cybernetics grew from the reaction in the scientific field to the unsettling implications of Heisenberg's uncertainty principle and the desire to return to the more orderly reality described by Newtonian and Cartesian physics (1985, 51). Porush then characterizes the main goals of cybernetics within the philosophical-scientific arena:

> cybernetics was still at its core a direct reaction to the contingent and uncertain view of the universe promoted by the New Physics. Its primary intention was and still is to reconquer chance by subordinating it within a larger system of mathematical logic, and to bring the world described by physics into conformity with the actual conditions of the natural and social structures which are the contexts for human experience. (1985, 54)

Cortázar's framing of cybernetics within the Cartesian rationalist camp, then, is nothing original. Cybernetics' declared enemy was the New Physics that we have seen Cortázar single out as a more accurate version of reality. For Cortázar, then, Descartes occupies a space in the past, the source of traditional ways of conceiving reality, while cybernetics acts as a complementary symbol that shows the threat of Cartesian thinking in the future, especially in the image of the coming "era cibernética." In the textual positioning of sciences that occurs in *Rayuela*, Heisenberg occupies a foregrounded space that opposes rationalistic theories from both the past and the present. We have, then, in the midst of an attack on a scientific theory (Cartesianism), the appearance of another science (quantum mechanics) as a powerful force in Cortázar's attack.

Cortázar takes his critique of cybernetics even further, using it as an expansion of his general attack on conformity. *Rayuela* itself is an answer to the perceived conformity of the traditional novel, a conformity that has acquired the negative qualities of machine and cybernetics thanks to a pattern of associations that has been established throughout *Rayuela*. Cortázar seems to use the novel to line up images of conformity and rationalism like ducks at a shooting gallery. These narrative ducks become interchangeable, in a sense, owing to their shared semiotic function as symbols of the evils of rationalism. For example, many critics have commented on the antinovel of *Rayuela*, showing how the second reading undermines the development of the traditional novel based in nineteenth-century standards.[28] Indeed, just as Oliveira's commentary infiltrates Benito Pérez Galdós's *Lo prohibido* in chapter 34, undermining its ability to act as a transparent window on reality, the "capítulos prescindibles" interrupt and undermine the development of a traditional novel. The traditional novel and the cybernetic era become markers for the same concept in Cortázar, an establishment that requires conformity, and by so doing, slowly destroys human beings. The positioning of Heisenberg and Morelli to which I referred earlier once again becomes important. The traditional novel, Descartes, cybernetics, rationalism, all serve as concepts against which Cortázar fights and against which he uses the philosophical implications of Heisenberg's theories as one of his weapons.

The association (albeit merely implied) between the traditional novel and cybernetics sets Cortázar's thought in opposition to the theories of critics studying cybernetics and literature. Porush, for example, has noted that the increased interest in the novel as self-aware literary artifact resulted in the modernist view of a mechanistic text, noting William Carlos William's statement to that effect: "The poem is a machine" (1985, 21). The implication is that when one highlights the mechanisms of the novel, one interrupts the novelistic illusion so carefully cultivated by the realist novelists of the nineteenth century. Also important in the modernist vision was the role of the reader, as Porush argues, and the relationship between the reader and the text becomes one that he would call cybernetic (1985, 21). Gary Stonum develops the cybernetic view of reading along a slightly different line, noting the similarities between the structuralist and poststructuralist view of the text as an object that is decoded and the theories of encoding and decoding that accompany cybernetic analyses of information exchange. While neither Porush nor Stonum includes a consideration of *Rayuela* in his discussion of cybernetics in literature, one would be hard pressed to find a better example of a text that continually exposes the literary techniques and mechanisms that make it a literary text and that requires a concerted decoding by the reader.

In fact, Cortázar seems to suggest such a reading with his presentation of the *Rayuel-O-Matic* in the essay "Otra máquina célibe" from *La vuelta al día en ochenta mundos*, a machine designed to facilitate the reading of its namesake novel. The *Rayuel-O-Matic* consists of an easy chair positioned parallel to a bureau with a series of numbered drawers that contain, individually, all of the chapters of the novel. There are also a panel with several buttons and a cabinet where one can keep *maté* (an Argentine tea) and/or gin. To operate the machine, the reader sits in the easy chair, causing the drawer containing chapter 73 to open. When the reader finishes the chapter and closes its drawer, the drawer for chapter one automatically opens. In fact, the machine turns into a cybernetic, biomechanical device, where the process of reading the chapters and interacting with the automatic drawers forms a feedback loop in which the machine responds to the actions of the reader as the reader responds to the information provided by the machine. This erasure of the boundary between the body of the reader and the mechanical apparatus of the text creates a metaphorical cyborg, or cybernetic organism, and anticipates subsequent literature that has explored this image. The link is further strengthened by the story that introduces it, a description of a fanciful meeting between Marcel Duchamp, whose Bachelor Machine provides the model for the title of the article, and Raymond Roussel, whose writing machine serves as the inspiration for the *Rayuel-O-Matic*. Cortázar then describes a subsequent meeting between himself and a mechanically inclined friend, the friend doubling for Duchamp and Cortázar for Roussel. The eventual product of the meeting is the *Rayuel-O-Matic*, the physical manifestation of the novel/machine whose nature becomes biomechanical with the insertion of the human reader.

At first glance, this merely confirms what we have seen in Cortázar's use of quantum mechanics, that is that he continually values and cultivates the participatory nature of the reading process. The novel and the reader create a dialogue between them not unlike a feedback loop in cybernetics where information is exchanged between two systems, the text challenging the reader with information that the reader processes and then imposes on the text.[29] This position, especially when taken in light of the *Rayuel-O-Matic*, would seem to undermine, at least philosophically, the anti-cybernetic position Cortázar takes both in the novel and in his essays. While the article presents itself as a gag (and is dismissed as such by the criticism that does mention it), it is also likely that Cortázar possessed only a cursory knowledge of cybernetic theory, viewing it rather as a simple symbol of a new rationalism. Even so, there appears a troubling tension as the playful image of the *Rayuel-O-Matic* stands apparently at odds with Cortázar's very serious critique of cybernetics and the rationalism that it represents.

Perhaps, however, this position could also lead us to a rethinking of Porush's conception of the cybernetic text. Let us revisit the *Rayuel-O-Matic*, considering its semiotic potential as image. It is indeed a machine designed to facilitate the reading of *Rayuela*, a comfortable recliner with a system of drawers and buttons that provide the desired chapters at the appropriate times. However, the image of the easy chair as a space for reading is not the ideal readerly area in Cortázar's work. In "Continuidad de los parques," one of Cortázar's most widely read stories in which a man becomes engrossed in a novel only to have its characters come hunting for him, the easy chair is the place where this reader meets his doom. Cortázar's reference to Foucault's book on Raymond Roussel at the beginning of "Otra máquina célibe" also raises suspicions, as Foucault's interpretation of Roussel's reading machine in that book emphasizes its connections with the death of Roussel. With those points in mind, and with the very clear antimechanical theme in *Rayuela*, the *Rayuel-O-Matic* becomes a very unstable image. In fact, a machine designed for the reading of a novel whose purpose is to undermine the past and coming mechanistic eras becomes a self-destructing device. The machine delivers the text that will question the very ideas that support its existence. In that sense, the *Rayuel-O-Matic* directly signifies Cortázar's concept of the cybernetic age, an age whose dependence on a Cartesian, rationalist system of thinking will be the cause of the destruction of human beings.[30] The machine becomes a torture chamber, designed to administer an intellectual discipline similar to the kind Borges exercised on Nietzsche.

While Cortázar mentions cybernetics in relatively few instances, one can appreciate the importance of his conception of the theory of information exchange and its mechanistic metaphor for society in his work. Cortázar employs extensively the mechanical metaphor and the coming of a cybernetic era, elements that figure prominently in popular descriptions of cybernetics.[31] However, he tends to exclude the information exchange theory that forms the basis of the science, preferring to strengthen cybernetics' connection with Cartesian modes of thought. Cybernetics becomes, then, an image of all that is wrong in contemporary society, the conformity and tradition that, through mechanization, robs humanity of what for Cortázar is the truly real. In a similar fashion, Cortázar's play with elements of quantum mechanics simultaneously argues that the new physics is an accurate description of reality, and that conversely, his descriptions of reality have a basis in scientific theory. What we see, then, in Cortázar's use of science is the appropriation of elements of scientific theories and practices he observes in popular culture, seeing metaphors in the various disciplines for his own vision of reality. The rhetorical power of the figurative test tube continues, as Cortázar uses his vision of Heisenberg's theories to disprove those of scientists and philosophers that came both before and after.

When analyzing a text as rich as *Rayuela*, one must choose and foreground specific aspects, while ignoring many other important and salient points in order to consider any fruitfully. It is by no means the case that the intellectual kinship between Cortázar's ideas and quantum physics acts as the one and only determining force in the novel. Nevertheless, the Descartes and Wiener versus Heisenberg dichotomy that functions as a textual and metaphorical opposition of historical figures and cultural paradigms illuminates aspects of Cortázar's antirationalism that have previously gone understudied. An understanding of the metaphorical roles Cartesianism, cybernetics, and quantum physics play in Cortázar's work and especially *Rayuela* uncovers an important dimension to his rich work and suggests a continuity with the nineteenth-century practice so prevalent in Argentina of appropriating scientists and the scientific theories they embody for their rhetorical and philosophical power.

One also perceives a continuity with Arlt's development of a scientific image. Just as Arlt uses scientific language to strengthen his attack on the horrors of science, Cortázar uses the scientific authority of Heisenberg against the evils he sees in scientific thinking. Additionally, in both twentieth-century authors, we see a use of scientific discourse within a metaphysical system, rather than the mainly political objectives of the nineteenth-century authors. Finally, each author focuses the influence their writing can be said to exercise on science on the redefinition of the cultural perception of science rather than on its actual practice, preferring to control the philosophical implications of science in its popular conception. The difference between the Arlt and Cortázar lies in the careful distinctions between scientific disciplines and theories Cortázar cultivates as he questions scientific tradition. Arlt sets chemistry against chemistry, proving his critique true by virtue of his ability to use the language of the discipline he attacks. Cortázar uses one scientific theory against another, developing the rhetorical authority of Heisenberg against that of Wiener and Descartes. In that, Cortázar builds scientific timelines not dissimilar to Borges's construction in "La doctrina de los ciclos," while avoiding Borges's subsequent abandonment of scientific discourse. Cortázar exhibits then, as the test tube envy seen previously in Arlt and early Borges as he exhibits the need for the authority of Heisenberg in order to carry out his philosophical project. In that sense, Cortázar is surprisingly less radical than his twentieth century cohorts. Arlt, and Sabato, set science against itself on its most basic level and Borges worked to abolish its authority outright. Cortázar merely mirrors the changing of the scientific guard, using the development in modern physics as a metaphor for the developments he saw as true in philosophy and metaphysics.

7
Test Tube Envy at the Turn of the Century: Convergences and Divergences

THE SO-CALLED POSTBOOM IN LATIN AMERICAN NARRATIVE HAS caused many different veins to converge and diverge, its variety serving as one of its key characteristics. The relationship between science and narrative is no exception. In this chapter I will look briefly at a group of authors who subvert the tradition of test tube envy through a recursion to science fiction, explicitly in the case of Ricardo Piglia and implicitly in the case of Ana María Shua and Angélica Gorodischer. I will then dedicate the majority of the chapter to a consideration of Mempo Giardinelli's *Imposible equilibrio*, a novel that attempts to embrace both the sociopolitical objectives of the first group as well as a markedly nineteenth-century version of test tube envy.

In *La ciudad ausente* (1993), Ricardo Piglia uses the science fiction trope of a mechanical female narrator (Elena) in an exploration of the trauma inflicted on Argentina by the recent dictatorship. Among the many narrative lines that intertwine in Elena's story is one that reflects on the role of science in Argentine history. One of the characters recounts the story of one Richter, a Swiss charlatan who fools Juan Perón into believing that he was a German physicist and into funding a nuclear energy program designed by Richter. Perón's response to Richter's claim provides an excellent example of the way in which science operated in Argentine culture:

> Nadie puede comparar mi descubrimiento con el invento de Richter, que le construyó a Perón una fábrica atómica sólo con palabras, con la sola realidad de su acento alemán. Le dijo que era un científico atómico que tenía el secreto de la bomba y Perón se lo creyó y cayó como un chorlito y le hizo edificar edificios subterráneos, laboratorios inútiles con tubos y turbinas que jamás se usaron. Un decorado maravilloso por el que Perón se paseaba mientras Richter, con un fuerte acento alemán, le ex-

plicaba sus planes enloquecidos de producir la fisión nuclear en frío. Le hizo el cuento, era apenas un pobre profesor secundario de física y ni siquiera era alemán, en realidad era suizo y Perón, que se pasó la vida pasando a todo el mundo, . . . le creyó su historia fantástica y la defendió hasta el fin. (1993, 140–41)

[You cannot compare my discovery with Richter's invention, he built an atomic plant for Perón using only words, just with the reality of his German accent. He told him he was an atomic scientist and that he had the secret to make the bomb, and Perón believed him and fell like a fool, and had underground buildings and useless labs with pipes and turbines built for him that were never used. Perón would stroll through the marvelously decorated facilities while Richter, with a strong German accent, explained his wild plans of how he would produce nuclear fission in a cold environment. He won him over with his story, he was just a poor high school physics teacher, and he was not even German, he was actually Swiss, and Perón, who spent his life surpassing everyone . . . believed Richter's fantastic story and defended it to the end.] (2000, 116)

Richter serves as a model of the writer who similarly manipulated cultural discourse, exercising real political power because of its supposed basis in science. The unmasking of the process that occurs as Piglia describes who Richter really was functions simultaneously as an unmasking of Argentine discourse, revealing the author behind the curtain of scientific reference. Piglia's example describes not only the literary workings behind Richter's façade, it shows the way in which the intersection of literature and science affected important policy decisions. The anecdote also reminds one of Sabato's complaint that enthusiasm for science stems directly from a failure to understand it. While Piglia rejoices in the fictional nature of Richter's subterfuge, he also describes clearly the practice of test tube envy that runs through elements of Argentine culture.

Piglia, however, tends not to suffer the same envy that we see in other authors. In that sense, Idelber Avelar's observation that Piglia writes the novels that Borges never did finds confirmation in Piglia's inheritance of Borges's demolition of scientific authority. This is an ironic turn of events if we remember Piglia's relegation of Borges to the nineteenth century. At the same time, we see Piglia confront the power relationships between science and literature head on. Immediately following the relation of Richter's story, we find the following observation:

7: TEST TUBE ENVY AT THE TURN OF THE CENTURY

Vea, dijo, los políticos les creen a los científicos (Perón-Richter) y los científicos les creen a los novelistas (Russo-Macedonio Fernández). Los científicos son grandes lectores de novelas, los últimos representantes del público del siglo XIX, los únicos que se toman en serio la incertidumbre de la realidad y la forma de un relato. Los físicos, decía Macedonio, le pusieron *quarks* a la partícula básica del universo, en homenaje al *Finnegans Wake* de Joyce; el único amigo que tuvo en Princeton, su único confidente, fue el novelista Hermann Broch, cuyos libros, sobre todo *La muerte de Virgilio*, citaba de memoria. (1993, 141)

["Look," he said, "politicians believe scientists (Perón-Richter), and scientists believe novelists (the Russian-Macedonio Fernández). Scientists are big readers of novels, the last representatives of a nineteenth-century public, the only ones who really consider the uncertainty of reality and the form of a story. Physicists, Macedonio would say, added the *quarks* to the basic particle of the universe, in homage to Joyce's *Finnegans Wake*. The only friend Einstein had at Princeton, his only confidant, was the novelist Hermann Broch, whose books, especially *The Death of Virgil*, he could quote from memory."] (2000, 116)

The claim that scientists are great readers of novels is a rather broad generalization, but the gesture itself is worthy of discussion. We have seen in previous chapters the narrative attempt to influence the nature of scientific discourse by defining what is and what is not science even as it appropriate the cultural authority enjoyed by science. Here, Piglia attempts a similar strategy. As Piglia places writers at the source of a flow of authority that runs from writer to scientist to politician, he responds to 150 years of a power dynamic that has influenced some of the most influential texts of Argentine narrative. He also participates in the gesture that we saw occur in the critical reinsertion of Borges within "test tube envy." Piglia's claim for the importance of literary authority here stems directly from its ability to influence the scientists who have, in turn, the ears of the politicians. While Piglia's work in general does not exhibit the kind of test tube envy that we have seen in the other works in this study, this observation certainly recognizes a dynamic that exists in Argentine narrative albeit alongside other practices.

In fact, Piglia's literary relationship with science is better understood in his development of the science fiction so evident in his 1993 novel. As I mentioned in the introduction, I have not included science fiction in this study. Although it is of great importance in Argentine narrative, harking to as far back as Eduardo Holmberg and including many of the authors that figure in this study, its relationship with science is different from the dynamic at issue here. While this difference in strategy does not preclude a committed position by any means, the flow of cultural power operates differently as science is used to aid in the suspension of belief rather than an attempt to garner cultural authority for a particular literary position. In fact, the tradition of science fiction in Argentine letters could be seen as an attempt to circumvent the power structures that we have seen active in our story of test tube envy. By using a scientific reality clearly labeled as fantastic, the authors are able to sidestep certain discourses of power while simultaneously tapping into a public interest in scientific advancement. Borges's own "Tlön, Uqbar, Orbis Tertius" is an excellent example of just such a strategy, where Borges needs no scientific proof for the antiscientific themes of his story. Piglia's use of science fiction goes one step further, incorporating a statement against the necessity of test tube envy that complements his characterization of the line of authority that runs from writer to politician. (Of course, nineteenth century figures like Sarmiento or Mansilla who attempted to function as writer, scientist, and politician simultaneously destabilize Piglia's position somewhat.)

This view of science fiction also suggests a way for understanding why women authors in Argentina do not seem to evince the same need for the cultural authority of science. Aside from the fact that test tube envy only describes the dynamics at play in a specific set of novels, it is still curious that women do not seem to participate more fully in this dynamic. The strategy is not necessarily gender specific; Charlotte Brontë was known to use phrenology extensively in her writing as I noted in the first chapter. Nevertheless, the leading women writers in Argentina do not seem to share their male counterparts' desire to employ scientific discourse as a means for bolstering their literary agendas. Piglia's use of science fiction to undermine the power dynamic may help suggest a way for understanding the two women who are connected with science in Argentine narrative by way of their interest in science fiction. I refer to Angélica Gorodischer and Ana María Shua.

These two are the only women to appear in the recent anthology of Argentine science fiction *Historias futuras*, one of several such anthologies to appear in the last several years. Both are recognized for their work in science fiction although when one examines the entirety of their work neither can be considered solely a science fiction writer. The stories that appear in this recent anthology provide an excellent example of the way in which these two authors use science fiction and, simultaneously, avoid the test tube envy that runs through the work of many of their male counterparts. I choose this particular anthology as it presents Shua and Gorodischer as the leading female science fiction writers, placing the stories side by side like an island amid the rest of the stories all written by men.[1]

Ana María Shua is probably better known for her writing in other genres, but is, as her introduction in the anthology reminds, recognized for her commitment to the genre (2000, 147). She has published a series of stories in science fiction reviews, but has not dedicated entire collections or novels to the genre.[2] Her story "Octavio el invasor" is an exploration of childbirth and the bond between mother and child as told from the perspective of an alien who is attempting an invasion of Earth by inhabiting the body of a fetus who is then born and lives in a human home. The story functions within science fiction because its use of extraterrestrials but has very little to do with the discourse of science. Note, for example, the initial paragraph of the story in which the alien first confronts the new reality of the human body:

> Estaba preparado para la violencia aterradora de la luz y el sonido, pero no para la presión, la brutal presión de la atmósfera sumada a la gravedad terrestre, ejerciéndose sobre ese cuerpo tan distinto del suyo, cuyas reacciones no había aprendido todavía a controlar. Un cuerpo desconocido de un mundo desconocido. (2000, 149)
>
> [He was ready for the terrifying violence of the light and the sound, but not for the pressure, the brutal atmospheric pressure made heavier by Earth's gravity, pressing upon this body that was so distinct from his own with reflexes and responses he had not yet learned to control. An unfamiliar body in an unfamiliar world.]

The passage immediately marks the story as unreal, the idea of possession of bodies serving as a marker of the fantastic nature of the narrative. As the story proceeds to identify the presence as part of an alien invasion team, it clearly enters the realm of science fiction. What is missing, however, is any use of scientific reference or discourse to advance the story or even to make the narrative seem more possible. Shua is interested in other things, namely, using the fantastic nature of the situation to defamiliarize the mother/child relationship in such a way as to invite further exploration. Indeed, the end of the story emphasizes the triumphant role of motherhood:

> Y por fin, llegó la palabra. La primera palabra. La utilizó con éxito para llamar a su lado a la mujer que estaba en la cocina. Octavio había dicho "Mamá." Y ya era, para entonces, completamente humano. Una vez más, la milenaria, infinita invasión había fracasado. (2000, 158)

> [And finally, the word arrived. The first word. He used it successfully to call the woman in the kitchen to his side. Octavio had said "Mama." And, from then on, he was completely human. Once more, the millennial, infinite invasion had failed.]

While Shua ends the story on its science fiction context of alien invasion, it casts the mother/child relationship as the real motor for the events of the story with Octavio's first words acting as the event that endows him with humanity. The story ends championing the importance of motherhood, in this particular case as an essential line of defense against the continuing effort to conquer the earth. What we see, then, is a kind of science fiction that works as fantasy, where the exotic nature of the other, be it future being or alien, allows for an exploration of common themes. It does not, however, depend on scientific discourse as a method for gaining believability. Instead, it exploits the unbelievable nature of the narrative to increase the impact of the story.

Angélica Gorodischer uses science fiction in a similar manner. Her work is also quite varied, although she does have more of a reputation in Latin American science fiction circles. Indeed, with Ursula K LeGuin's recent translation of Gorodischer's novel *Kalpa Imperial*, she will gain even more international recognition in fantasy and science fiction genres. She tends, as do many writers in the genre, to use science fiction settings as lens for the exploration of contemporary themes and issues. Her story "Los circuitos, las ondas, los ejes, los tableros de control, Equis y Gama" from the collection *Opus dos*, for example, uses a postapocalyptic world as a setting for a condemnation of racism. The world is an inversion of the racial situation of the 1960s with "blancos" excluded from education while the "negros" occupy the positions of power. As the main characters converse, they learn of the story of nuclear war caused by a society in which the "blancos" held power and repressed their darker-skinned counterparts. While the story makes reference to scientific experiments and several of the main characters are scientific technicians, those details are merely background details that contribute to the creation of a futuristic world. They do not serve the same disciplinary or power functions that we see in the other texts we have studied. Even Cortázar, whose cultivation of the fantastic is renowned, used physics as justification for particular theories. Gorodischer leaves the scientific background of her stories deep in the background.

Her story in the anthology under discussion is another example of a tendency to write science fiction but avoid science envy. "A la luz de la casta luna electrónica" presents the story of an interstellar trader Trafalgar who tells his friend of an erotic encounter on the matriarchal planet Veroboar ruled by a group of beautiful women known as "Las Mil." The story comes from a collection of related stories Gorodischer published called Trafalgar that center on the main character of "A la luz." The narrative is marked by gender confusion (Trafalgar is unsure about the sex of the "woman" he encounters) likely brought on by the inversion of gender hierarchies on this planet. The story revolves around that issue and, as in the previous story, suggests the theme that power corrupts and that it does not matter which gender or which race holds power, it will inevitably result in oppression. Gorodischer uses the story to question sexual identity as well, a theme that critics have identified throughout an oeuvre that contains hermaphrodite generals and homosexual interstellar traders.[3]

In the case of "A la luz de la casta luna electrónica," as well as the rest of her science fiction work, science does not appear as a discursive force in service of ideology. Certainly Gorodischer has her agenda, one that she revisits continually. However, she does not use scientific reference or an imitation of scientific discourse as the source of textual authority. Rather she uses science in the building of fantastic situations that allow her to explore her themes from varied perspectives. In that sense, Gorodischer follows Capanna's observation about the lack of scientific detail in Argentine science fiction. Andrea Bell and Yolanda Molina Gavilán follow up on that argument noting that not only does the genre avoid detail, the majority of Hispanic science fiction "do[es] not aim for scientific plausibility" (Bell and Gavilán 2003, 14). In fact, the two critics identify this lack of scientific plausibility as an important factor in Hispanic science fiction's ideological objectives. They note:

> In addition to its general tendency to avoid technical and scientific details, Spanish and Latin American SF's emphasis on the sociopolitical has earned it the reputation of being "soft." In times of political repression, for example, the science fiction mode has proven to be an excellent tool to foreground a particular ideological position or to disguise social criticism from government censors. (2003, 14)

If the majority of texts that we have considered in this study do use scientific detail as a method to build cultural power, science fiction cultivates a different kind of power. While the clear invocation of scientific discourse provides a more direct route to certain modes of political and philosophical power as we have seen, science fiction allows the authors to achieve particular political aims without confronting the machines of political power directly. In fact, one could argue that the political and social objectives of science fiction writers like Piglia, Shua, and Gorodischer reconnect them with the nineteenth-century writers we have studied. If test tube envy in the twentieth century appears more involved in philosophical and metaphysical debates as we see in Arlt, Sabato, Borges, and Cortázar, science fiction tackles more political and social issues like state terror in the case of Piglia, racial and sexual power hierarchies in Gorodischer and the interpretation of gender roles in Shua. In that, they share the nineteenth century's interest in using some configuration of literature and science to influence sociopolitical issues. They simultaneously enjoy a textual and cultural space made stronger by Borges's critique of the power of scientific discourse and his relegation of science to the realm of antiutopian themed stories.

This is not to say that science fiction never uses science in a way that suggests the dynamics explored in this study, indeed, the use of scientific detail to enhance the plausibility of the fantasy is an important part of the science fiction genre generally. Even Bell and Molina Gavilán note that some science fiction writers in Spain and Latin American employ such a strategy. Its general lack, however, highlights the distinctive role of science in the science fiction cultivated by these three authors. It also suggests a way for understanding Gorodischer, Shua, and even Piglia in their relationship with an Argentine canon that does exhibit test tube envy in several of its most revered texts. When we look at Gorodischer and Shua's work in science fiction through the lens provided by Piglia, we can perceive as well a veiled reaction to the power wielded by science. In a sense, writing science fiction allows for the conversion of science into fiction in a way that silences its cultural authority rather than exploiting it. That is, Sarmiento, Mansilla, Arlt, and Cortázar all exploit cultural expectations of science as a method of privileging their own ideas, depending on the valuation of science as authoritative for their texts to exercise power. Gorodischer and Shua silence that authority by inserting science within a completely literary world where science acts as one more cog in a narrative reality unconcerned with the support that it might provide. Borges's dismissal of such support proves beneficial in their own, more politically and sociologically motivated, literary agendas.

Such a case does not invalidate the concept of "test tube envy," but it certainly shows one of the many alternatives to the strategy as literary texts negotiate the power relationships between Argentine narrative and culture. It also shows how women in particular have exploited alternative strategies in that negotiation. While I hesitate to call "test tube envy" an exclusively masculine mode of discourse, the appearance of writers like Gorodischer and Shua who consciously opt toward a science fiction that eschews the cultural power of science suggests a situation similar to the dynamics described by feminist critics like Elaine Showalter. Excluded from traditional discourses of power, these women have cultivated a form of writing that at once imitates and subverts the dynamic that runs through a significant portion of Argentine narrative.[4] At the same time, these women are participating in a separate tradition that continues to be male dominated. In the many Argentine science fiction anthologies that have been published, it is rare to find more than two stories by women, nearly always Gorodischer and Shua. While women science fiction writers may be doubly marginalized, they also help us appreciate better the subversive potential of Argentine science fiction.

The example of Borges extends beyond his critique of scientific power and his use of scientific antiutopias in science fiction. Ironically, we also see the same critical phenomenon that reinserted Borges within the tradition of test tube envy appear in relation to Luisa Valenzuela, a writer who has not cultivated an obvious interest in either science or science fiction. Gwendolyn Díaz has studied the chaotic structures in Valenzuela's *Novela negra con argentinos*, arguing that the narrative itself operates as a chaotic system (Díaz 1994, 178). Díaz presents a compelling argument that is similar to those made in any number of studies that look for chaotic structures in literature, including the Weissert article on Borges and Hayles's book on the very subject of chaos theory and literature. Díaz is clearly participating in that tradition in her assessment of Valenzuela's work. At the same time, when read in relationship to the criticism we saw in Borges, we can interpret the argument as another in a series of such efforts that in some way connect a text's literary value with its ability to enunciate a scientifically valid observation on reality.

While the preceding authors, if not certain critics, make the case for a marked weakening of test tube envy in the final decades of the twentieth century, we find that the tendency is not completely gone in contemporary Argentine narrative. Indeed, we find a resurgence of the use of scientific epigraph generally absent in the twentieth-century texts that we have considered. The same Mempo Giardinelli that commented on the *vigencia* of *Facundo* opens his 1995 novel, *Imposible equilibrio*, with the following epigraph from Ilya Prigogine:

> Un mundo en equilibrio sería caótico, el mundo de no equilibrio alcanza un grado de coherencia que, para mí al menos, es sorprendente . . . No hay sistema estable para todas las fluctuaciones estructurales, no existe fin para la historia. (Giardinelli 1995, 8)

> [A world in equilibrium would be chaotic, a world in a state of nonequilibrium reaches a state of coherence that is, for me at least, surprising. There is no stable system for all structural fluctuations, there is no end to history.]

Giardinelli's choice of title, a direct allusion to Prigogine's theories on far from equilibrium systems, reinforces the importance of the epigraph by this Nobel Prize winning chemist and popularizer of chaos theory with the title of the novel.

Mempo Giardinelli, like the other writers of his generation, has cultivated many different genres and styles. His early work centers on fostering a specifically Argentine expression of the hard-boiled genre, his award-winning *Luna caliente* (1983) serving as the best known example of that interest. The 1991 novel *Santo oficio de la memoria* that won the 1993 Rómulo Gallegos award cultivates a Faulknerian family epic, deftly intertwining the voices of twenty-four family members in a reflection on Argentine history. He even has a science fiction story in "La máquina de dar besitos" that revisits the mad scientist stories popular in Argentina during the first half of the twentieth century. Given the broad range in style and genre, Giardinelli's work is likely best characterized by its constant reinvention. Such is certainly the case with *Imposible equilibrio*. The novel begins with the arrival of four hippopotami in Corrientes, the capital of the northern Argentine province of El Chaco. Water hyacinths are currently choking the Paraná river, and the hippos form an integral part of a program that the provincial government has created to resolve the problem. The real excitement begins when a group of friends, upset with the ecological implications of introducing nonindigenous organisms in the environment as well as the moral problems implicit in the use of the hippos, abduct the animals amidst a series of explosions designed to facilitate the getaway. The novel the develops along two separate lines, one following the adventures of the fugitives, the other reporting the reactions of the friend of these fugitives among whom figures the narrator. The car chase across northern Argentina and the philosophical discussions of the friends left behind result in several other twists and bifurcations that combine helicopter rescues with discussions about Latin American postmodernity and that culminate in a fantastic ending with two of the fugitives flying off in a balloon with Jules Verne. Giardinelli ably combines humor, cinematic narrative technique and the precepts of the genre of the *novela ecológica* in a novel that has enjoyed a good deal of success in Argentina and several editions throughout Spain and Latin America.

With a plotline that reminds the North American reader more of movies like *Thelma and Louise* than of a treatise on chaos theory, one wonders at an epigraph from a Nobel Prize winning chemist.[5] The conjunction of the title *Imposible equilibrio* and Prigogine's words is especially intriguing as one reads the novel and finds only one other reference to Prigogine and just two references to the title, all three in the same one-page conversation. In fact, the as yet unpublished English translation of the novel carries the title "The Dance of the Hippos," further distancing the text from Prigogine's ideas so forcefully suggested in the epigraph.[6] Nevertheless, we cannot and should not dismiss the importance of the epigraph and the original title in a critical engagement with the novel. Indeed, the two combine to suggest a poetics for the novel itself, since their inclusion loads the text from the beginning with an implied invitation to read it through the theories of Prigogine. As we do so, we find a system of plot devices and dialogic commentary that presents Giardinelli's conception of a postmodern world in terms of Prigogine's popularization of chaos theory. Initially, I will briefly discuss salient aspects of Prigogine's work, and then turn to *Imposible equilibrio* and its aesthetization of those principles. Finally, I will examine the way in which the novel integrates Prigogine's theories with Giardinelli's particular conceptions of *posmodernidad* as developed both in the novel and elsewhere in his writings.

After winning the Nobel Prize in 1977 for his work on thermodynamics in nonequilibrium systems, Ilya Prigogine has turned his attention in part to making these theories more accessible to lay persons as well as proposing their cultural power as explanations of all levels of systems, from the chemical to the ecological and to the societal. In his widely read book, *Order Out of Chaos* (written with Isabelle Stengers and based on their *La nouvelle alliance*), he dedicates a great deal of space to situating his work within the history of thermodynamics, extending afterward the theory's explanatory power from chemical relations to universal levels. Owing in part to this extension, Prigogine's work has been especially provocative for scientists and nonscientists alike, and his worked has been quoted and studied by scientists, philosophers, and literary critics. Prigogine's work has been especially influential in Argentina and Latin America, where his books have enjoyed several editions and continue to find space in bookstores long after disappearing from North American shelves. The epigraph comes from *Tan sólo una ilusión*, a collection of essays by Prigogine that has stayed in print in Spanish to the present date, years longer than its English version.

One figure who has embraced the popular and philosophical implications of Prigogine's work is the futurist Alvin Toeffler, whose description of key elements in the chemist's thought provides an effective introduction to the ideas that concern us in this study:

> What makes the Prigoginian paradigm especially interesting is that it shifts attention to those aspects of reality that characterize today's accelerated social change: . . . In Prigoginian terms, all systems contain subsystems, which are continually "fluctuating." At times, a single fluctuation or a combination of them may become so powerful, as a result of positive feedback, that it shatters the preexisting organization. At this revolutionary moment—the authors call it a "singular moment" or a "bifurcation point"—it is inherently impossible to determine in advance which direction change will take: whether the system will disintegrate into "chaos" or leap to a new, more differentiated, higher level of "order" or organization, which they call a "dissipative structure." (Toeffler 1984, xiv–xv)

Toeffler's observation provides an accurate explanation of the important concept of bifurcation in Prigogine's theories, the idea that far from equilibrium systems can reach levels of chaos that produce a situation in which one knows bifurcation is imminent but cannot predict the path it will follow once it has passed that point. To the theory of bifurcation, Prigogine adds the concepts of irreversibility and the creation of order within otherwise chaotic systems. Irreversibility occupies an important space in Prigogine's argument as it refutes Newton's (and Einstein's) concept of time, one in which natural reactions and processes could run backward or forward, while it guarantees the essential unpredictability of specific chaotic reactions.[7] Prigogine's concept of "order out of chaos" suggests a solution to the oddity of the appearance of highly organized living organisms within an entropic system that according to the second law of thermodynamics should be moving towards disorder.[8] Prigogine's theories have been compared to the dynamics of societal change and have gained authority in Western culture as explanations of reality.[9] The epigraph Giardinelli uses for his novel activates specifically the concepts of order developing out of chaos while proposing the universality of far from equilibrium systems with their entailing unpredictability and bifurcation points.

Such an activation within a work of fiction evokes another important point in Prigogine's argument: literature as an accompanying conceptualization of chaotic reality. Not only do Prigogine and Stengers incorporate various literary references as they build their argument, but the original title of *Order Out of Chaos*, *La nouvelle alliance*, refers to just this combination. Prigogine and Stenger's refutation of the current attempt to divide literary and scientific knowledge reveals the same attitude:

> One of the reasons for the opposition between the "two cultures" may have been the belief that literature corresponds to a conceptualization of reality, to "fiction," while science seems to express objective "reality." Quantum mechanics teaches us that the situation is not so simple. On all levels reality implies an essential element of conceptualization. (Prigogine and Stengers 1984, 225–26)

Prigogine and Stengers end their book with a further fusion of art and science, commenting on the examples of a time dependent, chaotic reality provided by music and Greek tragedy. By so doing, they accord a privileged space to art and literature in which the conceptions of reality offered by literature exist side by side with Prigogine's scientific theorems. In such a conception, we can appreciate an idea similar to that of the laboratory of literature we saw earlier, where art serves as an intellectual and cultural space in which scientific ideas are proven and disproved. In that sense, Prigogine's theories could act as the unspoken support for Piglia's description of the flow of influence between writers and scientists. The difference between Prigogine and the expressions of test tube envy that we have observed, of course, is that such a space for Prigogine is disinterested in the question of cultural and political power. Science and literature produce similar knowledge simply because they do, not because of a dynamic between the two that negotiates and constructs cultural truth. Nevertheless, the position afforded to literature in Prigogine's thought makes it remarkable among popularizations of science.

It is perhaps for these reasons that Prigogine has figured so prominently in studies of literature and science. Matei Calinescu highlights *Order Out of Chaos* specifically as the scientific version of theories of postmodernism:

> Even so, the critics' new interest in theoretical-epistemological issues comes from a real sense that important changes have occurred in the ways science views itself and the legitimacy of its procedures of inference. And this interest is enhanced by a belief that such changes in scientific paradigms cannot be without analogies on the level of artistic consciousness. Significantly, this belief seems to receive recognition or encouragement when a philosopher of science, borrowing the controversial cultural label postmodernism, will speak of a "postmodern science" almost as a matter of course. But even a more cautious position, like the one taken by Ilya Prigogine and Isabelle Stengers when they elaborate their distinction between a "modern science" and a "new science," can be quite relevant to the larger debate about postmodernism. (Calinescu 1987, 269–70)

Calinescu reflects the literary and cultural appropriation of Prigogine's ideas for the purposes of postmodernism. The concept of a scientific discipline that succeeds and goes beyond "modern" science strengthens Prigogine and Stenger's ability to function as icons in the attempt by some postmodernists to find scientific equivalents of their own questioning of modernism. What we see occur is similar to Sarmiento's inscription of Humboldt within *Facundo* or Cortázar's representation of Heisenberg in *Rayuela*, albeit

7: TEST TUBE ENVY AT THE TURN OF THE CENTURY   203

with more cooperation on the part of the scientists whose work and image are appropriated by literature and philosophy.

On this cultural level, Prigogine is not without his critics. Paul Gross and Norman Levitt criticize him for a lack of scientific rigor, and through him take to task those self-defined postmodernist critics who claim Prigogine's theories of proof of their own. Even N. Katherine Hayles, while recognizing his importance, admits that the evidence Prigogine offers as proof for his theories is, at times, somewhat scanty (92–93). Yet the power of Prigogine's scientific and cultural personae depends not so much on the complete accuracy of his science as on his ability to suggest a model for reality that can be readily incorporated into philosophical, cultural, and literary artifacts. *Imposible equilibrio* acts as just such an artifact, one in which Giardinelli creates a world based on Prigogine's theories and implies that this is the world in which we all live. To our purpose, whether Prigogine is scientifically correct at all times is less important than the fact that Giardinelli manages to integrate his theories into a literary representation of a chaotic system.[10]

As noted before, Prigogine seems to have enjoyed particular success in Argentina. The science fiction novel *El libro de la tierra negra* by Carlos Gardini uses Prigogine as a place name in his portrayal of a postapocalyptic world in which science has been outlawed and religion has reestablished itself as the central discourse of power. Giardinelli's own best-selling analysis of Argentine culture, *El país de las maravillas*, contains several references to Prigogine that draw on the power of the chemist's ideas, not only in science but in philosophy as well. The following passages from Giardinelli's book reveal this allegiance:

> La Filosofía de la Resistencia que nos propone Fracchia, por cierto, tiene un parentesco con la teoría del caos determinista de Ylia [*sic*] Prigogine, acerca del cual cabe hacer una breve referencia: "El orden a partir del caos" es una de las conferencias más impresionantes de Prigogine, y en ella explica su teoría del equilibrio inestable. Para él, aplicado a la Física, el movimiento interno es el que determina la inestabilidad propia de las estructuras de no equilibrio. De ahí su *teoría del orden del desorden*. Para Prigogine "es evidente que la relación entre desorden y orden es uno de esos interrogantes que cada generación se plantea y resuelve con arreglo al vocabulario y los intereses de su época." (Giardinelli 1998, 32)

> [The philosophy of resistance that Fracchia proposes, of course, shares a relationship with the theory of deterministic chaos of Ilya Prigogine,

about which we should make a brief reference. "The order out of chaos" is one of Prigogine's most impressive lectures, and in it he explains his theory of unstable equilibrium. For him, applied to physics, internal movement is what determines the instability of nonequilibrium structures. From that he gets his theory of order out of disorder. For Prigogine "it is evident that the relationship between disorder and order is one of those questions that each generation asks itself and resolves according the vocabulary and interests of its time period."]

Giardinelli's deployment of Prigogine's theories on chaos in this essay about the Argentine philosopher Eduardo Fracchia indicates that the ideas of this relatively unknown philosopher can be related to the theories of a well-known scientist. Giardinelli begins the passage by building both the scientific and rhetorical power of Prigogine, referring to his theories on chaos as well as his *"conferencias impresionantes."* Giardinelli presents him not only as a renowned scientist, but also as an able ambassador of science, one who can make his scientific ideas accessible to the layperson. Prigogine's authority as scientist and communicator is then used to fortify Fracchia's philosophical position. If, according to Prigogine, each generation tries to understand the relationship between order and chaos, then both Prigogine's and Fracchia's theories are manifestations of that attempt. Fracchia (and the musing that Giardinelli bases on Fracchia's thought) gain status through the aspirations they share with Prigogine of understanding order and chaos in reality.

Imposible equilibrio presents the literary aesthetization of the ideas Giardinelli advances in his cultural criticism. By the end of the novel, Giardinelli has woven Prigogine's thought not only into the philosophical discussions held by several characters but also into the very structure of the narrative. One of the more striking structural elements in *Imposible equilibrio* appears in the constant divisions in plot development. The explosions that accompany the abduction of the hippos at the end of the first chapter have the effect of exploding the development of the novel. After the first chapter, we find a system of alternating chapters in which we read of the fugitives Victorio, Clelia, Frank, and Pura in one chapter, only to return to Cardozo, Rafa, and the group at the bar *La estrella* in the next. Giardinelli maintains interest and suspense as he forces the reader to switch between plot lines, frustrating a readerly desire to continue with a particular story. While the principal division controls most of the structure of the novel, several other splits occur in the plot as well. Frank and Pura are divided from Victorio and Clelia by their capture, Cardozo and Rafa leave the Estrella group in order to search for Victorio, and Clelia; Rafa, Cardozo, Frank, Victorio, and Clelia all reunite at the end, only to split once again before Victorio and Clelia experience a final separation from the narrative reality of the Chaco in favor of a universal literary reality in Jules Verne's balloon. The novel ends with the line: "Aquí nunca, nadie, los va a joder. Están entrando en la literatura" (1995, 235). [Here no one will ever mess with them. They are entering in literature.] On one level, this narrative pattern of switching between story lines functions as a strategy to maintain the reader's attention. On another level of interpretation, these divisions in the structure of the novel also imitate Prigogine's theory on the points of bifurcation in far from equilibrium systems. It is important to recognize certain differences between the plot devices and Prigogine's ideas. Whereas in Prigogine the two options exist only as possibilities, the system choosing one unpredictably at the point of bifurcation, in the novel both possibilities happen in many of the narrative situations.[11] Nevertheless, the peculiar structure of the novel clearly evokes patterns that Prigogine traces in thermodynamic systems. If both possibilities happen, the event only underlines the fact that there was indeed a pronounced bifurcation point in the narrative.

Giardinelli advances the idea of far from equilibrium systems on several levels in *Imposible equilibrio*. The ecological question at the root of the decision to bring the hippopotami to the Chaco initially hints at the idea of chaos, since ecosystems are widely noted for their chaotic behavior.[12] The question of the balance of the Chaco ecosystem serves, however, as more of an excuse for the subsequent development of the novel than as a major element. The far from equilibrium system that the Chaco natural environment represents shifts then to the group of friends at the bar *La Estrella*. This group of friends comes to symbolize this same nonequilibrium system through a metonymic identification fueled by their constant discussion of the hippopotami. In a sense, they become what they discuss. Giardinelli then uses the arrival of the hippopotami as a Prigoginian fluctuation that causes the bifurcations to ensue. This is especially evident in the first chapter, as Cardozo flashes back one year in order to trace the buildup that led to Victorio's decision to use explosives to disrupt the arrival of the hippopotami.

Giardinelli underscores the unpredictability of this bifurcation through several comments made by various characters. The first voice in the novel suggests the approach of this bifurcation point as the American Frank Woodyard remarks in his broken Spanish, "En cualquier momento, empezando quilombo . . . Este asunto traer cola . . ." (1995, 9). [Any moment now, all hell will break loose. This thing is going to cause problems.] Cardozo reinforces this sense of anticipation on the following page with his reflective, "La algarabía, de hecho fomentada a lo largo de casi todo el año por una incesante propaganda, era completa" (10). [The whole affair, encouraged throughout the year by an unending propaganda, was complete.] While these recurring remarks alert the reader to an imminent momentous event, they proffer no clue as to the nature of what will transpire. The last scene of the introductory section that prefaces Cardozo's recounting of the year leading up to that day fortifies the sense of an impending, unknown event.

> —¿Qué hace Victorio allá, junto al palco?—preguntó Martina, que parecía buscarlo como si fuera su hijo. Ninguno de nosotros entendía qué le había dado por ubicar a Victorio justo este día.
> —¿Por qué no te dejás de joder con ese muchacho?—dijo Rafa—. Es grande y sabe lo que hace.
> —Ninguno de ustedes sabe lo que hace—replicó Martina—. Empezando por mi marido.
> Y se largó a caminar resueltamente hacia el palco.
> (1995, 11–12)

> ["What is Victorio doing there next to the stand?" Marina asked, as she looked for him as if he were her child. None of us understood what had made her decide to look for Victorio just that day.
> "Why don't you stop bothering with that boy?" said Rafa, "he's a big boy and knows what he's doing."
> "None of you know what he's doing," replied Martina, "especially my husband."
> And she began to walk resolutely toward the stand.]

The image of Martina walking resolutely toward an event that no one can foretell evokes precisely the far from equilibrium system that moves inexorably toward a bifurcation point that one can anticipate but not predict. Giardinelli reiterates this state of not knowing as he saturates the first chapter with several references to the complete ignorance on the part of Cardozo and the members of the *La Estrella* group as to what Victorio and friends would do. Indeed, the section that immediately follows the passage quoted above builds the expectation of an unknown event as it narrates Negro Flores's idea to bring the hippos:

> Desde luego que todos debimos haber sido conscientes de los problemas que se avecinaban, pero no lo fuimos. Apenas el Negro Flores lanzó la idea, más o menos un año antes de ese momento en que el tiempo parecía haberse detenido en Barranqueras, tras la sorpresa y las primeras bromas forzosamente teníamos que haber advertido que las consecuencias iban a ser muy graves. Pero todos aceptamos la proposición alegremente. (1995, 12)

> [Of course we should have been aware of the problems that were coming, but we weren't. As soon as Blackie Flores suggested the idea, about a year before the moment in which time seemed like it had stopped in Barranqueras, after the surprise and the initial jokes we were forced to realize that the consequences would be very serious. But we all happily accepted the proposition.]

Giardinelli strengthens the connection between the novel and Prigogine's ideas by emphasizing the string of events that lead to the instant described while reiterating the characters' ignorance of what would develop. The reference to stopped time foregrounds the event's importance as a moment that defines reality, contributing simultaneously to the creation of a narrative point that will control the structure of the novel.

In the final scene of the first chapter, Giardinelli activates additional aspects of Prigogine's theories. Cardozo's observation, "Nosotros, alejados de la muchedumbre, presentíamos que la historia torcería su curso en aquel momento" (1995, 32) [All of us, far away from the crowd, sensed that history would turn from its path in that moment] underlines again the sense of anticipation of bifurcation while simultaneously invoking Prigogine's work on time and irreversibility. In the same way that Prigogine suggests that chemical reactions find similarities in the development of time, Giardinelli provides examples of this same suggestion.[13] The term "historia" in the passage can be translated into English in two ways, both important for an interpretation of the event. The history of the Chaco would certainly change forever with the bombing of a public event, while the history of the *La Estrella* group would be permanently altered by the actions of three of its members. At the same time the *historia* or story of the novel is also going to twist and bifurcate irreversibly with the subsequent developments.

The theme of the irreversibility of events appears again more forcefully a few lines later with the narration of the explosion,

> Ni Rafa ni yo habíamos tenido la convicción suficiente para detener la locura en que se embarcaron Victorio Lagomarsino, Pura Solanas y Frank Woodyard y que se manifestó a pleno—violenta, irreversible y trágica—a partir del momento en que estalló la primera bomba junto al palco de honor. Ese primer estallido . . . nos cambió la vida. (1995, 32)

> [Neither Rafa nor I had had enough conviction to stop the insanity on which Victorio et al had embarked and that manifested itself completely—violently, irreversibly, and tragically—at the moment in which the first bomb exploded near the seat of honor. That first explosion changed our lives.]

The key word "irreversible" followed by the phrase "nos cambió la vida" establishes clearly the relationship both Giardinelli and Prigogine see between the irreversibility of thermodynamic phenomena on the chemical level and events that occur on an individual and societal level. Victorio's bombs, then, act as the bifurcation point of a Prigoginian nonequilibrium system, a system that Giardinelli will continue to develop and divide throughout the rest of the novel.

Giardinelli loads this specific point of narrative bifurcation with various references to chaos theory and Prigogine's ideas. As the narrator describes the group's physical departure from Resistencia, hippos in tow, we see phrases such as "el caos generalizado" and "La impericia camionera de Victorio sumó confusión al caos" (34). [Vicotorio's driving added confusion to the chaos.] The specific use of the word chaos in a text whose epigraph quotes Prigogine acts as an important marker, further emphasizing the characteristics of unpredictability in Prigogine's theory of bifurcations. Prigogine's description of the period of bifurcation makes the relationship clear:

> One of the most unexpected results of recent research is that this situation changes drastically when we move to nonequilibrium situations. First, when we come close to bifurcation points the fluctuations become abnormally high and the law of large numbers is violated. . . . Local events have repercussions throughout the whole system. (1984, 180)

The general chaos described illustrates both the wild fluctuations as well as the repercussions of local events. The addition of the new character Clelia to the getaway group acts as another such fluctuation. While she seems to join Victorio in the truck on a whim, her action develops the theme of repercussions as this rather extraordinary event converts her into a central character in both Victorio's life and in the development of the novel. The act of a split-second moves her from the periphery of the action as an unnamed "jovencita" to one of the main characters that end up in Jules Verne's balloon.

Giardinelli continues to develop the themes of bifurcation and unpredictability. I have already mentioned the various plot divisions that in the light of Prigogine's thought can now be read as bifurcations in a nonequilibrium system. To these bifurcations, Giardinelli repeatedly adds not only the total unpredictability of the first, major bifurcation but also a general sense of not knowing the outcomes of subsequent narrative crossroads. Victorio and Pura provide an example of this situation in the following exchange, "—Tenemos que decidir si tomamos la ruta 7—dice Victorio. —Cuando lleguemos al cruce—dice Pura—. Ahora préndanme un pucho" (1995, 130–31). [We have to decide if we should take route 7, says Victorio. When we get to the crossroads, says Pura, now light me a cigarette.] The simultaneous postponement of decision until the time of bifurcation with the foreknowledge that such a bifurcation will occur, in this case a quite literal fork in the road, depicts a reality that follows exactly the one described in chaos theory. On a broader scale, Clelia's interrogatory, "¿Pero vos tenés algún plan más o menos claro o improvisás todo sobre la marcha?" [But do you have some kind of clear plan, or are you improvising as you go?] suggests a level of indeterminacy that Victorio augments with his noncommittal reply, "Las dos cosas" (1995, 68). [Both.] This response increases the instability by suggesting that the future includes the planned and the unpredictable, denying Clelia's desire to understand what awaits her.

Giardinelli completes his appropriation of Prigogine's thought for the purposes of fiction with a complex evocation of the principle that order arises out of chaotic behavior. Just as Prigogine and Stengers look to literature as an alternate conceptualization of reality, literature in *Imposible equilibrio* becomes the path to order within a chaotic reality. Giardinelli begins to introduce a metaliterary subtext with the characters' growing awareness of their fictional state, ending with a final chapter in which the characters take their places among such authors and fictional characters as Kafka, Dostoyevsky, Virginia Woolf, Borges, Don Quixote, and Sancho Panza. Victorio's comment near the end of the novel as Victorio and Clelia enter literature proper reflects the soothing effect their literary surroundings have on him: "—Quizá te suene un poco irresponsable lo que voy a decir, pero es como si de pronto sintiera que el mundo se empieza a calmar, como si algo se estuviera acomodando" (1995, 232). [It might seem to you a little irresponsible what I'm going to say, but it is as if I suddenly felt that the world was beginning to calm down, as if something were settling in.] This calming of what has been until then a chaotic existence acts as an invitation to rethink the various remarks the characters make as they compare their experiences to literature and film. At the beginning of the novel, shortly after Clelia joins Victorio in the truck, he asks her: "—¿Y cuál se supone que es tu papel en esta milonga?" Clelia responds: "—La chica que acompaña al héroe" (1995, 37). ["And what, do you suppose, is your role in this dance?" "The hero's girlfriend."] Clelia's use of a narrative cliché in her definition of self suggests a situation in which characters find meaning in relation to the roles they represent. After that point, we see the group of fugitives make several references to their literary/cinematic situation.

This metaliterary discourse culminates in the above-mentioned calming effect that the entrance to the world of literature in the final chapter exercises on Victorio and Clelia. In the culmination, we see a suggestion of order that springs from the chaotic bifurcations we have witnessed up to this point. That is, the very act of fleeing so fraught with chaotic fluctuations and unpredictable events also provides literary roles for the fugitives that will eventually provide the order and tranquility found in Jules Verne's balloon. The bifurcations also end tragically in Pura's death, but the love Clelia and Victorio find and the stabilizing guarantee of literature imitate the way in which nonequilibrium systems create pockets of order. The fantastic end of the novel becomes the "grado[s] de coherencia" referred to in the epigraph, an orderly pocket within otherwise chaotic systems.

At the same time, the character's self-awareness as literary creations seem somewhat similar to the theories of the postmodern novel we see developed by Linda Hutcheon on the metafiction she sees as crucial to the definition of postmodern literature.[14] This phenomenon has also been connected to the contemporary Latin American novel, both among "Boom" novels as well as more recent texts in which metaliterary situations, cinema, and popular culture create a sense of artificiality that has become an identifying feature in much of Latin American narrative as well as in Western literature in general. *Imposible equilibrio* reinforces these ideas both with the use of characters who find solace in cinematic tropes as well as in images of television and literature that influence the way in which these characters attempt to find meaning in their lives. What is particularly important about the novel is that Giardinelli uses these elements of postmodernism and the contemporary Latin American novel in conjunction with his development of a narrative reality based on the model of Prigogine's theories.

Giardinelli continues this adaptation of Prigogine's thought in an idiosyncratic presentation of *posmodernidad* that he develops in *Imposible equilibrio*. The character Rafa serves as the ideological spokesperson for the novel in one of his theoretical discussions with Cardozo:

> En este contexto social insolidario, decadente y cada vez más violento que para muchos es la inevitable posmodernidad, es imposible alcanzar el equilibrio . . . Porque en la posmodernidad todas las fuerzas se han desatado con exageración . . . Lo cual no deja de provocar un maravillante desequilibrio: el que nos lleva a aferrarnos a esos pequeños valores que todavía le dan sentido a la vida, Cardozo: la amistad, por ejemplo; el amor, cuando se presenta, y por fortuna todavía se presenta de vez en cuando; las tranquilas y sabrosas conversaciones; el no tener televisor, artefacto que usted apreciará que en esta casa no hay . . . Y la literatura, claro, como posibilidad de encuentro con aquellos viejos valores universales y también como estímulo para la imaginación y el sentido del humor, y como potencia de las posibilidades de la ironía. No hay mucho más. (1995, 121)

> [In this social context of insolidarity, decadent and everyday more violent that for many is the inevitable postmodernity, it is impossible to achieve equilibrium. . . . Because in postmodernity all forces have come undone in an exaggerated fashion. . . . Something that does not cease to produce a marvelous desequilibrium: that which makes us cling to those small values that still help one make sense of life, Cardozo: friendship for example; love, when it happens, and luckily it still happens once in a while; tranquil and flavorful conversations, not having a television, an artifact you will note that does not exist in this house . . . And literature, of course, as a possibility of encountering those old universal values and

as a stimulant for the imagination and the sense of humor, and as a power for the possibilities of irony. There's not much else.]

The key phrase "es imposible alcanzar el equilibrio" occupies an important space in Rafa's discussion of postmodern culture. The reference to the title immediately highlights the passage as a key moment in the novel. By referring to the title, it also introduces the influence of Prigogine's theories into the debate, suggesting that the impossible equilibrium associated with Prigogine's ideas on chaos theory are an essential part of the postmodern conception of reality. As Rafa develops a related idea about chaos and postmodernity, he remarks: "Prigogine cita a un tal Carl Rubino, que dice que según Horacio los dioses son los únicos seres que llevan una vida sin riesgos" (1995, 121). [Prigogine quotes a Carl Rubino, who says that, according to Horace, the gods are the only beings who lead a risk free life.] Rafa and Cardozo's conversation becomes at this point a microcosm of the novel as Prigogine and his ideas appear as implicit and explicit rhetorical supports for what Rafa and Giardinelli argue. In a clear display of test tube envy, Giardinelli reinforces the philosophical positions of the characters and the novel with a loaded reference to a popular science of the time.

The conception Giardinelli develops of a postmodernity based on Prigoginian ideas of chaos and order brings us back to Calinescu's description of Prigogine's place in postmodern thought. Indeed, Calinescu describes a situation that could easily be defined using the concept of test tube envy. One need not infer too much from his argument to observe a situation in which artists and critics perceive patterns in science that seem to support their epistemological assumptions and then appropriate these patterns as a proof of those assumptions. While Calinescu specifically uses Prigogine and Stengers's work as an illustrative point rather than a rhetorical proof, his discussion of their work clearly suggests the connection between Prigogine's thought and postmodernism that we see developed in *Imposible equilibrio* as well.

Calinescu and Giardinelli are not the only cultural observers to examine the relationship between chaos theory and postmodern thought. Indeed, the theme has been the subject of a serious critical debate. Hayles supports the position of Calinescu and Giardinelli in a cogent study of the connections between chaos and the postmodern world. She specifically identifies similarities between deconstruction and chaos, noting the preference for complexity that one finds in the expressions of poststructuralist thought. Her conception of postmodernity differs somewhat from Giardinelli and Calinescu. She emphasizes the connections with deconstruction while Giardinelli and Calinescu seem to stress the renovating role of postmodernism. Such a difference is of fundamental importance for Giardinelli, who appears to embrace an optimism implicit in a theory that argues that order emerges unexpectedly from chaos, that political and social disorder might, perhaps, produce some kind of meaning. Nevertheless, her analysis strengthens the theoretical link many have observed between chaos theory and the idea of a complex, multivalent reality that we see associated many times with postmodernism.[15]

Alexander Argyros disagrees sharply with this linking, taking issue specifically with Hayles. His careful examination of chaos theory focuses on the patterns of order that are spontaneously produced within complex, chaotic systems. This focus leads him to reject a philosophical connection between the two theories. He notes a preference for disordered realities in deconstruction and postmodernism that for him do not support the pockets of order that paradoxically appear in chaotic systems. He also objects to this preference, noting that it does not coincide with what he perceives as a scientific interest in these manifestations of order (236–38):

> On the one hand, deconstruction [a term he equates with postmodern discourse] seeks to affirm the destabilizing effects of undecidability; on the other hand, chaos theorists are intrigued by the appearance of order in apparently random systems. Deconstruction sees itself as a sentry watching for recrudescence of order, whereas chaos scientists tend to be fascinated by the strange paths chosen by nature to order, universality, and beauty. (1991, 238–39)

Argyros clearly limits his critique of postmodernism and deconstruction first by implying (earlier) that the two are identical. Secondly, and more importantly, he seems to miss a joy in the beauty of disorder that one finds in the writings of critics like Derrida that would at least answer a portion of his criticism. Nevertheless, he highlights an important difference in attitude in which one side prefers chaos in itself, while the other sees chaos as a pathway to order in nature. From another perspective on this debate, Gross and Levitt deny any connection outright. They reject the positions of both Hayles and—mysteriously—Argyros, arguing that any perceived similarities are the result of a misunderstanding of the mathematics involved in nonlinear equations.

The question at the heart of this debate is the definition of postmodernity. It is clear that Argyros's objection to the connection of chaos theory and postmodern thought is embraced by the presentation of Prigogine we see in *Imposible equilibrio*. Indeed, Giardinelli fosters the idea of order out of chaos as a key element in his presentation of the narrative reality in the novel. For the purposes of this chapter, the definition of the notoriously difficult-to-define concept of postmodernity must come from Giardinelli himself. In an essay on postmodernity written in 1990, the Argentine novelist provides just such a definition of what for him is a Latin American *posmodernidad*:

> Y es que no comparto el escepticismo como pose seudonitzscheana. No comparto la iconoclastia ni el espíritu "pasota," esencialmente nihilista. Antes bien, creo en la posmodernidad como modernidad de la modernidad pero con espíritu recomponedor, con propuestas que no maten por decreto a las utopías sino que las re-piensen a fin de actualizarlas y adecuarlas—es decir, modernizarlas—a los tiempos que vivimos. Si me dicen que posmodernidad es caer en reducciones, como si ser posmo fuera sólo ser minimalista, me opongo. . . . Pero sí me confieso posmoderno y acepto sus postulados si la posmodernidad se entiende como una actitud de rebeldía y disconformidad propositiva. (1990, 31)

> [I do not believe in skepticism as a pseudonietzschean pose. I do not believe in iconoclasts or in the essentially nihilist spirit of the past. Rather, I believe in postmodernity as modernity of modernity but with a renewing spirit, with proposals that do not kill utopias by decree but rather rethink them with the goal of bringing them up to date and making them adequate, that is, modernizing them, for the times in which we live. If someone tells me that postmodernity means falling into reductionism, as if being postmodern means just being minimalist, I am opposed. But I do claim to be postmodern and accept its postulates if postmodernity is understood as an attitude of rebellion and a disconformity with purpose.]

One immediately notices in this quotation a sense of postmodernity like that developed by Calinescu, that is, an attitude in which one reexamines and, in effect, "modernizes" modernism. This rebellious, proactive disconformity with reality that Giardinelli describes as his postmodernity also bears a passing resemblance to Santiago

Colás's discussion of Argentine postmodernity. Colás develops a concept of postmodernity that emphasizes the sociopolitical aspects of a rebellion against society that forms, for him, the basis of postmodernity in Argentina.[16] Giardinelli seems to reflect this attitude somewhat in his rejection of the deconstruction assumed by Argyros in his critique of postmodern chaos theory, embracing rather an almost existential struggle for meaning within an admittedly chaotic reality.[17] The power of Prigogine's theories as a metaphorical description of social reality within Giardinelli's paradigm becomes clearer at this point. Prigogine's theories of far from equilibrium systems in which apparently chaotic fluctuations can produce both unpredictable instability and cohesive order along with his vindication of the representational role of literature finds its aestheticization in Giardinelli's depiction of a chaotic reality that, while unsettling and even threatening, can also be survived.

As Giardinelli draws upon the cultural authority of Prigogine's thought as a rhetorical and philosophical support for the narrative reality he constructs in *Imposible equilibrio*, he positions his novel within a tradition of test tube envy that endures despite the alternate directions in science and literature we see in Piglia, Gorodischer, and Shua. Giardinelli's use of scientific reference and allusion differs on many levels from that of his nineteenth-century counterparts, but the fundamentals of the process by which the literary borrows from the cultural prestige enjoyed by science remains the same. For example, Giardinelli's presentation of Fracchia's philosophy of resistance as well as his exposition of a theory of Latin American postmodernity depend to a large extent, both in his novel and in his other writings, on the comparisons he draws between these theories and the scientific (or at least perceived as scientific) work of Prigogine. In that sense, Prigogine's work on thermodynamic systems functions as a guarantor of the philosophical position elaborated in *Imposible equilibrio*. At the same time, it contributes to an inscription of Prigogine as scientist within Argentine culture that casts his work as important not so much because of its scientific rigor, but because of its ability to explain sociocultural reality.

Giardinelli's novel serves, then, as the latest chapter in this literary tradition and as a testament to its endurance in Argentine letters as it simultaneously explores literary themes and issues of the 1990s. It serves well as an ending point to this study as it combines Sarmiento's strategies with those of Arlt and Cortázar as it intertwines the use of the epigraph with the modeling of narrative reality on the principles of popular science as well as the literary construction and redefinition of science and the scientist within the power structures Argentine culture employs as it makes sense of its situation. Its own bifurcating structure also suggests a model for understanding the changing shape of science and literature relations as we see what could be termed a bifurcation point in Borges's work where test tube envy veers off toward test tube disdain. That swerve would then strengthen the writing of Piglia, Gorodischer, and Shua among others. By reemphasizing the strategies that we see run through the nineteenth and twentieth centuries, *Imposible equilibrio* effects, in fact, an impossible equilibrium as it brings into convergence the various manifestations of test tube envy in 150 years of Argentine narrative.

Conclusion

With the balance of chapters focusing on the twentieth century in an examination of the appropriation of science by Argentine narrative, this study diverges somewhat from the groundwork laid out in *Myth and Archive*. González Echevarría proposes a shift in the mediating "masterstory" for Latin American narrative in the early twentieth century from science to anthropology, from political discourse based on science to narrative based on anthropological models designed to uncover the myths and beginnings of Latin American reality. He highlights the telluric novels of the 1920s and 1930s that most clearly show the anthropological aspirations of those novelists and then presents what for him is the mythic substructure of the novels of Miguel Ángel Asturias through Gabriel García Márquez and Jorge Luis Borges. In this way, he forms a tripartite division in the history of Latin American narrative with the legal paradigm dominating colonial writing, the scientific traveler influencing the nineteenth century and the twentieth century borrowing from anthropological models and objects of inquiry. González Echevarría's proposal for understanding the discursive structure of the Latin American canon has proved to be extraordinarily influential in contemporary criticism. As recently as 2000, Jerry Hoeg based his *Science and Technology in Latin American Literature*, on the premise of the archive(s) González Echevarría constructed, arguing that Latin American writing had moved from the anthropological archive proposed by the Cuban critic to an archive based on information systems.

The Argentine example provides a somewhat different perspective on the scientific discourses that mediate the narrative discussed here. The modeling of literary discourse on scientific paradigms of writing appears as a tendency that transcends the narrative and philosophical shifts that occur in the Argentine literary tradition near the beginning of the twentieth century. The case is not merely one where Sarmiento and Mansilla use the scientific travel model while Julio Cortázar's *Rayuela* serves as an archival narrative mediated by an anthropological interest in beginnings and myth. The authorial evocation of the cultural prestige of science withstands the changes of the century that separates the texts we have considered. It is for that reason that we should not stop at an analysis of the influence of scientific travel writing in the nineteenth century or one of the mythic substructure of twentieth-century narrative, at least in Argentina. Sarmiento, Mármol, and Mansilla's rhetorical use of phrenology in their writings provides an accompanying model that anticipates the use of science in twentieth-century Argentine narrative. When considered from that perspective, the "masterstory" of science in the nineteenth century implied by González Echevarría serves as a unifying element between the narrative of the nineteenth and twentieth centuries rather than one that distinguishes the literary phenomena of the two time periods.

González Echevarría's anthropological masterstory presents other complications as well. The critic argues that Latin American narrative exhibits a shift in methodological conception that mirrors the early twentieth-century developments in the discipline of anthropology:

> Revealingly, anthropologically mediated Latin American narratives lead, through a process analogous to one that takes place within anthropology itself, to a crisis in anthropological knowledge. If in the novel we move from a Gallegos to a Borges, a Carpentier and a García Márquez; in anthropology we go from Bronislaw Malinowski and Marcel Griaule to Clifford Geertz, James Clifford, George Marcus, Talal Asad, Vincent Crapanzano, James Boon, Michael Taussig, and several others who are subjecting anthropological discourse to a radical critique. Latin American narrative may well be the design on the reverse side of the picture, or the mirror image of the crisis in anthropology as a discipline. (1990, 151)

González Echevarría's analysis here is persuasive as applied to the shifts in narrative between the telluric novels and the narrative of the Boom. However, his argument places both traditions of the Latin American novel together under the anthropological model for narrative and implicitly opposes them to the texts of the nineteenth century. If we are to look at anthropology as a mediating discourse for Latin American narrative, it cannot figure as something new for the twentieth century. Mansilla's *Una excursión* presents an excellent example of a nineteenth-century text that mirrors the shifts in anthropology as a discipline with its emphasis on the importance of the fieldworker in authoritative ethnography. To be sure, González Echevarría presents the development of anthropology as a discipline through the nineteenth century and by so doing implies a sense of continuity. However, that continuity, strengthened by what we see in *Una excursión*, suggests an alternative vision of the framework proposed in *Myth and Archive*.

This opposite flow of discursive power and authority that we have seen in the course of the study complements González Echevarría's idea of the literary archive. In both centuries, we see writing exercise a profound influence on the way science as a discipline and as a cultural entity is conceived and constituted. From Sarmiento's influence on the phrenological practices of late nineteenth-century Argentine science to Mansilla's redefinition of Argentine ethnology and anthropology, we see the essential role of literature in the construction of science and scientific practice. While science appears to have provided cultural authority for the rhetorical aims of these texts, the texts themselves helped define the very nature of that science. Writing in the nineteenth century, then, not only availed itself of the archive of knowledge González Echevarría proposed, it actively participated in the construction of that archive. The twentieth-century writings studied in this book may not have exercised as extensive an impact on the actual practice of chemistry, quantum mechanics, and chaos theory, but we do see a similar effect in which literature reconfigures the cultural definitions of science and what science can say about reality. That is, not only does literature appropriate the image and methodology of science as an attempt to bolster its own cultural prestige, but it also uses that image in the construction of the place and function of science in the cultural imaginary. This particular effect, the literary reconfiguration of science and the theories it produces serves as another connection between the narratives of the two centuries.

And yet this is not to say that the narratives of the nineteenth and twentieth centuries are the same, obviously not. One of the goals of this study has been to trace a narrative tendency through one hundred and fifty years and several authors of diverse styles and temperaments. If I have highlighted the test tube envy that links these narratives, my focus has also revealed the profound differences that do indeed separate the twentieth-century narratives from their nineteenth-century predecessors. Through the nineteenth century, we see science in the employ of politics. That is, Sarmiento, Mansilla, the Argentine naturalist authors, all use references to the sciences of their times as a way to privilege and make culturally authoritative the sociopolitical positions they advance in their writings. Sarmiento's inclusion of references to Humboldt in name and in style, his use of the physiognomic/phrenological model, both operate as rhetorical mechanisms that serve his political intentions of defaming Quiroga and Rosas. Indeed, his writing exercised real, disciplinary authority on the bodies of Rosas and his other enemies by using scientific discourse to define them as contrary to civilization. Mansilla's use of phrenology and anthropological theory function as a support for what is essentially a critique of Sarmiento's national policy, as is the Argentine naturalists' use of a medical discourse in their attack on a policy of open immigration. In all cases we see scientific authority created, manipulated, and appropriated in attempts to exercise political and social authority over particular communities and individuals. In those cases, scientific discipline is part and parcel of political and social discipline.

The shift we see beginning with Arlt is one in which science is put to the service of the metaphysical and philosophical goals implicit (or explicit) in the novels rather than the more political objectives of the nineteenth century. Arlt's use of Darwin in *El juguete rabioso* does not have as its principal objective a political critique of urban sprawl. Rather, the novelist uses the authority of Darwin to aid his depiction of a universal reality in which humans are no different from animals, without purpose or meaning other than survival. His critique of science in *Los siete locos/El lanzallamas* reflects a similar metaphysical anguish. It is not just the science that defeats itself, but an important element of modern society that mirrors the breakdown of belief systems and meaning that Arlt so keenly senses. The scientific discourse so readily apparent in Arlt's fiction privileges, then, the metaphysical crisis many critics have observed in his work. Arlt's literary laboratory works, then, not to reconstruct scientific practice, but to display the function of science in a broader experiment; one that "proves" the failure of a modern, urban civilization. While Arlt sees science as an integral part of that failure, he maintains the discursive structures, this literary laboratory, as the vehicle for his portrayal of the broken test tube. Sabato only presents, then, part of what makes Arlt an important presence in the Argentine literary tradition. Not only does his metaphysical concern distinguish him, his marriage of scientific discourse and metaphysics suggests his role as a key turning point in the evolution of test tube envy. In that sense Borges acts more as a continuation of Arlt than of the nineteenth century as we saw Piglia argue. Borges follows Arlt's use of scientific authority on a more metaphysical and philosophical stage in his use of thermodynamics against Nietzsche. When he then embraces a metaphysical angst sans scientific authority, he enunciates a dissatisfaction with science that Arlt had already set in motion. If Borges could successfully divorce the two concepts, Arlt had already enunciated the faults and fissures in positivistic thinking. In both cases, scientific discipline can be seen as a tool for the construction of an authoritative philosophy of the human condition.

Cortázar's use of science similarly reflects philosophical concerns. He presents quantum physics as a scientific example of what for him is the true, irrational reality in sharp contrast to the Cartesian rationality he sees throughout Western culture. His use of Heisenberg as an authoritative scientific figure in addition to his what-if narratives based on the theories of quantum mechanics provide a scientific referent for his surrealist conception of reality. While one might argue that Cortázar's iconoclastic stance versus traditionally perceived reality mirrors his revolutionary politics, the philosophical implications of his use of a scientific referent more closely link his work to that of Arlt and Borges than to the political uses of science we see in the nineteenth century. Even so, Cortázar's use of scientific reference in his critique of rationalist thought is also much more complex than Arlt's and certainly more than Borges's brief expression of test tube envy or even in his dismissal of scientific authority. Arlt, and Sabato for that matter, uses discursive structures allusive to science in order to show science's failings. Borges merely lumps science in with all philosophy in a generic attack on systems of thought. Cortázar constructs an image of science that he then splits, exploiting the revolutionary discourse employed by Heisenberg to set particular scientific disciplines against others. Such a strategy is at once more complicated and more optimistic than what we see in Arlt's turning of science against itself. For Arlt, the truth of science is that human beings live as animals in a world ruled by natural selection. For Cortázar, the truth of science confirms his view of an irrational reality that rejects authoritarian logic and embraces freedom. In both cases, we see a use of scientific authority that is simultaneously inherent in Argentine culture and newly constructed by the literary texts that employ it. That optimism may help explain why we could later find further expressions of test tube envy in Giardinelli despite the other directions we see literature and science take.

The counterexamples of Piglia, Gorodischer, and Shua also show the other directions that science and narrative could take while continuing to operate amidst the power structures of scientific discourse. In that sense they inherit both a literary landscape in which science continues to exercise power and the post-Borges critique of science that erodes its ability to enunciate objective truth. While they, and many other authors, show that test tube envy is not the only authoritative mode of writing, their particular approach to science attests to its continuing importance in contemporary Argentine writing, especially when examined alongside Giardinelli's novel. Indeed, Giardinelli's use of science also functions along lines similar to his nineteenth-century predecessors where Prigogine's theories on chaos are used as rhetorical support for the Argentine author's views on postmodernity and reality. Additionally, Giardinelli's reconfiguration of the Russian chemist as a postmodern theorist exhibits a dynamic similar to Cortázar's recasting of Heisenberg, both use literature to reshape the cultural image of science and its practitioners even as they invoke their authority. While Giardinelli's use of the epigraph reminds us of Sarmiento and Humboldt or Mansilla and Comte, his use of science to privilege his conception of the nature of reality firmly situates his work within the tradition of Arlt and Cortázar. Indeed, in all our twentieth-century authors that display a brand of test tube envy, we see science as an explanation and an example of the conceptions of reality instead of an explanation of the political and social situations of our nineteenth-century authors. In this sense, my study of the development of scientific discourse in Argentine narrative reveals what critics already knew: As Latin American literature moved from the nineteenth to the twentieth century, there occurred the development of a profound questioning of the nature of reality. The intriguing element of this study is the way in which twentieth-century authors with very different ideological concerns from their nineteenth-century predecessors employ similar tools in their questioning and critique of a reality that these same nineteenth-century authors generally took for granted.

Foucault's vision of the régime of truth serves, then, as a particularly appropriate description of the dynamics we see between narrative and science in Argentina. While the focus of the book has highlighted literature's use of the cultural authority of science, we are also able to perceive that this régime of truth, this archive, is not some immaterial entity from which literature withdraws discursive power by presenting the correct structures or strategies. Both literature and science participate in the construction of the régime, with power and authority created in the negotiations between disciplines that serve to shape each other simultaneously. Michel Serres has argued that literature and science can be construed as two modes of thought that reflect, sometimes differently, sometimes similarly, a shared reality. Such may be, but what we see in these texts is a much more unstable situation, one in which discursive power is constantly constructed and reconstructed, where literary, political, philosophical, and scientific authority can be seen as the result of complex negotiations between disciplines. Models are followed, archives invoked, to be sure, but only after these models and archives have been created and defined by the texts that invoke them. Furthermore we see the exercise of real political and philosophical power in both centuries as science forms an integral part of an attempt to discipline the bodies and minds of the Argentine people and the philosophers and authors they read.

Calinescu's views on postmodernism and science quoted in the final chapter particularly apply to this situation. I repeat the passage here, including the beginning of the paragraph:

> The more comprehensive presentations of the issues of postmodernism sometimes include references to epistemological problems and concepts, such as the crisis of determinism, the place of chance and disorder in natural processes, Heisenberg's principle of indeterminacy, the question of time and particularly irreversible time (whose recognition has displaced the powerful classical clockwork model of the universe), . . . and Thomas Kuhn's "paradigms" and "scientific revolutions." That such ideas can easily be misunderstood and distorted by literary critics and artists goes without saying. Even so, the critics' new interest in theoretical-epistemological issues comes from a real sense that important changes have occurred in the ways science views itself and the legitimacy of its procedures of inference. And this interest is enhanced by a belief that such changes in scientific paradigms cannot be without analogies on the level of artistic consciousness. (1987, 269)

What we observe in the work of many of these twentieth-century writers is, in a sense, just what Calinescu describes; a situation in which authors reflect and borrow the changing paradigms of science and the concomitant effects of those changes on epistemological issues. Calinescu's linking of quantum physics and Heisenberg would also contribute to the current critical debate on whether to classify Cortázar as a modern or postmodern Latin American writer.[1] His incorporation of quantum physics and Heisenberg's uncertainty principle would seem to suggest a pronounced postmodernity in the Argentine author's work, at least according to Calinescu. But an interest in the epistemological implications of contemporary science is hardly new to the postmodern era Calinescu attempts to describe. Daniel Albright identifies similarities, for example, between quantum physics and the modernist poetry of Yeats, Eliot, and Pound.[2] Furthermore, if the search for scientific analogy and support is not new to the twentieth century, indeed, Sarmiento and Mansilla show that it is not, then can we assume Calinescu's description of the relationship of art and science as unique to postmodernism?

The answer would have to be the ultimately unsatisfying perhaps. If the postmodern view of the science-art relationship is that both are equally insightful and flawed discourses, literature is then brought to an equal footing with science. The power relationship inherent in González Echevarría's archive, or even in the phrase "test tube envy" would be subverted. That would indeed, seem to be unique. Even so, there exist two, almost contradictory objections to such a position. The subversion of a science-art hierarchy would not be new with postmodernity, as the nineteenth century is rife, as we have seen, with examples of a literary discourse that expose the malleable nature of scientific practice. The influence of literary discourse on the perception of scientific practice in the early twentieth century would also seem to anticipate Calinescu's characterization of postmodern science. This "new" postmodern emphasis on the leveling of scientific and literary discourse suggests, then, a paradoxically new form of test tube envy, as it implicitly suggests that an unequal power relationship currently exists between science and art. What seems to be happening, then, is the reverse of the old cliché, if you can't join them, beat them; if art cannot wield the authority of science, why not remove science's authority? Ricardo Piglia, in his attribution of scientific inspiration to literature appears to be just such a gesture. However true it may be, such an attempt simultaneously confirms the perception of scientific authority in a world where actors dress in lab coats to sell shampoo and the evening news continues to announce the latest scientific discoveries. It also seems to ignore the negotiations of cultural authority we have observed through some 150 years of Argentine narrative. The microcosm we have observed in Argentine letters would certainly seem to shed light on the science/literature dynamic in other contexts as well.

From that perspective, Calinescu's analysis of the integral nature of chaos theory in postmodern epistemological thought suggests a pattern for approaching literary and artistic thought. The science that the artist chooses as an authoritative expression of his or her thought reveals much about the author as well as the intellectual and historical milieu in which the text is produced. To understand the nature of the interplay between science and ideology, one needs to consider the philosophical and epistemological implications not only of the fact that science is used, but which science is used and how it is interpreted within the novel in which it appears. By so doing, we can understand issues of literary tradition in a better fashion. Understanding how phrenology relates to manifestations of Latin American romanticism, for example, could help to illuminate differences and similarities between the European model of romanticism that used phrenology extensively and the profoundly altered version we see in Latin America. If the Argentine or Latin American situation can teach us about the construction of literary and discursive strategies on the local level, what can we learn as we compare those manifestations with other localities?

There remains much to be investigated in the relationship between science and Argentine literature. Indeed, any of the authors, or at least any of the literary movements, surveyed in this book could serve alone as the topic of separate books examining the role of scientific discourse in each work or set of works. The perspectives provided by a survey of texts from various time periods suggest possible approaches to different critical issues as they delineate an enduring element in Argentine narrative that survives the very different narrative styles, epistemological configurations, and authorial idiosyncrasies over 150 years of Argentine literature.

Notes

INTRODUCTION

1. As we will see in the course of the chapter, I use the terms "discursive fields" in much the same way as Foucault. My conception of a discursive field is as a textual space created by the intersection of various cultural discourses. For example, the interweaving of scientific discourse with Sarmiento's political anti-Rosas discourse and the socioeconomic discourse of Buenos Aires trade interests create the discursive field that controls Sarmiento's *Facundo*. I propose to follow the thread of the scientific discourse as it intertwines with the other discourses functioning in the text.

2. Alonso identifies this *deseo* as central to the discursive strategies Sarmiento uses in *Facundo* (Alonso 1979, 129).

3. John Davies makes this claim (Davies 1955, xi).

4. *Historias futuras* (2000) is one of the more recent in many such anthologies published in the last twenty years.

5. See Alonso (1979) for an examination of the power structures in *Facundo* on a wider scale.

CHAPTER 1. BUTTING HEADS: PHRENOLOGY AS WEAPON IN *FACUNDO* AND *AMALIA*

1. Throughout the book, I have used published translations where possible, my own where necessary. Published translations will be indicated with parenthetical references, translations that are my own will not include those references.

2. While González Echevarría purposefully uses "tiger" to translate *tigre*, I have decided to use "jaguar," the animal signified by the Argentine use of *tigre*.

3. One should note Shaw (1980) where he argues for the general cohesion of the text on the basis of its novelistic structure, an argument González Echevarría does not take into account.

4. Cooter (1984), Colbert (1997), and Shuttleworth (1996) all make this remark.

5. See Martha Krow-Lucal (1983) for more information on Cubí y Soler's work in Spain.

6. Two such examples are Pierre Flourens's *Examen de la frenología* published in Mexico in 1845 and Sabino de Losada y Rocheblave's *Lecciones de frenología*, published in Havana in 1849.

7. See Silva Gruesz (1996).

8. Both Davies (1955) and Cooter (1984) give excellent examples of this strategy.

9. The main thrust of Cooter's book is to explore the way in which the middle and lower classes tended to appropriate phrenology as a "science" of the masses. In the United States, Colbert and Davies both note the growing phrenological societies made up of scientists, intellectuals, and others who accepted phrenology as science.

10. See Cooter (1984) for a further exploration of this situation.

11. This phenomenon has been studied by critics and scholars from various disciplines. Sommer (1991), for example, studies the patterns of borrowing that mark both Sarmiento's *Facundo* and Mármol's *Amalia*. Salomón (1984) also remarks on this tendency in Sarmiento: "El Sarmiento 'europeizante,' convencido admirador de Francia y de Inglaterra, ha sido para la Argentina décimonónica un espíritu 'ilustrado'—como solía decirse en la España del s.XVIII" (2). Rock 1987 has also noted the pro-Europe and pro-U.S. tendencies of the Unitarios specifically that would also suggest a motive for their incorporation of a discipline like phrenology that was so popular in Europe (114).

12. This relationship is the most likely source of Sarmiento's comments on phrenology as well as a likely conduit for ideas from Combe's *On the Constitution of Man*. Davies (1955) notes that Horace Mann was very close with George Combe (he named his son after Combe), impressed with his work and instrumental in the introduction of the book into the United States (85–86). A friendship with Sarmiento undoubtedly would have given rise to discussions of phrenology generally and Combe's work specifically.

13. His 1841 article "El diarismo" is one such example, where he surveys the impact of newspapers throughout the world, displaying in that survey a broad familiarity with the journalism of other countries.

14. While the determinism suggested by aspects of phrenology might make one wonder as to its usefulness for reform, the phrenologists argued that the foreknowledge of character that the discipline afforded could act as the basis for the reform of societal institutions. Rather than a society based on class, it would be based on abilities, as evidenced by the characteristics of their craniums.

15. Where Sarmiento would see phrenologic indications to barbarism in the gaucho as a condemnation of the gaucho's ability to progress, the English phrenologist would see it as a clue as to the most appropriate style of education needed to improve the individual. For example, while a developed organ of destructiveness would damn Sarmiento's gaucho, Combe would merely find alternate activities that would allow the destructive gaucho to exercise his negative tendency in an acceptable manner. See chapter 4 of *On the Constitution of Man* for a presentation of Combe's ideas.

16. Besides González Echevarría and Pratt and their specific studies of travel literature, comments on the taxonomic nature of the first part of *Facundo* appear throughout *Facundo* criticism.

17. Silva Gruesz (1996) examines how the use of the term *fisonomía* by the Generation of 1837 invokes a physiognomic and phrenological metaphor in which these authors applied the physiognomic link between human appearance and character to the Argentine land. She especially highlights the link forged by these writers between the face of the land and the spirit of the people.

18. Silva Gruesz (1996) notes, in fact, that this colloquial use of *fisonomía* can be seen in Humboldt as well (5).

19. In fact, Shaw (1980) shows how Taine's three categories act as the structural model for the text, where Sarmiento first describes the "race" of the Quiroga and the gauchos, then moves to their "milieu" and ends on the "moment" in Argentina.

20. These descriptions appear with near redundant consistency. Some examples can be found on pp. 14, 22, 25, 33, 36, 37, 42, 46, 64, 121, 123, 176, 221, 290, and 331. This kind of black and white distinction between the Unitarios and the Federalistas has also been studied by Lander 2003, she examines in particular the characters' adhesion to manners and standards of conduct as the point of differentiation.

21. It is also possible that this passage repeats Sarmiento more than alludes to phrenology. If so, the passage would still carry scientific authority, even if a step removed.

22. Amalia's intriguing reference to "escoceses" would seems to evoke the shadow of Combe, but such a connection is muted by the much older superstition of a telepathic power called "second sight" attributed to the Scots.

23. The "prestigious science" to which I refer is, as I have said, the resultant conflation of phrenology and physiognomy that we first see in Sarmiento. By following the pattern established in *Facundo*, Mármol both situates his text within the tradition and reaffirms the cultural authority of such a tradition.

24. That idea that such a tendency exists forms the basis of González Echevarría's *Myth and Archive*.

Chapter 2. A Dandy New Scientist: Lucio V. Mansilla

1. I will refer to *Una excursión a los indios ranqueles* as *Una excursión* throughout the rest of the chapter.

2. There were two more editions in Mansilla's lifetime, the final in 1890, see Blas Matamoro's introduction to his 1993 edition of *Una excursión*.

3. Various critics comment on this quotation, proving it more and more untrue with each repetition. One might also note that Martínez Estrada's own formidable reputation helped to correct the injustice he saw in *Una excursión*'s lack of readership.

4. See Area, Crisafio, Lojo, Mathieu-Higginbotham, Rodríguez, and Stern for examples of the varying criticism on *Una excursión*.

5. Alonso's chapter on *Una excursión* in *The Burden of Modernity* enlightens our study on several levels. While he does not examine the use of scientific discourse in the text, his analysis of the creation and interplay of cultural discourse on a textual level complements the study of the creation of other discourses as well. His basic argument on the nature of the discourse of modernity in Latin America is especially interesting. He argues for a contradictory position of Latin American writing vis-à-vis the concept of modernity in which writers would employ the discourse of modernity to privilege positions and views about Latin America that were decidedly not modern. While Alonso's attention is drawn to discourses other than that of science specifically, we can see a similar dynamic at work in the ap-

pearance of scientific discourse. In Sarmiento, Mármol, and to a lesser extent in Mansilla, we see a sometime indiscriminate inclusion of scientific terminology to privilege clearly nonscientific concepts, even by the standards of nineteenth-century science. Alonso's analysis of *Una excursión* is also provocative for its description of Mansilla's self-fashioning as a dandy and its study of Mansilla's oedipal relationship with Sarmiento's writings, especially *Facundo*. Indeed, the workings Alonso identifies in his treatment of Mansilla's text are all dynamics I see at play in the Mansilla's systematic deployment of scientific references.

David William Foster's thoughtful article on knowledge in *Una excursión* also examines Mansilla's self-fashioning as someone who can relay truth about the Argentine condition. Foster identifies an especially important dynamic in Mansilla's text: the creation of an authorial "yo" that has the rhetorical and cultural power necessary to teach Argentines about their own culture. While Foster does not extend his analysis to Mansilla's use of scientific discourse in that self-fashioning, he does begin a critical path that opens up the study of the role that ethnographic and phrenological discourses play in the construction of the work.

6. See Carlos Alonso's 1999 book *The Burden of Modernity*, especially his chapter on Mansilla where he delves into Mansilla's use of the discourse of modernity as another source of rhetorical power. Also Mirta Stern's article on the creation of textual authority in the work.

7. I refer, of course, to Sarmiento's generation of writers in Argentina, including both him and Mármol as well as others like Juan Alberdi. Esteban Echeverría is considered to be the one of the heads of this group.

8. Area and Parodi's article analyzes this relationship well.

9. For a recounting of this episode, see Popolizio, Also for a novelesque biography of Mansilla, one should examine Lanuza.

10. See Operé, as well as either of the two biographies to which I refer in note 8.

11. This topic has been the subject of various studies, Raul Crisafio's article on foundational autobiography, Alonso's chapter on *Una excursión*, and Goodrich's *Facundo and the Construction of Argentine Culture* all deal with this aspect of Mansilla's work.

12. José Ramos, for example, studies the text as a travel-tourist document, focusing on that particular aspect of travel literature. While he does not examine the scientific basis of travel literature in his article, he does analyze fruitfully the way Mansilla manipulates the tourist aspect of travel literature. Also see George Schade's article that examines the travel narrative of the Generation of 1880 in general, with a particularly good section on Mansilla.

13. For more analysis of the situation of anthropology in the nineteenth century as well as the developing importance of fieldwork in anthropology, see Evans-Pritchard, especially the introduction; as well as studies by Honigmann; Stocking; Herbert; Pratt; Lowie. Clifford Geertz's work in general has been most instructive on the epistemology of anthropology.

14. Mansilla's *causeries* were a series of journalistic articles written between 1880 and 1895 on a variety of subjects. His use of satire and wit remind one of Mariano José de Larra's journalism from earlier in the nineteenth century. These *causeries* were later collected into the work *Entre nos*, first published in 1895.

15. The difference between the two terms being that the ethnographer is the one

who writes about the culture and the ethnologist is the interpreter of both that culture and that writing. While the two are often now found in the same person, in the nineteenth century the distinction was much clearer and important.

16. For an in-depth study of the various scientific travelers that influenced Mansilla and the Argentine model of discourse, see Guzzo's dissertation, specifically her chapter on *Una excursión*.

17. Ramos Mejía uses a version of phrenology based on Paul Broca's late nineteenth-century adaptation of various phrenological principles. Ramos Mejía's description of Juan Manuel Rosas's cranium is especially interesting and appears to be trying to lend scientific credence to Mármol's description of the narrow foreheads of the *Federalistas* and the wide foreheads of the *Unitarios* (182–84). In any case, the appearance of phrenological assumptions in a book characterized as "un libro de ciencia pura" indicates the continuing authority of the discipline as science (Vicente López, in his introduction to *Las neurosis*, 69).

18. Cooter notes:

> It was above all in popular working-class culture that phrenology was most faithfully preserved and pursued in the second half of the century. . . . Already, by the 1850's, works such as that by "Gall the Younger" on *The Practical Uses of Phrenology Exemplified in the application of the Science to Everyday Life* (Glasgow, 1856) or John Mill's *A Catechism of Practical Phrenology* (Leeds, 1851) were becoming more available and sought after. (259)

19. John Davis notes in his description of phrenology:

> For purposes of classification the human race was divided into four psychological types: the "nervous," distinguished by a large brain, delicate health, and emaciation; the "bilious," marked by harsh features and firm muscles; the "sanguine," characterized by large lung capacity and moderate plumpness; and the "lymphatic," with rounded form and heavy countenance. (3)

20. I refer to this phenomenon in the first chapter.

21. Miriam Gárate has an analysis of this *causerie* that, while not pertinent for this particular study, is an excellent study of Mansilla's article.

22. One might also argue that he makes himself into the Quijote. The phrase could well come from don Quijote's remarks to Sancho:

> De allí a poco descubrió don Quijote un hombre a caballo, que traía en la cabeza una cosa que relumbraba como si fuera de oro, y aun él apenas le hubo visto, cuando se volvió a Sancho y le dijo: "Paréceme, Sancho, que no hay refrán que no sea verdadero, porque todos son sentencias sacadas de la misma experiencia, madre de las ciencias todas, especialmente aquel que dice: «donde una puerta se cierra, otra se abre». (281)

The contrast between scientist and country philosopher becomes even greater with the intertext, but also captures the dual nature to which I refer. Mansilla paints himself as accessible as don Quijote and as knowledgeable as a scientist. It is also interesting to note that Borges quotes this section of the Quijote in "Pierre Menard."

23. We know that Mansilla was an avid enough reader of Darwin to have a copy of some of Darwin's works in his library. See María Montero's listing of the books in Mansilla's library.

24. The parenthetical remark is likely a jab at the *Unitarios* for whom the word *colorado* carried political connotations.

25. Such a position certainly reminds one of the sentiments that led Mansilla's contemporaries and later intellectuals to conceptualize and embrace eugenics, although Mansilla's ideas were of a more inclusive nature, miscegenation acting as a solution rather than the threat that later Latin American intellectuals like Alcides Arguedas would denounce it as.

26. See chapter 6, "The Religion of Humanity" of Comte's *A General View of Positivism*, for example.

27. This creation served him personally better than it did the Indians whom he sought to protect. We see Mansilla attending various scientific conferences on behalf of the Argentine government throughout his life as the interpreter of science that he had shown himself to be in his writings.

CHAPTER 3. ARGENTINE NATURALISM'S TEST TUBE ANXIETY

1. See specifically her *Ficciones somáticas: Naturalismo, nacionalismo y políticas médicas del cuerpo (Argentina 1880–1910)*, and her articles on Argentine Naturalism and medicine. Her 1997 article in *MLN* is an excellent synopsis of her argument in this regard, her 1996 article in *LALR* positions the use of a pathological discourse against Doris Sommer's work on the national romances of nineteenth-century Latin America.

2. Jorge Salessi has worked on issues of control and medical discourse in Argentine naturalism as it was applied to sexuality and specifically the control and subjugation of homosexuals. See especially Salessi 1995. See also Benigno Trigo 2000 for his treatment of medical discourse as it related to race and sexuality.

3. I choose Zola as the main example of French naturalism, well aware of the other authors who figure importantly in the movement, among whom figure the Goncourt brothers and, as many would argue, Gustave Flaubert. Nevertheless, Zola serves as what J. A. Cuddon has called the "high priest of the naturalistic movement in literature" (575). Zola's theories on the naturalist novel were the most widely read and distributed, and Argentines particularly responded to Zola specifically in their written reactions to naturalism.

4. I would be remiss not to mention Georg Lukacs's criticism of Zola's failings as a marxist or socialist writer. Especially in Fredric Jameson's analysis of Lukacs's critique of Zola, we see the idea that the French novelist's desire to depict the lowest of society tended toward the melodramatic and, in Lukacs's (and Jameson's apparently) view, did more damage than good to the socialist cause.

5. Indeed, as Berg and Martin note, environment held a much more prominent position than heredity in Zola's scientific ideology:

> Of the three main "determinants" of human behavior [heredity, moment, and milieu], certainly the one that most dominates the novels is environment. Zola repeatedly stresses the role of milieu in justifying the often overwhelming amount of description in his works . . . (12)

Chapter 4. Test Tube Terror: Science and Society in Roberto Arlt

1. An excellent review of the criticism till 1995 is Omar Borré's book. Bravo de Rueda also gives a review of pertinent Arlt criticism. See Flint, Hayes, and Nuñez for their similarly titled discussions of Arlt's narrative strategies. Raúl Larra's book has become a classic in Arlt criticism, while Zubieta and Amícola, among many, study the function of the dystopia in Arlt.

2. Scari's article on Arlt the inventor gives important biographical information on this point. Dapia and Gregorio investigate Arlt's incorporation of pseudoscience, as does Jarkowski. Rufinelli touches on it in his more general study of *El juguete rabioso*. We will examine the studies that deal with science in Arlt specifically in the body of the chapter.

3. See Ortiz's historical article on science in Argentina. Lugones himself is an important figure in Argentine science fiction, his *Las fuerzas extrañas* is a classic in the Argentine genre. His stories are traditional science fiction fare in which a scientist comes to a messy end because of his experiments. He, with Quiroga and Arlt form a triad of writers who used the classic Frankenstein plot in a series of stories that forebode a science run amok.

4. This is not to say that positivism enjoyed unanimous support in the nineteenth century. Nevertheless, the horrors of World War I strengthened a questioning of the view of science as wholly beneficial.

5. For more information on Darwinism's influence in Argentine culture, see articles by Montserrat, Ortiz, and Marún.

6. See for example, Rodríguez, Ainsa, Gilman, Matamoro, Giordano, among many.

7. Arlt's position as precursor both to the Latin American urban novel and the Boom has been remarked by a variety of critics. Gnutzman and Leland figure among many, but it is difficult to find a study that does not mention this idea.

8. Various critics have commented on *El juguete rabioso* as a picaresque novel. Among them we find, Hernández, Gnutzman, and Canepa. Indeed, Arlt himself names Quevedo as an important influence on his work.

9. Rufinelli and many others note this.

10. Darwin dedicates a major portion of *The Descent of Man* to a phenomenon he calls "Selection in Relation to Sex," relating it in several instances to natural selection and the struggle for life.

11. Gostaustas and others have examined this episode, interpreting it as a function of Arlt's criticism of marriage as a bourgeois convention. While it certainly performs such a function, room still exists for its interpretation along Darwinian lines.

12. We see in the conversation noted above a passing reference to phrenology, now used solely as a device to mark Souza as decidedly nonscientific: "—Remolinos de cabello, carácter indócil . . . , cráneo aplanado en occipucio, temperamento razonador . . . ; pulso trémulo, índole romántica . . . (1981, 52)." Here Souza uses references to phrenological language, but instead of privileging him as a scientist, this language brands him as a theosophical philosopher.

13. Shaw's *Nueva narrativa hispanoamericana* highlights Arlt's metaphysics as central to his fiction. Larra's book also develops this theme.

14. Piglia's work on Arlt is extensive, from his treatment in *Respiración artificial* to the critical work Piglia has devoted to him, to the literary prank Piglia pulled in presenting the translated story "Luba" as an unpublished Arlt text. See McCracken's article for the uncovering of the prank as well as an excellent analysis of the relationship between Piglia and Arlt.

15. In a 1988 interview with La Nación, Sabato complained of "el imperialismo de la ciencia" in literary criticism and argued that "la creación artística es exactamente al revés" of scientific investigation (1). Chavarri also discusses this subject in some depth, looking specifically at Sabato's interest in metaphysics as a cause of his abandonment of science.

16. "Informe sobre ciegos" has probably received more critical attention than all the rest of the novel and nearly as much as *El túnel*. Foster calls the section "the most captivating segment of the work" and remarks that "it has rightly been recognized as perhaps the most creative of Sabato's efforts" (1975, 84).

17. Holzapfel argument that the Darwin references in "Informe sobre ciegos" form an interpretative key for understanding the text suggests another link with Arlt although the deprecating tone with which they are presented undermine the more supportive role that Darwin's theories serve in Arlt (147).

18. Villalobos dedicates an article to this phenomenon, distinguishing between Sabato the man and Sabato the character. Sabato would later renounce the accent altogether, further muddying the difference between the two.

19. Of particular interest on that level is his attack on Darwinism and phrenology, two modes of thinking that, as we have seen, held particular sway in Argentine letters:

> La reducción del Universo a Materia-en-Movimiento dio origen a las doctrinas más peregrinas. Primero fue la tentativa de localizar el alma en una glándula. Luego, la investigación del alma con amperímetros y compases; mientras algunos se dedicaban a medir con tales aparatos la inteligencia y la sensibilidad; otros, como Fechner, organizaban desfiles de señores delante de diversos rectángulos, para decidir estadísticamente la esencia de la belleza; y otros, en fin, exponían bruscamente una lámina a la mirada de un sujeto, anotando el tiempo, de reacción tomado con un cronómetro. Al mismo tiempo Gall y Lavater perpetraban su frenología y su fisiognómica —¡Oh, espíritu de Balzac!—. Y al llegar al siglo XX, Pavlov midió la salivación de un perro ante un trozo de carne, con y sin tortura. (2002b, 43)

Note that even in this vituperative attack, Sabato increases his stature through his knowledge of the history of science, his ability to produce a detailed history of science's absurdities empowering his critique of science in general.

CHAPTER 5. BORGES'S SCIENTIFIC DISCIPLINE

1. See Serres's *Feux et signaux*. Also see Weissert's discussion of Serres in the context of Borges (1991, 223), and Assad's discussion of Serres's idea (1991, 296).

2. See the collection of essays *Borges y la ciencia*, a book edited by Borges's widow María Kodama that contains essays by several Latin American scientists.

3. Borges's tendency to tear down systems has been well documented. See, in particular, Alazraki, Bell-Villada, and Shaw for the standard critical reaction.

4. Renzi remarks: "Borges . . . es un escritor del siglo XIX. El mejor escritor argentino del siglo XIX. . . . su ficción sólo se puede entender como un intento consciente de concluir con la literatura argentina del siglo XIX" (2001, 130). [Borges . . . is a nineteenth century writer. The best Argentine writer of the nineteenth century . . . his fiction can only be understood as a conscious attempt to conclude with nineteenth century Argentine literature.]

5. He explains: "Crear ideas literarias y poéticas, ése era el único interés de Borges al escribir sus cuentos. Si de alguna manera las ideas científicas, así como las metafísicas o teológicas, podían ofrecer un punto de partida para ello, Borges no dudaría en usarlas aún sin tratar de entenderlas a fondo, o sin entenderlas del todo" (31) [Creating poetic and literary ideas, that was Borges only interest in writing his stories. If, somehow, scientific ideas, just like metaphysical or theological ideas, can offer a starting point for them, Borges would not hesitate in using them without understanding them completely or even at all].

6. Ortiz notes: "nevertheless, Einstein's visit had a considerable impact, and it acted as a catalyst in a number of intellectual concerns which had been brewing in Argentina since the end of the First World War. This impact was not only felt in science. But also in philosophy" (1998, 115). In light of Balderston's work on Borges's connection with history, this suggests another connection (Balderston 1993).

7. See vol. 4, 394. Also see Corry's discussion of the review, p. 28.

8. See Molloy's discussion of the two texts for an excellent description and analysis of their treatment of the paradox (1994, 101–2).

9. Capobianco (1982) provides a list of texts in which Borges uses mathematical expressions in his "Mathematics in the *Ficciones* of Jorge Luis Borges." See also Merrell, who comments extensively on Borges's use of math throughout *Unthinking Thinking* and Amaral.

10. As with most subjects, a good deal of criticism has been dedicated to Borges's disdain for Nietzsche's philosophy as well as possible influence that the German philosopher may have exercised on Borges despite the intellectual antipathy. See, in particular, Selnes and Halpern.

11. Cantor developed the notion of transfinite numbers as descriptors of infinite sets. Cantor showed the infinite correspondences could be constructed from apparently finite sets, proving, for him, the reality of infinity. For further study into Borges's use of Cantor, see Selnes, also Hernández, Corry, and Merrell. Merrell's discussion of Cantor's theories is especially useful for understanding Borges (1991, 60–61).

12. It also creates a Borgesian dilemma for me, Foucault's impact on my work is obvious and, with Borges' influence on Foucault, I find myself in an interpretative circle.

13. See Donald Shaw's *Jorge Luis Borges: Ficciones* for a standard interpretation of the story. Also see Ludmer, Sosnowski, and Stark as a good cross-section of recent and classic criticism.

14. There are several articles dedicated to this subject. See especially Clark, Grau, and Mosca.

15. He comments in the prologue to *El informe de Brodie*, "el curioso lector advertirá ciertas afinidades íntimas. Unos pocos argumentos me han hostigado a lo

largo del tiempo soy decididamente monótono" [the curious reader will not certain intimate affinities. A very few plots have followed me for a long time, I am decidedly monotonous] (Vol. 3, 399).

16. The most thorough, popular, discussion of Gödel appears in Hofstadter's *An Eternal Golden Braid*. I refer here, of course, to Gödel's particular theorem that holds that in any set, there exists an element that disproves its truth. See also Schmidt-Emans's work on the connections between Gödel, Escher and Borges.

17. There are nearly too many to name. In addition to Weissert, Hayles, and Merrell's relatively early work on the subject, Schreiber and Umansky, Rivero-Potter, Gómez, Mosher, Zanelli, Capobianco (1989), Rojo, Brandão, and Höfner have all written on "El jardín" and science. While some end up repeating the same ideas, Rivero-Potter and Screiber and Umansky are quite good. Rojo is interesting for the more personal perspective of a scientist reader as is Cerejido.

18. For a more detailed, popular, description of Everett's work, see Gribbin (1984, 235–54).

19. Weissert argues, "In an almost Freudian trope, Albert is killed at the end of the story. Dr. Tsun, the terminator whose commitment to his mission is stronger than his humanity, identifies the premeditated act with an exemplary chaotic one: 'I swear that his death was instantaneous, as if he had been struck by lightning'" (101). Seen as chaotic event, Mr. Albert's assassination seems to prophesy the coming paradigm shift from global to local theorizing, from modernity to postmodernity (1991, 232).

20. See Ted Lyon's series of articles on Borges's manipulation of the literary interview as its own genre.

21. Heisenberg's description of what for him was philosophy's march toward the ideas of quantum physics emphasizes the anticipatory roles of Hume and Berkeley, especially as anti-Cartesians who would lend credence to Heisenberg's destabilization of Newtonian/Cartesian thought (1958, 76–92).

22. Once again, while discussing Bertrand Russell, Borges resorts to mathematical notation (he also confuses Russell with Cantor, popularizing someone who was, in fact, popularizing someone else. Note the final references indicating that the idea is valid because mathematicians have accepted it.

Bertrand Russell lo explica así: hay números finitos (la serie natural de los números 1,2,3,4,5,6,7,8,9,10 y así infinitamente). Pero luego consideramos otra serie, y esa otra serie tendrá exactamente la mitad de la extensión de la primera. Está hecha de todos los números pares. Así, al 1 corresponde el 2, al 2 corresponde el 4, al 3 corresponde el 6 . . . Y luego tomemos otra serie. Vamos a elegir una cifra cualquiera. Por ejemplo, 365. Al 1 corresponde el 365, al 2 corresponde el 365 multiplicado por sí mismo, al 3 corresponde el 365 multiplicado a la tercera potencia. Tenemos así varias series de números que son todos infinitos. Es decir, en los números transfinitos las partes no son menos numerosas que el todo. Creo que esto ha sido aceptado por los matemáticos. (Vol. 4, 201)

[Bertrand Russell explains it this way: There are finite numbers (the natural series of numbers . . . and so on infinitely). But then we consider another series, and that other series will have exactly half the length of the first. It is made up of all the even numbers. So, 1 corresponds to two, two to 4, 3 to 6 . . . And then we take up another series. We are going to choose any number. For example 365. So 1 corresponds 365, 2 corresponds to 365 multiplied by itself, 3 corresponds to 365 to the third power. We have many series of numbers that are all infinite. That is to say in transfinite numbers, the parts are not less numerous than the whole. I believe that this has been accepted by mathematicians.]

23. There are endless articles dedicated to this subject (that of Borges's connection to detective fiction). See Irwin's book as a good beginning point.

Chapter 6. Cortázar's Quantum Values

1. For critical work that centers on the ludic in Cortázar, see Yurkievich's article on the ludic element in *Rayuela*, also Ramos-Izquierdo, Luchting, the entire *Coloquio Internacional: Lo lúdico y lo fantástico en la obra de Cortázar*, and Blanco Arnejo's recent study of the ludic in Cortázar novels.
2. For a cogent, albeit popularized, description of Everett's theory as well as its historical context, see Gribbin (1984, 235–47).
3. The best descriptions of Cortázar's *cronopio* would be in his collection of short stories and other observations: *Historia de Cronopios y de Famas*. The following, from "Viajes" of that text, provides a flavor for the cronopio personality type:

> Cuando los cronopios van de viaje, encuentran los hoteles llenos, los trenes ya se han marchado, llueve a gritos, y los taxis no quieren llevarlos o les cobran precios altísimos. Los cronopios no se desaniman porque creen firmemente que estas cosas les ocurren a todos, y a la hora de dormir se dicen unos a otros: «La hermosa ciudad, la hermosísima ciudad.» Y sueñan toda la noche que en la ciudad hay grandes fiestas y que ellos están invitados. Al otro día se levantan contentísimos, y así es como viajan los cronopios. (1996, 113–14)

> [When cronopios travel, they find the hotels full, the trains having left, that it is raining cats and dogs and the taxis won't pick them up or charge them too much. Cronopios don't get down because they firmly believe that these things happen to everyone and when it's time to go to sleep they say to each other "The beautiful city, the extraordinarily beautiful city." And they dream all night that in the city there are great parties and they are all invited. The next day the wake up happy and that is how cronopios travel.]

As one can infer from the passage, the *cronopios* are irrational dreamers, do not plan trips and live in the moment. (As opposed to the anal-retentive *Famas*). Cortázar uses the term *cronopios* throughout his work (especially in *Último round*, *La vuelta al día en ochenta mundos*, and *Los autonautas de la cosmopista*) to refer to himself and his friends.

4. Note, for example, his *Teoría del túnel*, esp. For a critical perspective of this phenomenon in his work, see Sosnowski (1973).
5. For an in-depth study of surrealism in Cortázar, see Evelyn Picón Garfield, see also Rosario Ferré's brief study of symbolism and surrealism in Cortázar's work as well as his *Teoría del túnel*.
6. I am indebted to Patricio Lizama, as he was the first to note the mention of quantum physics both in *Teoría del túnel* and the interview with Castro-Klarén (1995, 178–79)

7. Michael Capobianco—whose article forms the basis of Patricio Lizama's subsequent study—finds elements of quantum physics in several of Cortázar's novels and short stories, especially in *62: Modelo para armar* and stories such as "Axolotl" and "La noche boca arriba." In his analysis, Capobianco makes use of the Copenhagen interpretation of quantum physics in order to suggest similarities between Cortázar's fiction and quantum theory. As Capobianco argues, the Copenhagen interpretation shows an obvious kinship to Cortázar's project because of its insistence upon John Wheeler's notion of a participatory universe, one in which the nature of reality is fundamentally related to one's observation of it (8). Capobianco's study then focuses on self-other relationships and acts of observation that change reality in Cortázar's work.

8. For a detailed discussion of this experiment, see Gribbin (1984, 14–17, 162–63). Also, see Capello's description, 50–53.

9. See Gribbin's explanation, 168–71.

10. For a study of the vampiresque in *62*, see Hernández, in fact her treatment of the same issues of the basilisk and blood suggest the polyvalent nature of the images employed that evoke simultaneously the vampire theme and the aesthetization of quantum physics.

11. Sara Castro-Klarén has remarked on this tendency generally in Cortázar's fiction, calling the practice of participator-based reality ontological fabulation. She relates Cortázar's reading of the new physics to this practice as well (1978).

12. Schrödinger first proposed this experiment in print in 1935, John Gribbin's treatment of the experiment is enlightening, see 203–8.

13. Richard Young's study of *Octaedro* in its entirety is a notable exception to this lack of critical attention.

14. I use the word "seriously" here consciously. In this case it invokes Cortázar's aforementioned sense of serious play, as taking a mockery seriously creates a humorous situation, yet is used simultaneously to deal with the very serious issue of the death of a friend.

15. Amorós mentions Descartes briefly in his critical introduction and notes, others seem to include him implicitly in their discussions of Cortázar and irrationality. Bibliographical searches for studies analyzing the two have produced nothing.

16. Studies of Cortázar's metaphysics abound. Castro-Klarén's concept of ontological fabulation suggests Cortázar's basis for this other reality. See also Curutchet, Sosnowski, and Planells among others.

17. Cortázar's questioning of the novelistic structure is also a well-studied theme. See, for example, Amorós, Lezama Lima, and many others.

18. For further discussion of Cortázar's attitude toward language, see Amorós, Salazar, and Gallo among many others.

19. The similarity between this group and the group of scientists and philosophers that create Tlön in Borges's story "Tlön, Uqbar, Orbis Tertius" written earlier is an intriguing coincidence.

20. See Hayles 2000, also Porush 1985 for characterizations of the development of cybernetics as a discipline and the impact of that development on literature.

21. The idea of the antinovel, some times called the other novel has been studied from several perspectives. Lezama Lima provides a worthwhile study of "la otra novela" as does José Emilio Osses in his article about "la novela morelliana."

22. Margery Safir's article on transgressive behavior in *Rayuela* clearly outlines the importance of Oliveira's attempt to break with traditional values.
23. Again, this point has been the focus of several critical studies. See, for example, Curutchet's book, also Sosnowski, Planells, and Amorós's introduction.
24. Wiener describes it several times, but first develops the idea completely in *The Human Use of Human Beings*.
25. See especially his final chapters of *The Human Use of Human Beings*.
26. Santiago Colás has argued that this focus on international capitalism develops the representation of modern alienation he finds as central to the novel's project (1994, 50).
27. Porush investigates this tendency more fully in his book, *The Soft Machine*.
28. Barrenechea argues this point specifically:

La doble lectura muestra una superposición de dos diseños: el diseño superficial, que corresponde más o menos a una interpretación o una experiencia superficial del vivir, y el diseño profundo, que denuncia las secretas conexiones. (1972, 231)

[The double reading shows a two designs superimposed: the superficial design, that corresponds more or less an interpretation or a superficial experience of living, and the profound design, that denounces secret connections.]

Shaw has also outlined this effect (1981, 95).
29. I have found studies by Zunilda Gertel and Alfred MacAdam examining the important position of the reader in the elaboration of *Rayuela* to be especially instructive.
30. Ironically, hypertext enthusiasts have appropriated the *Rayuel-O-Matic* as indicative of Rayuela's place in a genealogy of hypertext pioneers. A Web version of *Rayuela* is, in fact, called *Rayuel-O-Matic Universal Digital*. I discuss the contradiction between Cortázar's anti-cybernetic stance and his nascent hypertextual tendencies with their concomitant embrace of new technology in "Reading *Rayuela* in the *Rayuel-O-Matic*."
31. One can perceive in this antimechanistic, antirationalist position the echoes of Romantic thought in Cortázar. His writings on Keats and other romantics are widely commented and certainly suggest a propensity toward the ideas that he develops with the images of cybernetics against quantum physics.

Chapter 7. Test Tube Envy at the Turn of the Century

1. For an informative discussion of Hispanic women science fiction writers, see Molina-Gavilán's book.
2. See Rhonda Buchanan's edition of essays devoted to Shua's work for a glimpse at the author's varied literary pursuits.
3. We see those characters appear in the novel Kalpa Imperial and the story "Los embriones del violeta" respectively. Claudia Sánchez Arce and Yolanda Molina-Gavilán provide solid analyses of much of Gorodischer's work.
4. Such was the reaction of Reina Roffé who dismissed any feminine envy of science, arguing that women do not need to look outside of themselves for authority (personal conversation with the author).

5. That is not to say, however, that chaos theory has not figured strongly in popular culture. One need merely remember the description of chaos theory in *Jurassic Park* provided by Jeff Goldblum's character, an explanation that was used to make (somewhat) plausible the subsequent attack of the dinosaurs.

6. I refer to Gustavo Pellón's unpublished translation of the novel. The English translations of the novel that appear later are based in part on that translation.

7. See all of book 3 in *Order Out of Chaos*.

8. See Prigogine's discussion of the three stages of thermodynamics in chapter 5.

9. See statements by Toeffler in his introduction to *Order Out of Chaos* as well as remarks by Matei Calinescu in *Five Faces of Modernity*.

10. This is exactly the situation against which Gross and Levitt argue and the reason they see the postmodern appropriation of Prigogine as dangerous. Nevertheless, these situations arise and as a critic one must examine and analyze their function in literature. While Giardinelli's use of Prigogine and chaos theory, for example, may not accurately reflect chaos theory as a science, his incorporation of the Russian chemist and his theories constitute a narrative device in the text.

11. In that sense, the novel also seems to produce a narrative version of the ideas of time Borges develops in "El jardín de senderos que se bifurcan," although an extension to Hugh Everett's "Many Worlds Theory" in quantum mechanics would be rather forced.

12. Prigogine identifies ecosystems as principally chaotic systems (192–95). Gleick, in his widely read popularization of chaos theory has argued this point in his chapter "Life's Ups and Downs," 57–80 in his *Chaos*.

13. For Prigogine's discussion see his chapters 5 and 6.

14. See in particular Hutcheon's book *A Poetics of Postmodernism*.

15. See specifically her chapter on "Chaos and Poststructuralism," 175–208, and her conclusion "Chaos and Culture: Postmodernism(s) and the Denaturing of Experience," 265–96.

16. See Colás's book *Postmodernity in Latin America*.

17. Giardinelli embroiders on his reading of Fracchia's ideas concerning the philosophy of resistance with the elaboration of his concept of Latin American postmodernity. See Giardinelli's discussion of the Argentine philosopher in *El país de las maravillas*, 28–34. Also see Fracchia's book for further study.

Conclusion

1. Colás describes this debate most fully, arguing for Cortázar's place as a modernist author who anticipates, but does not fully embrace, the position of Latin American postmodernity (1994, 23–75). See also Larsen's article and my "Reading *Rayuela* in the Rayuel-O-Matic."

2. See his book, *Quantum poetics*.

Works Cited

Ainsa, Fernando. 1993. "La provocación como antiutopía en Roberto Arlt." *Cuadernos Hispanoamericanos* Supp. 11: 15–22.

Alazraki, Jaime. 1983. *La prosa narrativa de Jorge Luis Borges*. 3rd ed. Madrid: Gredos.

Albright, Daniel. 1997. *Quantum Poetics: Yeats, Pound, Eliot, and the science of modernism*. Cambridge: Cambridge Univ. Pres.

Alonso, Carlos. 1979. "Facundo y la sabiduría del poder." *Cuadernos Americanos* 12.226: 116–30.

———. 1998. *The burden of modernity: The rhetoric of cultural discourse in Spanish America*. Oxford: Oxford Univ. Press.

Amaral, Pedro. 1971. "Borges, Babel y las matemáticas" *Revista Iberoamericana* 37, 421–28.

Amícola, José. 1984. *Astrología y fascismo en la obra de Arlt*. Buenos Aires: Weimar.

Amorós, Andrés. 1991. "Introducción" in his edition of *Rayuela*. Madrid: Cátedra.

Area, Lelia, and Cristina Parodi. 1995. "Lucio V. Mansilla: El peso de una 'conciencia histórica mortificada.'" *Revista de crítica literaria latinoamericana* 21.41: 177–92.

Argyros, Alexander. 1991. *A blessed rage for order: Deconstruction, evolution and chaos*. Ann Arbor: Univ. of Michigan Press.

Arlt, Mirta, and Omar Borré. 1985. *Para leer a Roberto Arlt*. Buenos Aires: Torres Agüero.

Arlt, Roberto. 1981. *Obra completa, Roberto Arlt: Prefacio de Julio Cortázar*. Vol. 1. Buenos Aires: C. Lohlé.

———. 2002. *Mad Toy*. Trans. Michele Aynesworth. Durham: Duke Univ. Press.

Assad, Maria. 1991. "Michel Serres: In search of a tropography." *Chaos and order: Complex dynamics in literature and science*. Ed. N. Katherine Hayles. Chicago: Univ. Chicago Press, 278–98.

Balderston, Daniel. 1993. *Out of context : historical reference and the representation of reality in Borges*. Durham: Duke Univ. Press.

Barrenechea, Ana María. 1972. "La estructura de *Rayuela*." *La nueva novela hispanoamericana*. Ed. J. Lafforgue, Buenos Aires, 222–47.

Bell, Andrea, and Yolanda Molina-Gavilán. 2003. "Introduction: Science fiction in Latin America and Spain." *Cosmos Latinos: An anthology of science fiction from Latin America and Spain*. Middletown, CT: Wesleyan Univ. Press.

Bell-Villada, Gene. 2000. *Borges and his fictions: A guide to his mind and art*. Austin: Univ. of Texas Press.

Benjamin, Walter. 1968. *Illuminations.* Ed. Hannah Arendt. New York: Schocken Books.

Berg, William J., and Laurey K. Martin. 1992. *Emile Zola revisited* New York: Twayne.

Bessières, Georges Louis. 1837. *Nueva clasificacion de las facultades cerebrales, ó La frenología.* Trans. José Gerber de Robles. Valencia : Imprenta de Cabrerizo.

Blanco Arnejo, María Dolores. 1996. *La novela lúdica experimental de Julio Cortázar.* Madrid: Editorial Pliegos.

Borges, Jorge Luis. 1996. *Obras completas.* 4 vols. Buenos Aires: Emecé.

———. 1998. *Collected Fictions.* Trans. Andrew Hurley New York: Viking.

———. 1999. Selected Non-Fictions. Ed. Eliot Weinberger. Trans. Esther Allen, Suzanne Jill Levine, and Eliot Weinberger. New York: Viking.

Boruchoff, David. 1985. "In pursuit of the detective genre: 'La muerte y la brújula' of J. L. Borges." *Inti* 21 (Spring): 13–26.

Brandão Tiago de Oliveira, José Carlos. 1989. "Borges, o matemático." *Ometeca* 1.1: 53–61.

Bravo de Rueda, José. 1996. *El cuerpo humano: un nexo entre la narrativa y la dramática de Roberto Arlt.* Diss., Univ. of Maryland.

Bretón de los Herreros, Manuel. 1845. *Frenología y magnetismo en un acto.* Madrid: Impr. de J. Repullés.

Brown, J. Andrew. "Reading *Rayuela* in the Rayuel-O-Matic," *Revista Canadiense de Estudios Hispánicos* 28.3 (Spring 2005).

Bunge, Mario. 1987. "Borges y Einstein, o la fantasía en arte y en ciencia." *Revista de Occidente* 73 (June): 45–62.

Calinescu, Matei. 1987. *Five faces of modernity.* Durham: Duke Univ. Press.

Cambaceres, Eugenio. 1984. *En la sangre.* Ed. Claude Cymerman. Madrid: Editora Nacional.

Cánepa, Mario A. 1994. "El 'Pícaro' y la novela picaresca en Buenos Aires." *Crítica Hispánica* 16.2:211–22.

Capanna, Pablo. 1995. *El cuento argentino de la ciencia ficción.* Buenos Aires: Nuevo Siglo.

Capello, Jean. 1994. *Reader response to the unbelievable story: The fantastic, non-verifiable truth claim, and the physics.* Diss., Rutgers University.

———. 1995. "'El Aleph' read as new Physics realism" *Revista Canadiense de Estudios Hispánicos* 19.3 (Spring): 463–78.

———. 1997. "Science as story: Julio Cortázar and Schrödinger's cat." *Revista de Estudios Hispánicos* 31.1 (Jan.): 41–60.

Capobianco, Michael. 1982. "Mathematics in the *Ficciones* of Jorge Luis Borges." *International Fiction Review* 9.1 (Winter): 51–54.

———. 1989. "Quantum theory, spacetime, and Borges' bifurcations." *Ometeca* 1.1:27–38.

———. 1994. "Julio Cortázar and the various interpretations of quantum theory." *Taller de Letras* 22:7–16.

Castro-Klarén, Sara. 1978. "Ontological fabulation: Toward Cortázar's theory of literature." in *The final island: The fiction of Julio Cortázar.* Ed. Jaime Alazraki and Ivar Ivask. Norman: Univ. Oklahoma Press, 140–50.

Catalá, Rafael. 2002. "Jorge Luis Borges." *Encyclopedia of literature and science.* Ed. Pamela Gossin. Westport, CT: Greenwood Press.

Cereijido, Marcelino. 1994. *Ciencia sin seso, locura doble.* Mexico City: Siglo Veintiuno.

———. 1997. *¿Por qué no tenemos ciencia?* Mexico City: Siglo Veintiuno.

———. 1999. "Borges visto por un científico." in *Borges y la ciencia* Buenos Aires: Eudeba. 33–50.

Cervantes, Miguel de. 1996. *Don Quijote de la Mancha. Obras completas de Miguel de Cervantes Saavedra.* Electronic ed. Fred F. Jehle. http://users.ipfw.edu/jehle/wcdq.htm. West Lafayette, Indiana: Purdue Research Foundation.

Clark, John R. 1995. "Idealism and dystopia in 'Tlön, Uqbar, Orbis Tertius.'" *International Fiction Review* 22.1–2:74–79.

Clifford, James. 1988. *The predicament of culture: Twentieth-century ethnography, literature, and art.* Cambridge, MA: Harvard Univ. Press.

Colás, Santiago. 1994. *Postmodernity in Latin America: The Argentine paradigm.* Durham: Duke Univ. Press.

Colbert, Charles. 1997. *A measure of perfection: Phrenology and the fine arts in America.* Chapel Hill: Univ. North Carolina Press.

Combe, George. 1835. *On the constitution of man* Boston: Marsh, Capen and Lyon.

Comte, Auguste. 1975. *A general view of positivism.* Trans. J. H. Bridges. New York: Robert Speller and Sons.

Cooter, Roger. 1984. *The cultural meaning of popular science: Phrenology and the organization of consent in nineteenth-century Britain.* Cambridge: Cambridge Univ. Press.

Corry, Leo. "Algunas Ideas Científicas en la Obra de Borges y su Contexto Histórico." http://www.tau.ac.il/~corry/texts/chapters/borges-ciencia.pdf.

Cortázar, Julio. 1956. "Continuidad de los parques." In *Final del juego.* México: Los Presentes.

———. 1963, 1991. *Rayuela* Ed. Andrés Amorós. Madrid: Cátedra.

———. 1966. *Hopscotch.* Trans. Gregory Rabassa. New York: Random House.

———. 1967. *La vuelta al día en ochenta mundos.* Mexico City: Siglo XXI.

———. 1980. Julio Cortázar, Lector con Sara Castro-Klarén. *Cuadernos Hispanoamericanos* 364–66:11–36.

———. 1981. "Prefacio" *Obra completa, Roberto Arlt: Prefacio de Julio Cortázar.* Vol. 1. Buenos Aires: C. Lohlé.

———. 1986. *Around the day in eighty worlds.* Trans. Thomas Christensen. San Francisco: North Point Press.

———. 1994a. *Cuentos completos I.* Madrid: Alfaguara.

———. 1994b. *Cuentos completos II.* Madrid: Alfaguara.

———. 1994c. *Obra crítica/1. Teoría del túnel.* Ed. Saúl Yurkievich, Madrid: Alfaguara.

———. 1996a. *62: Modelo para armar.* Madrid: Alfaguara.

———. 1996b. *Historias de Cronopios y de Famas.* Madrid: Alfaguara.

Crisafio, Raul. 1988 . "Sarmiento-Mansilla: Una excursión a la biografía autofundacional." *Romanticismo 3–4: Atti del IV Congresso sul romanticismo spagnolo e ispanoamericano.* Ed. Ermanno Caldera. Genoa: Biblioteca de Lett, 30–37.

Crow-Lucal, Martha. 1983. "Balzac, Galdós and phrenology." *Anales Galdosianos* 18:7–14.

Cubí y Soler, Mariano. 1846. *Sistema completo de frenolojía: con sus aplicaziones al adelanto i mejoramiento del hombre, individual i sozialmente considerado.* Barcelona : J. Oliveres.

Curutchet, Juan Carlos. 1972. *Julio Cortázar o la crítica de la razón pragmática.* Madrid: Editora Nacional.

Dahl-Buchanan, Rhonda. 1996. "El género negro como radiografía de una sociedad en *Luna caliente* de Mempo Giardinelli." *Narrativa hispanoamericana contemporánea: Entre la vanguardia y el posboom.* Ed. Ana María Hernández de López. Madrid: Pliegos, 155–66.

Dapia, Silvia, and Guillermo Gregorio. 1995. "Roberto Arlt y los saberes marginales." *Romance Languages Annual* 7:441–45.

Darwin, Charles. 1993a. *Origin of species. The Portable Darwin.* Ed Duncan Porter and Peter Graham. New York: Penguin.

———. 1993b. *The descent of man. The Portable Darwin.* Ed. Duncan Porter and Peter Graham. New York: Penguin.

Davies, John. 1955. *Phrenology: fad and science.* New Haven: Yale Univ. Press.

De Costa, René. 1999. *El humor en Borges.* Madrid: Cátedra.

de Giustino, David. 1975. *Conquest of mind: Phrenology and Victorian social thought.* London: Croom Helm.

Díaz, Gwendolyn. 1996. "Estructuras caóticas en novella negra con argentinos de Luisa Valenzuela." In *La palabra en vilo: narrativa de Luisa Valenzuela.* Ed. Gwendolyn Díaz and María Inés Lagos. Santiago, Chile: Cuarto Propio, 177–90.

Dubner, Carlos. 1983. "Sábato y compañía: Algunas meditaciones sobre Ciencia y Literatura." *Cuadernos Hispanoamericanos* 391:681–85.

Espinoza, Pilar. 1997. "*Luna caliente* de Mempo Giardinelli y *Lolita* de Vladimir Nabakov." *Atenea* 475 (Jan.–June): 187–97.

Evans-Pritchard, Sir Edward. 1981. *A history of anthropological thought.* New York: Basic Books.

Ferré, Rosario. 1987. "Cortázar: sombras del simbolismo y del surrealismo." *Revista de Estudios Hispánicos* 21.2 (May): 101–10.

Ferrer, Caroline. 1998. "Chaos theory and Latin American dictatorships: A narrative form against political exile and repression" presented at the Conference for the Society of Literature and Science, November 6, 1998, Gainesville, Florida.

Fishburn, Evelyn. 1981. *The portrayal of immigration in nineteenth century Argentine ficion (1845–1902).* Berlin: Colloquium Verlag.

Flint, Jack. 1985. *The prose works of Roberto Arlt.* Durham, UK: Univ. of Durham Press.

Flourens, Pierre. 1844. *Examen de la frenología.* Trans. M. Andrade. Mexico, Impr. de V. Garcia Torres.

Flynn, Thomas. 1994. "Foucault's mapping of history." *The Cambridge companion to Foucault.* Ed. Gary Gutting Cambridge: Cambridge Univ. Press, 28–46.

Foster, David William. 1975. *Currents in the contemporary Argentine novel.* Columbia: Univ. of Missouri Press.

———. 1988. "Knowledge in Mansilla's *Una excursión a los indios ranqueles.*" *Revista hispánica moderna* 41.1:19–30.

Foucault, Michel. 1970. *The order of things.* New York: Vintage.

———. 1972. *The archaeology of knowledge.* New York: Pantheon.

———. 1977. *Discipline and punish : the birth of the prison.* New York: Pantheon.

———. 1980. *Power/Knowledge: selected interviews and other writings 1972–1977.* Ed. Colin Gordon. New York: Pantheon.

———. 1984. *The Foucault reader.* Ed. Paul Rabinow. New York: Pantheon.

———. 1990. *The history of sexuality: an introduction, volume 1.* New York: Vintage.

Fracchia, Eduardo. 1997. *Apuntes para una filosofía de la resistencia.* Chaco, Argentina: Universidad Nacional del Nordeste Univ. Press.

Gallo, Marta. 1986. "Los nombres de *Rayuela.*" *Coloquio internacional: Lo lúdico y lo fantástico en la obra de Cortázar.* Madrid: Editorial Fundamentos.

Gárate, Miriam V. 1992. "'El famoso fusilamiento del caballo': Un espisodio revelador en la literatura argentina de fronteras. Apuntes sobre una causerie de Lucio v. Mansilla. *Remate de Males: Revista do Departamento de Teoria Literaria* 12:57–64.

Garcia-Chichester, Ana. 1993. "Jerarquía de los géneros sexuales en *Luna caliente* de Mempo Giardinelli." Romance-Notes 34.2 (Winter 1993): 169–76.

Gardini, Carlos. 2001. *El libro de la tierra negra.* Madrid: Sirius.

Gertel, Zunilda. 1988. "*Rayuela*, la figura y su lectura." *Hispanic Review* 56.3 (Summer): 287–305.

Giardinelli, Mempo. 1984. *Luna caliente.* Buenos Aires: Bruguera.

———. 1985. *Qué sólos se quedan los muertos.* Mexico D.F.: Diana Literaria.

———. 1990. Variaciones sobre la posmodernidad *Puro cuento* 23. 30–33.

———. 1991. *Santo oficio de la memoria.* Bogotá: Norma.

———. 1993. *El castigo de Dios.* Buenos Aires: Norma.

———. 1995. *Imposible equilibrio.* Barcelona: Planeta.

———. 1998. *El país de las maravillas.* Buenos Aires: Planeta.

Gilman, Claudia. 1993. "Los siete locos: novela sospechosa de Roberto Arlt." *Cuadernos Hispanoamericanos* Supp. 11 :77–94.

Giordano, Jaime. 1985. "Roberto Arlt: Escritura expresionista." *Revista de Estudios Hispánicos* 19.1 (Jan.): 55–70.

Gleick, James. 1987. *Chaos: Making a new science.* New York: Viking.

Gnutzman, Rita. 1984. *Roberto Arlt o el arte del calidoscopio.* Bilbao: Univ. País Vasco del Press.

———. 1995. Introducción a *Juguete rabioso.* Madrid: Cátedra.

Goloboff, Gerardo. 1988. *Genio y figura de Roberto Arlt.* Buenos Aires: Univ. of Buenos Aires Press.

Gómez, Michael A. 1999. "Borges' fantastic stories? Borges' relation with theories of physics." *Tropos* 25:15–20.

González Echevarría, Roberto. 1990. *Myth and archive: A theory of Latin American narrative.* Cambridge: Cambridge Univ. Press.

Gorodischer, Angélica. 1967. *Opus dos.* Buenos Aires: Minotauro.

———. 2000. "A la luz de la casta luna electrónica." In *Historias futuras: Antología de la ciencia ficción argentina.* Ed. Adriana Fernández and Edgardo Pígoli Buenos Aires: Emecé. 127–46.

———. 2001a. *Kalpa Imperial.* Buenos Aires: Emecé.

———. 2001b. "Los embriones del violeta." In *Los universos vislumbrados: Antología de Ciencia Ficción Argentina*, 2nd ed. Buenos Aires: Andrómeda, 151–96.

Gostautas, Stasys. 1977. *Buenos Aires y Arlt: (Dostoievsky, Martínez Estrada y Escalabrini Ortiz).* Madrid: Insula.

Grau, Cristina. 1996. "Tlön o la utopía cósmica." *Variaciones Borges* 2:116–24.

Gribbin, John. 1984. *In search of Schrödinger's cat: quantum physics and reality.* New York: Bantam.

———. 1995. *Schrödinger's kittens and the search for reality.* Boston: Little, Brown and Company.

Gross, Paul R., and Norman Levitt. 1994. *Higher superstition: The academic left and its quarrels with science.* Baltimore: Johns Hopkins Univ. Press.

Gutting, Gary. 1994. "Michel Foucault: A user's manual." *The Cambridge companion to Foucault.* ed. Gary Gutting Cambridge: Cambridge Univ. Press, 1–27.

Guzzo, María Cristina. 1997. *El híbrido argentino, el testimonio de Lucio v. Mansilla y el modelo americano.* Diss., Arizona State University.

Halpern, Paul. 1991. "Borges, Nietzsche and Poincaré recurrence" *Ometeca* 2.2:71–77.

Haraway, Donna J. 1982. "The high cost of information in post–world war II evolutionary biology: Ergonomics, semiotics, and the sociobiology of communication systems." *The Philosophical Forum* 13.2-3 (Winter–Spring 1981–1982): 244–74.

———. 1991. *Simians, cyborgs, and women.* New York: Routledge.

Hayes, Aden. 1981. *Roberto Arlt: La estrategia de su ficción.* London: Tamesis.

Hayles, N. Katherine. 1984. *The cosmic web: Scientific field models and literary strategies in the twentieth century.* Ithaca: Cornell Univ. Press.

———. 1990. *Chaos bound: Orderly disorder in contemporary literature and science.* Ithaca: Cornell Univ. Press.

———. 1999. *How we became posthuman: Virtual bodies in cybernetics, literature, and informatics.* Chicago: Univ. of Chicago Press.

Heisenberg, Werner. 1952. *Philosophic problems of nuclear science.* New York: Pantheon.

———. 1958. *Physics and philosophy: The revolution in modern science.* New York: Harper and Brothers.

Herbert, Christopher. 1991. *Culture and anomie: Ethnographic imagination in the nineteenth century.* Chicago: Univ. of Chicago Press.

Hernández, Ana María. 1978. Vampires and vampiresses: A reading of *62 in the final island. The Fiction of Julio Cortázar.* Ed. Jaime Alazraki and Ivar Ivask, Norman: Univ. of Oklahoma Press, 109–14.

Hernández, Domingo Luis. 1982. "Los modelos culturales en *El juguete rabioso.*" *Revista de filología de la Universidad de la Laguna* 1:59–74.

Hernández, Juan Antonio. 2000. "Biografía del infinito: La noción de transfinitud en Georg Cantor y su presencia en la prosa de Jorge Luis Borges." *Signos literarios y lingüísticos* 2.2 (July): 131–39.

Hoeg, Jerry. 2000. *Science, technology, and Latin American narrative in the twentieth century and beyond.* Bethlehem, PA: Lehigh Univ. Press.

Höfner, Eckhard. 1999. Les Allusions aux modèles scientifiques et leurs fonctions dans l'oeuvre de J. L. Borges. In *El siglo de Borges Vol. I: Retrospectiva-Presente-Futuro.* Ed. Alfonso de Toro and Fernando de Toro. Vervuert: Iberoamericana, 73–102.

Hofstadter, Douglas. 1979. *Escher, Gödel, Bach: An eternal golden braid.* New York: Basic Books.

Holzapfel, Tamara. 1973. "El «Informe sobre ciegos» o el optimismo de la voluntad." In *Homenaje a Ernesto Sábato: Variaciones interpretativas en torno a su obra.* Ed. Helmy F. Giacoman. Madrid: Anaya.

Honigmann, John J. 1976. *The development of anthropological ideas.* Homewood, IL: Dorsey Press.

Hutcheon, Linda. 1988. *A poetics of postmodernism: History, theory, fiction.* London: Routledge.

Irwin, John T. 1994. *The mystery to a solution: Poe, Borges, and the analytic detective story.* Baltimore: Johns Hopkins Univ. Press.

Jameson, Fredric. 1972. *Marxism and form: Twentieth-century dialectical theories of literature.* Princeton, NJ: Princeton Univ. Press.

Jarkowski, Aníbal. 1993. "La colección Arlt: Modelos para cada temporada." *Cuadernos Hispanoamericanos* Supp. 11:37–46.

Jitrik, Noé. 1968. *Los argentinos V: El 80 y su mundo.* Buenos Aires: Editorial Jorge Álvarez.

Katra, William. 1996. *The Argentine generation of 1837: Echeverría, Alberdi, Sarmiento, Mitre.* Madison: Fairleigh Dickinson Univ. Press.

Kellert, Stephen H. 1996. "Science and literature and philosophy: The case of chaos theory and deconstruction." *Configurations* 4.2 (Spring): 215–32.

Kirkpatrick, Gwen, and Francine Masiello. 1994. "Introduction: Sarmiento between history and fiction." In *Sarmiento: author of a nation* Ed. Tulio Halperín, Iván Jaksic, Gwen Kirkpatrick, and Francine Masiello. Berkeley: Univ. of California Press, 1–16.

Knight, David. 1986. *The age of science.* Oxford: Basil Blackwell.

Kodama, María. 1999. "Prólogo" in *Borges y la ciencia*. Buenos Aires: Buenos Aires Univ. Press.

Krakusin, Margarita. 1997. "Ciencia y arte: El quantum y los agujeros cortacianos en 'La isla a mediodía'." *Hispanic Journal* 18.2 (Fall): 317–26.

Krow-Lucal, Martha G. 1983. "Balzac, Galdós and phrenology." *Anales Galdosianos* 18:7–14.

Kuhn, Thomas. 1970. *The structure of scientific revolutions*. 2nd ed. Chicago: Univ. of Chicago Press.

Lander, María Fernanda. 2003. *Modelando corazones: Sentimentalismo y urbanidad en la novela hispanoamericana del siglo XIX*. Rosario, Argentina: Beatriz Viterbo.

Lanuza, Lucio. 1965. *Genio y figura de Lucio V. Mansilla*. Buenos Aires: Buenos Aires Univ. Press.

Larra, Raúl. 1956. *Roberto Arlt: El torturado*. Buenos Aires: Alpe.

Leland, Christopher. 1986. *The last happy men: The generation of 1922, Fiction, and the Argentine reality*. Syracuse, NY: Syracuse Univ. Press.

Lezama Lima, José. 1972. "Cortázar y el comienzo de la otra novela." In *Homenaje a Julio Cortázar: Variaciones interpretativas en torno a su obra*. Ed. Helmy Giacoman. New York: Las Américas, 13–30.

Lindstrom, Naomi. 1992. "Argentina." In *Handbook of Latin American literature*. 2nd ed. Ed. David William Foster. New York: Garland, 1–64.

Lizama, A. Patricio. 1995. "Comentario a la ponencia del Profesor Michael Capobianco, 'Julio Cortázar and the various interpretations of quantum theory.'" *Taller de Letras* 23:177–91.

Lojo, María. 1992. A quinientos años, desde el país del monte. *Alba de América* 10.18–19: 77–92.

———. 1996. "El indio como 'prójimo,' la mujer como el 'otro' en *Una excursión a los indios ranqueles de Lucio V. Mansilla*." *Alba de America*, July 14 (26–27): 131–37.

Losada y Rocheblave, Sabino de. 1849. *Lecciones de frenología, esplicadas en el Liceo Artístico y Literario de La Habana*. Habana: Diario de la Marina.

Lowie, Robert. 1937. *The history of ethnological theory*. New York: Holt, Rinehart and Winston.

Luchting, Wolfgang. 1972. "Todos los juegos el juego." In *Homenaje a Julio Cortázar: Variaciones interpretativas en torno a su obra*. Ed. Helmy Giacoman, New York: Las Américas, 351–64.

Ludmer, Josefina. 1999. "Enciclopedias y colecciones: Otra lectura de Tlön, Uqbar y Orbis Tertius." *Ciberletras* 1 (Aug.) (no pagination)

Lukacs, Georg. 1978. *The historical novel*. Atlantic Highlands, NJ: Humanities Press.

Lyon, Ted. 1994a. "Put-On by Borges: The interview as play" *Confluencia* 10.1 (Fall): 57–66.

———. 1994b. "Jorge Luis Borges and the interview as literary genre." *Latin American Literary Review* 22.44 (July–Dec.): 74–89.

Lyotard, François. 1984. *The postmodern condition: A report on knowledge.* Trans. Geoff Bennington and Brian Massumi. Minneapolis: Univ. of Minnesota Press.

MacAdam, Alfred J. 1989. "*Rayuela*: La cuestión del lector." *Explicación de textos literarios* 17.1–2 (1988–1989): 216–29.

Maldavsky, David. 1968. *Las crisis en la narrativa de Roberto Arlt: Algunas contribuciones de las ciencias humanas a la comprensión de la literatura.* Buenos Aires: Editorial Escuela.

Mansilla, Lucio. 1936a. *Entre nos.* Vol 1. Buenos Aires: WM Jackson.

———. 1936b. *Entre nos.* Vol 2. Buenos Aires: WM Jackson.

———. 1978. *Mis memorias.* Buenos Aires: El Ateneo.

———. 1993. *Una excursión a los indios ranqueles.* Madrid: Ediciones de Cultura Hispánica.

———. 1997. *An Expedition to the Ranquel Indians.* Trans. Mark McCaffrey. Austin: University Texas Press.

Mármol, José. 1991. *Amalia.* 6th ed. México DF: Porrúa.

Martínez Cuitino, Luis and Norma Carricaburo. 1979. "Una picaresca porteña: *El juguete rabioso*, de Roberto Arlt." *La picaresca: Orígenes, textos y estructuras.* Ed. Manuel Criado de Val. Madrid: Fundación Univ. Española, 1137–43.

Marún, Gioconda. 1998. "Darwin y la literatura argentina." *La Torre* 3.9 (July–Sept.): 551–77.

Matamoro, Blas. 1993a. "El Astrólogo y la muerte." *Cuadernos Hispanoamericanos* Supp. 11:95–102.

———. 1993b. "Prólogo." *Una excursión a los indio ranqueles.* Madrid: Ediciones de Cultura Hispánica.

Mathieu-Higginbotham, Corina. 1987. "El concepto de 'civilización y barbarie' en *Una excursión a los indios ranqueles.*" *Hispanofila* 30.2:81–87.

McCracken, Ellen. 1991. "Metaplagiarism and the Critic's Role as Detective: Ricardo Piglia's Reinvention of Roberto Arlt" *PMLA* 106:5 (Oct.): 1071–82

McHoul, Alec, and Wendy Grace. 1993. *A Foucault Primer: Discourse, Power and the Subject.* New York: New York Univ. Press.

Merrell, Floyd. 1991. *Unthinking thinking: Jorge Luis Borges, mathematics, and the new physics.* West Lafayette, IN: Purdue Univ. Press.

Mesonero Romanos, Ramón de. 1993. "El Romanticismo y los románticos." In *Escenas y tipos matritenses.* Ed. Enrique Rubio Cremades. Madrid: Cátedra, 294–314.

Molina-Gavilán, Yolanda. 1999. "Alternate realities from Argentina: Angélica Gorodischer's 'Los embriones de la violeta.'" *Science Fiction Studies* 79.26:401–11.

———. 2002. *Ciencia ficción en español: Una mitología ante el cambio.* Lewiston, NY: Edwin Mellen.

Molloy, Sylvia. 1994. *Signs of Borges.* Trans. Oscar Montero. Durham: Duke Univ. Press.

Montero, María L. 1991. "Mansilla y sus bibliotecas" *Boletín Argentino de Artes y Letras* 66:103–28.

Montserrat, Marcelo. 1986. "La presencia evolucionista en el positivismo argentino." *Quipu: Revista Latinoamericana de Historia de las Ciencias y la Tecnología* 3 (Jan.–April): 91–102.

Mosca, Stefania. 1983. "Borges: Antiutopía." *Zona Franca* 6.34 (Mar.–Apr.): 29–33.

Mosher, Mark. 1994. "Atemporal Labyrinths in Time: J. L. Borges and the New Physicists." *Symposium* 48.1 (Spring): 51–61.

———. 1996a. "Los despacios y los destiempos en los wormholes de Cortázar." *Hispanófila* 2.116:69–82.

———. 1996b. "The Fusion of Opposites: Borges and Particle Physics." *Ometeca* 3–4:393–401.

Nouzeilles, Gabriela. 1994. *El romance patológico: Naturalismo, medicina y nacionalismo en Argentina (1880–1910)*. Diss., Univ. of Michigan.

———. 1996. "Pathological romances and national dystopias in Argentine naturalism." *Latin American Literary Review* 24.47 (Jan.–June): 23–39.

———. 1997. "Ficciones paranoicas de fin de siglo: naturalismo argentino y policía médica." *MLN* 112.2:232–52.

———. 2000. *Ficciones somáticas: Naturalismo, nacionalismo y políticas médicas del cuerpo (Argentina 1880–1910)*. Rosario, Argentina: Beatriz Viterbo.

Nuñez, Ángel. 1968. *La obra narrativa de Roberto Arlt*. Buenos Aires: Editorial Nova.

Operé, Fernando. 1987. *Civilización y barbarie en la literatura argentina del siglo XIX: El tirano Rosas*. Madrid: Conorg.

Ortiz, Eduardo. 1984. "La polémica del Darwinismo y la inserción de la ciencia en Argentina." *Actas II Congreso de la sociedad española de historia de las ciencias*, 89–108.

———. 1998. "The transmission of science from Europe to Argentina and its impact on literature: from Lugones to Borges." In *Borges and Europe Revisited*. Ed. Evelyn Fishburn. London: London Univ. Press, 108–23.

Osses, José Emilio. 1988. "La novela morelliana en *Rayuela* de Julio Cortázar." *Revista chilena de literatura* 31 (Apr.): 9–32.

Pellón, Gustavo. 1995. "Ideology and structure in Giardinelli's *Santo oficio de la memoria*." *Studies in twentieth-century literature* 19.1:81–99.

———. 1996. "The Spanish American novel: Recent developments, 1975–1990." In *Cambridge history of Latin American literature*. Ed. Roberto González Echevarría and Enrique Pupo Walker. New York: Cambridge Univ. Press.

Pennington, Eric. 1998. "Vestiges of empire: Toward a contrapuntal reading of Borges." *CLA Journal* 42.1 (Sept.): 103–117

Picon Garfield, Evelyn. 1975. *¿Es Julio Cortázar un surrealista?* Madrid: Gredos.

Piglia, Ricardo. 1992. *La ciudad ausente*. Buenos Aires: Seix Barral.

———. 2000. *The Absent City*. Trans. Sergio Waisman. Durham: Duke Univ. Press.

———. 2001. *Respiración artificial*. Barcelona: Editorial Anagrama. (Original published 1980).

Planells, Antonio. 1979. *Cortázar: Metafísica y erotismo*. Madrid: José Porrúa Turanzas.
Poe, Edgar Allan. 1836. *Southern Lit. Messenger* 2 (March) 286. q. in Cooter.
Popolizio, Enrique. 1985. *Vida de Lucio V. Mansilla*. Buenos Aires: Editorial Pomaire.
Porush, David. 1985. *The soft machine*. New York: Methuen.
Pratt, Mary Louise. 1986. "Fieldwork in common places." In *Writing culture: The poetics and politics of ethnography*. Ed. James Clifford and George Marcus. Berkeley: Univ. of California Press, 27–50.
———. 1992a. "Humboldt and the reinvention of America." In *Amerindian images and the legacy of Columbus*. Ed. René Jara y Nicholas Spadaccini. Minneapolis: Univ. of Minnesota Press.
———. 1992b. *Imperial eyes: Travel writing and transculturation*. London: Routledge.
Prigogine, Ilya, and Isabelle Stengers. 1984. *Order out of chaos: Man's new dialogue with nature*. New York: Bantam.
———. 1993. *Tan sólo una ilusión*. Barcelona: Tusquets Editores.
Ramos, Julio. 1986. "Entre otros: *Una excursión a los indios ranqueles* de Lucio Mansilla." *Filología* 21.1:143–71.
Ramos-Izquierdo, Eduardo. 1986. "La escritura lúdica en *Rayuela*." *Coloquio Internacional: Lo lúdico y lo fantástico en la obra de Cortázar*. Madrid: Editorial Fundamentos, 257–61.
Ramos Mejía, José. 1936. *Las neurosis de los hombres célebres en la historia argentina*. Ed. José Ingenieros. Buenos Aires: Ediciones Anaconda. 1st edition, 1878–1882.
Redd, Margaret. 1985. "'Report on the blind': Sábato's journey into the fantastic." In *The scope of the fantastic—culture, biography, themes, children's literature*. Ed. Robert Collins and Howard Pearce. Westport, CT: Greenwood Press.
Rivadavia, Manuel. 1823. *La abeja argentina*, no. 2, no. 13 (May 15, 1822).
Rivero-Potter, Alicia. 1997. "Complementariedad e incertidumbre en 'El jardín de senderos que se bifurcan' de Borges." *La Torre* 2.6 (Oct–Dec.): 459–74.
Rock, David. 1987. *Argentina 1516–1987: From Spanish colonization to Alfonsín*. Berkeley: Univ. of California Press.
Rodríguez, Fermín. 1996. "*Una excursión a los indios ranqueles*. Una novela de espionaje." *Filología* 29.1–2:181–90.
Rodríguez Persico, Adriana. 1993. "Arlt: Sacar las palabras de todos los ángulos." *Cuadernos Hispanoamericanos* Supp. 11:5–14.
Roffé, Reina. 1999. Personal conversation, April 14, 1999.
Rojo, Alberto G. 1999. "El jardín de los mundos que ramifican: Borges y la mecánica cuántica." In *Borges en 10 miradas*. Ed. Beatriz Borovich. Buenos Aires: Fundación El Libro, 185–98.
Rolón, Alicia. 1996. "Relectura y reescritura de la historia: La novelística de Mempo Giardinelli entre 1980 y 1991." Diss., Univ. of Colorado, Boulder.
Rufinelli, Jorge. 1981. "Arlt: Complicidad y traición de clase." *Escritura* 6.12 (July–Dec.):375–405.

Sabato, Ernesto. 1968. *Sobre héroes y tumbas*. Barcelona: Planeta.
———. 1975. *Abaddón el exterminador*. Buenos Aires: Alianza.
———. 2002a. *Antes del fin*. Barcelona: Seix Barral.
———. 2002b. *Hombres y engranajes* Madrid: Alianza Libros de Bolsillo.
Safir, Margery A. 1978. "An erotics of liberation: Notes on transgressive behavior in *Hopscotch* and *Libro de Manuel*." In *The Final Island: The Fiction of Julio Cortázar*. Ed. Jaime Alazraki and Ivar Ivask. Norman: Univ. of Oklahoma Press, 84–96.
Salazar, Béatrice. 1986. "Palabras que juegan, juegos con las palabras: Juego verbal y reflexión pragmática en la narrativa de Cortázar." *Coloquio Internacional: Lo lúdico y lo fantástico en la obra de Cortázar*. Madrid: Editorial Fundamentos, 71–76.
Salessi, Jorge. 1995. *Médicos maleantes y maricas: higiene, criminología y homosexualidad en la construcción de la nación argentina (Buenos Aires, 1871–1914)*. Rosario: Beatriz Viterbo.
Salomon, Noel. 1984. *Realidad, ideología y literatura en el Facundo de D. F. Sarmiento*. Amsterdam: Rodopi.
Sarlo, Beatriz. 1992. *La imaginación técnica: Sueños modernos de la cultura argentina*. Buenos Aires: Ediciones Nueva Visión.
———. 1995. *Borges, un escritor en las orillas*. Buenos Aires: Ariel.
Sarmiento, Domingo. 1883. "El diarismo." In *Artículos críticos i literarios* Tomo I. Buenos Aires: Government of Argentina.
———. 1991. *Facundo: Civilización y barbarie, vida de Juan Facundo Quiroga*. México D.F.:Editorial Porrúa, S.A. 1st ed., 1845.
———. 2003. *Facundo: Civilization and Barbarism*. Trans. Kathleen Ross. Berkeley: Univ. of California Press.
Scari, Robert M. 1971. "La novela moderna en Roberto Arlt." *Cuadernos hispanoamericanos* 255:581–88.
———. 1983. "Roberto Arlt: El periodista, el inventor, el polemista." *Revista chilena de Literatura* 22 (Nov.): 105–16.
Schade, George. 1984. "Los viajeros argentinos del ochenta." *Texto crítico* 10.28:82–103.
Schmidt-Emans, Monika. 2002. "Gödel, Escher, Borges on paradoxes and self-reflection in literature and art." In *Littérature, modernité, reflexivité: conférences du Séminaire de Littérature comparée dé l'Université de la Sorbonne Nouvelle*. Ed. Jean Bessière Paris: Champion.
Schreiber, Gabriel, and Roberto Umansky. 2001. "Bifurcations, chaos, and fractal objects in Borges' 'Garden of forking paths' and other writings." *Variaciones Borges* 11:61–79.
Selnes, Gisle. 2002. "Borges, Nietzsche, Cantor: Narratives of Influence." *Ciberletras* 6 (Jan.) http://www.lehman.cuny.edu/ciberletras/.
Serres, Michel. 1975. *Feux et signaux de brume, Zola*. Paris: Grasset.
———. 1982. *Hermes: Literature, science, philosophy*. Ed. Josué V. Harari and David F. Bell. Baltimore: Johns Hopkins Univ. Press.
Shaw, Donald L. 1976. *Borges, Ficciones*. London: Tamesis.

———. 1980. "Concerning the structure of *Facundo.*" *Ibero-Amerikanisches Archiv* 6.3:239–50.

———. 1981. *Nueva narrativa hispanoamericana.* Madrid: Cátedra.

Shua, Ana María. 2000 . "Octavio, el invasor." In *Historias futuras: Antología de la ciencia ficción argentina.* Ed. Adriana Fernández and Edgardo Pígoli. Buenos Aires: Emecé, 147–58.

Shumway, David. 1989. *Michel Foucault.* Charlottesville: Univ. of Virginia Press.

Shuttleworth, Sally. 1996. *Charlotte Brontë and Victorian psychology.* Cambridge: Cambridge Univ. Press.

Silva Gruesz, Kirsten. 1996. "Facing the nation: The organic life of "La cautiva."" *Revista de Estudios Hispánicos* 30.1:3–22.

Sommer, Doris. 1991. *Foundational fictions: The national romances of Latin America.* Berkeley: Univ. California Press.

Sorensen Goodrich, Diana. 1996. *Facundo and the construction of Argentine culture.* Austin: Univ. of Texas Press.

Sosnowski, Saul. 1973. *Julio Cortázar: Una búsqueda mítica.* Buenos Aires: Ediciones Noe.

———. 1979. "'Tlön, Uqbar, Orbis Tertius': Histórica y desplazamientos." In *The contemporary Latin American short story.* Ed. Minc, Rose. New York: Senda Nueva.

Stark, John. 1972. "Borges' 'Tlön, Uqbar, Orbis Tertius' and Nabokov's *Pale fire*: Literature of exhaustion." *Texas Studies in Literature and Language* 14:139–45.

Stepan, Nancy Leys. 1991. *The hour of eugenics: Race, gender, and nation in Latin America.* Ithaca: Cornell Univ. Press.

Stern, Mirta. 1985. "*Una excursión a los indios ranqueles*: Espacio textual y ficción topográfica." *Filología* 20.1:117–38.

Stocking, George. 1992. *The ethnographer's magic.* Madison: Univ. of Wisconsin Press.

Stonum, Gary Lee. 1989. "Cybernetic explanation as a theory of reading." *New Literary History* 20.2 (Winter): 397–410.

Toeffler, Alvin. 1984. Foreword in *Order out of chaos: Man's new dialogue with nature.* Ilya Prigogine and Isabelle Stengers. New York: Bantam.

Trigo, Benigno. 2000. *Subjects of crisis: Race and gender as disease in Latin America.* Hanover: Wesleyan Univ. Press.

Villalobos V, Carlos Manuel. 1994. "Las máscaras del escritor: Sabato hecho personaje." *Kañina* 18.2 (July): 63–70.

Weissert, Thomas P. 1991. "Representation and bifurcation: Borges's garden of chaos dynamics." In *Chaos and order: Complex dynamics in literature and science.* Ed. N. Katherine Hayles. Chicago: Univ. of Chicago Press: 223–43.

Wiener, Norbert. 1950. *The human use of human beings: Cybernetics and society.* Boston: Houghton Mifflin.

———. 1961. *Cybernetics or control and communication in the animal and the machine.* 2nd. ed. New York: MIT Press and John Wiley and Sons.

Young, Richard A. 1993. Octaedro *en cuatro tiempos: Texto y tiempo en un libro de Cortázar.* Ottawa: Dovehouse Editions.

Yurkievich, Saúl. 1978. "Eros ludens: Games, love and humor in hopscotch." In *The final island: The fiction of Julio Cortázar*. Ed. Jaime Alazraki and Ivar Ivask. Norman: Univ. of Oklahoma Press: 97–108.

Zanelli, Jorge. 1995. "Borges, la mecánica cuántica y otras rarezas . . ." *Taller de Letras* 23 (Nov.): 193–202.

Zola, Emile. 1927a. *Oeuvres critiques*, Vol. 45. *Documents Littéraires*. Paris: François Bernouard.

———. 1927b. *Oeuvres completes*. *Le Roman Expérimental*. Vol. 45. Paris: François Bernouard.

Zubieta, Ana María. 1987. *El discurso narrativo arltiano: Intertextualidad, grotesco y utopía*. Buenos Aires: Hachette.

Index

Abeja Argentina, La, 13, 31, 37, 41, 162
Adams, John Quincy, 36
Alazraki, Jaime, 234 n. 3
Alberdi, Juan, 229 n. 7
Albright, Daniel, 224, 239 n. 2
Alonso, Carlos, 15, 30, 56, 61, 226 nn. 2 and 5 (intro.), 228–29 n. 5, 229 nn. 6 and 11
Amícola, José, 232 n. 1
Amorós, Andrés, 175, 237 nn. 15 and 17, 238 n. 23
anthropology, 24, 59–64, 77, 79, 83, 101, 114–15, 149, 217–20, 229 n. 13. *See also* ethnography
anti-Semitism, 148
Arce, Claudia Sánchez, 238 n. 3
Area, Lelia, 228 n. 4, 229 n. 8
Argentina: absence of scientific tradition in, 13–14, 22; class in, 42; dictatorship in, 189; financial crisis in, 13; and independence/nationhood, 13, 31, 41; indigenous peoples of, 55–56, 62–63, 79–81, 83; and marginality, 22
Arguedas, Alcides, 231 n. 25; *Pueblo enfermo*, 83
Argyros, Alexander, 213, 215
Aristotle, 93, 128
Arlt, Roberto, 25, 26, 97–121, 123–24, 134, 140, 141, 160, 196, 197, 215, 222, 232 nn. 1, 2, 3, 7, 8, 11, 12, and 13, 232 nn. 14 and 17; ambivalence toward science of, 99, 102, 104, 108, 109, 115, 116, 118, 120, 123–24, 126, 131, 142, 146, 148, 158, 187–88, 220–21, 232 n. 3; deconstruction of *civilación/barbarie* dichotomy by, 111, 124, 220; influence of, 116–17,

123. Works: *El juguete rabioso*, 25, 101, 104–15, 142, 160, 220, 232 nn. 2, 8, and 12; *Los lanzallamas*, 25, 101, 102–4, 115, 117, 123–24, 148, 220; *Los siete locos*, 25, 101, 102, 104, 123–24, 148, 220
artificial intelligence, 152
Asad, Talal, 218
Assad, Maria, 233 n. 1
Asturias, Miguel Ángel, 217
Augustine, Saint, 137
Avelar, Idelber, 190

Balderston, Daniel, 234 n. 6
Barrenechea, Ana María, 238 n. 28
Beck, Guido, 121
Bell, Andrea, 195, 196
Bell-Villada, Gene, 234 n. 3
Benjamin, Walter, 182
Berg, William J., 231 n. 5
Berkeley, George, 157, 235 n. 21
Bernard, Claude, 66
Bessières, Georges Louis, 37
Bible, 137
Bierce, Ambrose: "The Occurrence at Owl Creek Bridge," 168
biology, 66, 73, 80, 177–80
Blanco Arnejo, María Dolores, 236 n. 1
Bretón de los Herreros, Manuel: *Frenología y magnetismo*, 37
Boas, Franz, 59
Boon, James, 218
Booth, Wayne C., 95
Borges, Jorge Luis, 25–26, 125–59, 197–98, 210, 217, 218, 233 nn. 1 and 2, 234 nn. 3–13, 234–35 n. 15, 235–36 n. 22, 236 n. 23; antiscientific stance of, 126–27, 131, 132, 142, 143, 146, 148–49, 151–52,

254

158–59, 188, 190–92, 196, 197, 216, 220–22; destabilization of textual authority by, 125–26, 134, 136, 140; and infinity, 133–36; and labyrinths, 139, 149, 153–55, 157; and mathematics, 25, 127–32, 136–38, 142, 143, 147, 149, 152, 158, 234 nn. 9 and 11, 235 n. 16, 235–36 n. 22; and Nietzsche, 25, 132–43, 145, 150, 159, 171, 186, 221, 234 n. 10. Works: "Avatares de la tortuga," 128, 131–32; "La biblioteca de Babel," 132, 152–53; "Continuidad de los parques," 186; *Discusión*, 126, 128; "La doctrina de los ciclos," 26, 132–43, 145, 148, 188; *El elogio de la sombra*, 143, 149; "El etnógrafo," 143, 146, 148–51; "Examen de la obra de Herbert Quain," 132; *Ficciones*, 143, 157; "Funes el memorioso," 153; *Historia de la eternidad*, 126, 132; *El Hogar*, 128; "El idioma analítico de John Wilkins," 132, 143–46, 149–51, 153; *El informe de Brodie*, 234–35 n. 15; "El jardín de senderos que se bifurcan," 126, 133, 152, 153–58, 163, 235 n. 17, 235 n. 19, 239 n. 11; "El libro de arena," 153; "La muerte y la brújula," 157; *Otras inquisiciones*, 143, 145; "La perpetua carrera de Aquiles y la tortuga," 25–26, 128–32; "Pierre Menard," 230 n. 22; "Las ruinas circulares," 133; "El tiempo," 157; "Tlön, Uqbar, Orbis Tertius," 143, 146–48, 192, 237 n. 19
Borré, Omar, 232 n. 1
Bradley, James, 157
Brandão Tiago de Oliveira, José Carlos, 235 n. 17
Bravo de Rueda, José, 232 n. 1
Broca, Paul, 230 n. 17
Broch, Hermann: *The Death of Virgil*, 191
Brontë, Charlotte, 36, 192
Buchanan, Rhonda, 238 n. 2
Buenos Aires, 13, 41, 98, 105, 128, 226 n. 1 (intro.)

Burroughs, William: *The Soft Machine*, 182

Calinescu, Matei, 202, 212–14, 223–25, 238 n. 9
Cambaceres, Eugenio, 24, 25, 84, 104; *En la sangre*, 89, 91–96; *Sin rumbo*, 95
Canepa, Mario A., 232 n. 8
Cantor, Georg, 133, 136–37, 139, 145, 234 n. 11, 235–36 n. 22
Capanna, Pablo, 195
Capello, Jean, 168, 237 n. 8
capitalism, 102, 121, 180, 238 n. 26
Capobianco, Michael, 153, 158, 234 n. 9, 235 n. 17, 237 n. 7
Carpentier, Alejo, 101, 218; *El reino de este mundo*, 33
Carroll, Lewis: *Jabberwocky*, 175
Castro-Klarén, Sandra, 164, 236 n. 6, 237 nn. 11 and 16
Catalá, Rafael, 152
Cereijido, Marcelino, 13–14, 235 n. 17
Cervantes, Miguel de: *Don Quixote*, 210, 230 n. 22
chaos theory, 26–27, 125, 126, 152, 154, 155, 197–201, 203–15, 219, 222, 225, 239 nn. 5, 10, and 12
Charcot, Jean-Martin, 66
Chavarri, Raúl, 233 n. 15
chemistry, 17, 18, 25, 98, 99, 101, 103–4, 115, 118, 147, 188, 200, 207, 208, 219
Clarín, El, 13
Clark, John R., 234 n. 14
Clifford, James, 59–60, 218
Colás, Santiago, 213–14, 238 n. 26, 239 nn. 16 and 1
Colbert, Charles, 226 n. 4 (chap. 1)
colonial writing, 217
Combe, George, 40–41, 51, 71, 81, 82, 228 n. 22; *On the Constitution of Man*, 35–36, 40–41, 45–46, 227 nn. 12 and 15
communism, 148
Comte, Auguste, 66, 81–82, 222, 231 n. 26
Cooter, Roger, 38, 39–40, 42, 66, 226

n. 4 (chap. 1), 227 nn. 8, 9, and 10, 230 n. 18
Copenhagen interpretation, 164–65, 167–68, 176, 237 n. 7
Corry, Leo, 128, 234 nn. 5, 7, and 11
Cortázar, Julio, 17, 26, 98, 159, 160–88, 195, 196, 197, 215, 222, 224, 236 nn. 1, 2, 4, 5, and 6, 237 nn. 7, 11, and 13–19, 238 nn. 22, 26, 29, 30, and 31, 239 n. 1; aestheticization of science by, 165–68, 173–74, 237 n. 10; attack on Cartesian rationality by, 160, 170–72, 175–76, 179, 182–84, 186–88, 221, 235 n. 15, 238 n. 31; attitude toward language of, 175, 237 n. 17; and cybernetics, 176–87, 238 nn. 30 and 31; imagery of, 167, 169–70, 174, 179–81, 186. Works: "Ahí pero dónde, como," 168–70; *Los autonautas de la cosmopista*, 236 n. 3; "Axolotl," 237 n. 7; "Del sentimiento de no estar del todo," 176–78; *Historia de Cronopios y de Famas*, 236 n. 3; "La isla al mediodía," 168, 170; "Julios en acción," 160–62, 167; "La noche boca arriba," 237 n. 7; *Octaedro*, 168, 237 n. 13; "Otra máquina célibe," 185, 186; *Rayuela*, 26, 160, 166, 170–87, 202, 217–18, 236 n. 1, 236 n. 4, 238 nn. 22, 26, 29, and 30; *62: Modelo para amour*, 160, 165–67, 170, 174, 237 nn. 7 and 10; *Teoría del túnel*, 163–64, 170, 173, 236 nn. 4, 5, and 6; *Último round*, 236 n. 3; "Viajes," 236 n. 3; *La vuelta al día en ochenta mundos*, 160, 176, 185, 236 n. 3
Crapanzano, Vincent, 218
Crisafio, Raul, 228 n. 4, 229 n. 11
Crítica, 13, 98, 99
cubism, 164
Cubí y Soler, Mariano, 36–37, 226 n. 5 (chap. 1)
Cuddon, J. A., 231 n. 3
Cunha, Euclides da: *Os Sertões*, 58
Curie Institute, 116, 119, 120, 121
Curutchet, Juan Carlos, 170, 237 n. 16, 238 n. 23

cybernetics, 176–87, 237 n. 20, 238 nn. 30 and 31

Dapia, Silvia, 232 n. 2
Darwin, Charles, 19, 25, 73, 87, 100, 105, 109–11, 113–15, 118, 124, 142, 220, 230 n. 23, 233 n. 17; *The Descent of Man*, 232 n. 10; *On the Origin of Species*, 110
Darwinism, 87, 88, 91, 92, 100, 110–14, 160, 232 nn. 5 and 11, 233 n. 19
Davies, John, 36, 226 n. 3 (intro.), 227 nn. 8, 9, and 12
Davis, John, 230 n. 19
deconstruction, 213, 215
DeCosta, René, 133
Derrida, Jacques, 213
Descartes, René, 17, 170–73, 175–76, 179, 183, 184, 187, 188, 235 n. 21, 237 n. 15
Díaz, Gwendolyn, 197–98
Donovan, Cornelius, 67–69
Dostoyevsky, Fyodor, 210
Dubner, Carlos, 123
Duchamp, Marcel, 185

Echeverría, Esteban, 229 n. 7; "La cautiva," 38, 41, 44
Eddington, Arthur, 122, 175
Einstein, Albert, 13, 98, 99, 109, 121, 128, 154, 155–58, 162–64, 176, 191, 201, 234 n. 6
Eliot, T. S., 224
Emerson, Ralph Waldo, 36
empire, Spanish, 31, 55
Enlightenment, 19, 39
Escher, M. C., 235 n. 16
ethnography, 56, 58, 59–63, 149, 219, 228–29 n. 5, 229–30 n. 15
ethnology, 59–60, 63, 64, 73, 229–30 n. 15
eugenics, 84, 85, 91–94, 231 n. 25
Evans-Pritchard, Edward, 229 n. 13
Everett, Hugh, 126, 154–55, 235 n. 18, 236 n. 2, 239 n. 11
evolution, 19, 89, 100, 113, 177
existentialism, 164

Facundo Quiroga, Juan, 28, 31–35, 41–44, 47, 50, 133, 159, 220

INDEX

Federalistas, 30, 35, 42, 48–53, 56, 81, 228 n. 20, 230 n. 17
Fernández, Macedonio, 191
Ferré, Rosario, 236 n. 5
field theory, 152
Fishburn, Evelyn, 42, 86, 88, 89, 92, 95, 96
Flaubert, Gustave, 231 n. 3
Flint, Jack, 232 n. 1
Flourens, Pierre, 226 n. 6
Foster, David William, 56, 228–29 n. 5
Foucault, Michel, 14–23, 30, 35, 52, 57, 90, 107, 114, 126, 127, 143–44, 150, 163, 176, 179, 186, 222, 226 n. 1 (intro.), 234 n. 12
Fracchia, Eduardo, 204, 215, 239 n. 17
fractal geometry, 126, 153–55
Franzini, Paolo and Juliet Lee, 160–61
Frazer, James, 59
Freud, Sigmund, 14, 19, 24, 164
futurism, 164, 200

Gall, Franz Joseph, 37–41, 43–45, 85
Gallegos, Rómulo, 218
Gallo, Marta, 237 n. 18
Galton, Francis, 84, 85, 92
Gárate, Miriam, 230 n. 21
García Márquez, Gabriel, 101, 217, 218; *Cien años de soledad*, 33
Gardini, Carlos: *El libro de la tierra negra*, 203
Garfield, Evelyn Picón, 236 n. 5
Geertz, Clifford, 218, 229 n. 13
gender, 195, 196
Generation of 1837, 24, 38, 41–43, 50, 56–58, 80, 83, 227 n. 17, 229 n. 7
Generation of 1880, 89, 229 n. 12
Gertel, Zunilda, 238 n. 29
Giardinelli, Mempo, 159, 222; *Imposible equilibrio*, 26–27, 189, 198–201, 203, 204–16, 222, 239 nn. 10 and 11; *Luna caliente*, 198; "La máquina de dar besitos," 198; *El país de las maravillas*, 28–29, 203–4, 239 n. 17; *Santo oficio de la memoria*, 198
Gleick, James, 239 n. 12
Gnutzman, Rita, 101–2, 232 nn. 7 and 8

Gödel, Kurt, 149, 235 n. 16
Goethe, Johann Wolfgang von, 43
Gómez, Michael A., 153, 235 n. 17
Goncourt, Edmond, 231 n. 3
Goncourt, Jules, 231 n. 3
González Echevarría, Roberto, 23, 29–35, 44, 47, 48, 54, 57–58, 100–101, 217–19, 224, 226 nn. 2 and 3 (chap. 1), 226 n. 16, 228 n. 24
Goodrich, Diana Sorenson, 66, 229 n. 11
Gorodischer, Angélica, 26, 189, 192–93, 194–97, 215, 216, 222, 238 n. 3; "A la luz de la casta luna electrónica," 195; "Los circuitos," 194; "Los embriones del violeta," 238 n. 3; *Kalpa Imperial*, 194, 238 n. 3; *Opus dos*, 194
Gostaustas, Stasys, 232 n. 11
Grau, Cristina, 234 n. 14
Gregorio, Guillermo, 232 n. 2
Griaule, Marcel, 218
Gribbin, John, 167, 175, 235 n. 18, 236 n. 1, 237 nn. 8, 9, and 12
Gross, Paul, 203, 213–14, 239 n. 10
Guiraldes, Ricardo, 116–17; *Don Segundo Sombra*, 105
Guzzo, María, 58, 230 n. 16

Haddon, A. C., 59
Halpern, Paul, 234 n. 10
Haraway, Donna, 177–78
Hayes, Aden, 232 n. 1
Hayles, N. Katherine, 22, 125, 155, 178, 197–98, 203, 212–13, 235 n. 17, 237 n. 20, 239 n. 15
Heisenberg, Werner, 26, 163, 164, 170–76, 179, 183, 184, 187, 188, 202, 222–24, 235 n. 21
Herbert, Christopher, 63, 229 n. 13
Herder, Johann, 43
Hernández, Ana María, 237 n. 10
Hernández, Domingo Luis, 232 n. 8, 234 n. 11
Hernández, José, 116–17
Historias futuras, 192–93, 195, 226 n. 4 (intro.)
Hoeg, Jerry, 217

258 INDEX

Höfner, Eckhard, 235 n. 17
Hofstadter, Douglas, 236 n. 16
Holmberg, Eduardo, 179, 191–92
Holzapfel, Tamara, 233 n. 17
homosexuality, 231 n. 2
Honingmann, John J., 229 n. 13
Houssay, Bernardo, 116, 121
Human Genome Project, 13
Humboldt, Alexander Von, 27, 29–31, 42, 44, 47, 56, 58, 63–65, 80, 134, 202, 220, 222, 228 n. 18
Hume, David, 157, 235 n. 21
Hutcheon, Linda, 210, 239 n. 14
hypertext, 238 n. 30

immigration, 25, 42, 86, 89, 91, 94, 95, 220
Incas, 61–62
International Geographic Congress, 55, 58
Irwin, John T., 236 n. 23
Isaacs, Jorge: *María*, 30

James, William, 130
Jameson, Fredric, 231 n. 4
Jarkowski, Aníbal, 232 n. 2
Jitrik, Noé, 89, 96
Joyce, James: *Finnegans Wake*, 191

Kafka, Franz, 210
Keats, John, 238 n. 31
Kirkpatrick, Gwen, 28–29
Knight, David, 38
Kodama, María, 233 n. 2
Krow-Lucal, Martha, 226 n. 5 (chap. 1)
Kuhn, Thomas, 171, 173, 223

La Mettrie, Julien: *L'homme machine*, 179
Lander, María Fernanda, 228 n. 20
Lanuza, Lucio, 229 n. 9
Larra, Mariano José de, 229 n. 13
Larra, Raúl, 232 n. 1, 232 n. 13
Larsen, Neil, 239 n. 1
Lavater, Johann, 38–39, 44, 45
LeGuin, Ursula K., 194
Leibniz, Gottfried Wilhelm, 147, 157
Leland, Christopher, 232 n. 7
Levitt, Norman, 203, 213–14, 239 n. 10

Lezama Lima, José, 237 n. 21
Lizama, Patricio, 236 n. 6, 237 n. 7
Lojo, María Rosa, 81–82, 228 n. 4
Lombroso, Cesare, 84, 85
López, Vicente, 230 n. 17
Losada y Rocheblave, Sabino de, 226 n. 6
Lowie, Robert, 229 n. 13
Luchting, Wolfgang, 236 n. 1
Ludmer, Josefina, 234 n. 13
Lugones, Leopoldo, 99, 146; *Las fuerzas extrañas*, 232 n. 3
Lukacs, Georg, 231 n. 4
Lyon, Ted, 235 n. 20

MacAdam, Alfred, 238 n. 29
Malinowski, Bronislaw, 218
Mann, Horace, 41, 227 n. 12
Mansilla, Lucio V., 24, 25, 87, 88, 90, 99, 101, 105, 108, 122, 124, 130, 163, 192, 197, 217–20, 222, 224, 229 nn. 9 and 12, 230 n. 23, 231 n. 27; relationship to Sarmiento of, 56–57, 60–61, 64–65, 82–83, 171, 220, 228–29 n. 5, 229 n. 11; self-fashioning of, 56–63, 71–78, 82–83, 106, 228–29 n. 5, 230 n. 22; use of phrenology by, 56–57, 65–73, 76–82, 96, 100, 114, 218, 220, 228–29 n. 5. Works: "¡Esa cabeza Toba!," 67–69, 72, 76–78; *Entre nos*, 60, 70, 72, 78, 229 n. 14; *Una excursión a los indios ranqueles*, 30, 38, 48, 55–66, 69–72, 78–83, 131, 149, 218–19, 228 nn. 2, 3, and 4, 228–29 n. 5, 229 nn. 6 and 11, 230 n. 16; "¿Por qué?," 71–76, 231 n. 24
Marcus, George, 218
Mármol, José, 25, 83, 229 n. 7; *Amalia*, 24, 30, 38, 48–54, 55–57, 65, 80–81, 87, 108, 124, 218, 227 n. 11, 228 nn. 22 and 23, 228–29 n. 5, 230 n. 17
Martí, José: "Nuestra América," 83
Martin, Laurey K., 231 n. 5
Martínez Estrada, Ezequiel, 56, 228 n. 3
Marún, Gioconda, 232 n. 5
Marxism, 182–83, 231 n. 4

Masiello, Francine, 28–29
Massachusetts Institute of Technology, 120–21
Matamoro, Blas, 228 n. 2
mathematics, 25, 101, 102, 122, 127–32, 136–38, 142, 143, 147, 149, 152, 158, 177, 183, 214, 234 nn. 9 and 11, 235 n. 16, 235–36 n. 22
Mathieu-Higginbotham, Corina, 228 n. 4
McCracken, Ellen, 233 n. 14
medicine/medical discourse, 17–19, 21, 24, 70, 84–85, 90–92, 95–96, 122, 220, 231 nn. 1 and 2
Merrell, Floyd, 125, 158, 234 n. 9, 235 n. 17
Mesonero Romanos, Ramón de, 37
metaphysics, 117–18, 123–24, 187, 188, 196, 220, 232 n. 13, 237 n. 16
Mexico, 14, 37
microbiology, 17, 18
Mill, John Stuart, 129, 137
modernity/modernism, 14, 56, 202, 214, 224, 228–29 n. 5, 229 n. 6, 239 n. 1
Molina-Gavilán, Yolanda, 195, 196, 238 n. 3
Molloy, Sylvia, 234 n. 8
Monde, Le, 162
Montero, María, 230 n. 23
Montserrat, Marcelo, 232 n. 5
Morgan, Lewis, 59
Mosca, Stefania, 234 n. 14
Mosher, Mark, 235 n. 17
Mundo, El, 99

natural history, 63–64
naturalism, 24–25, 83, 84–96, 97, 104, 219, 220, 231 nn. 1, 2, and 3; French vs. Argentine, 86–91, 93–96, 231 n. 3
Nazism, 148
neurology, 152
Newton, Isaac, 109, 156, 157, 158, 165, 171, 173, 183, 201, 235 n. 21
Nietzsche, Friedrich, 25, 127, 132–43, 145, 234 n. 10
Nouzeilles, Gabriella, 24, 84–86, 88, 89, 95, 96, 231 n. 1

novela ecológica, 199
Nuñez, Ángel, 232 n. 1

Operé, Fernando, 229 n. 10
Oppenheimer, J. Robert, 163, 164
Ortiz, Eduardo, 99, 128, 232 nn. 3 and 5, 234 n. 6
Osses, José Emilio, 237 n. 21

Parodi, Cristina, 229 n. 8
Payró, Roberto: *Las divertidas aventuras*, 95
Pérez Galdós, Benito: *Lo prohibido*, 184
Perón, Juan, 189–91
phrenology, 14–15, 17, 19, 24, 34–54, 56–57, 65–73, 76–82, 84, 85, 114, 192, 218–20, 227 nn. 9, 11, 12, 14, 15, and 17, 228 nn. 21 and 23, 228–29 n. 5, 230 nn. 17, 18, and 19, 233 n. 18; decline of, 65–67, 72; in the Hispanic and Latin American worlds, 36–38, 41, 66, 69, 225, 226 n. 6, 227 n. 11; origins of, 38; and romanticism, 42–43, 225; Western popularity of, 35–36, 39–41, 225, 227 nn. 9 and 11
Physical Review, 120
physics, 17, 19, 25, 26, 31, 98, 99, 101, 106, 116, 122, 125, 126, 128, 152–58, 160–77, 183, 187, 188, 191, 195, 204, 221, 237 n. 11. *See also* quantum mechanics; thermodynamics
physiognomy, 24, 34, 38–54, 228 nn. 18 and 23
physiology, 17, 18, 177
Piglia, Ricardo, 26, 123, 140, 189, 196, 202, 215, 216, 221, 222, 224, 233 n. 14; *La ciudad ausente*, 189–91; *Respiración artificial*, 115, 126, 234 n. 4
Planck, Max, 171–72
Planells, Antonio, 237 n. 16, 238 n. 23
Podestá, Manuel, 84, 90
Poe, Edgar Allan, 36; "The Fall of the House of Usher," 36
Poplizio, Enrique, 55, 67, 229 n. 9
Porush, David, 182–84, 186, 237 n. 20, 238 n. 27

postmodernity, 27, 199, 200, 202–3, 210–15, 222–25, 239 nn. 10 and 17, 239 n. 1
poststructuralism, 184, 213
Pound, Ezra, 224
Pratt, Mary Louise, 23, 30, 227 n. 16, 229 n. 13
Prigogine, Ilya, 26–27, 198, 199–205, 207–9, 211–12, 214–15, 222, 239 nn. 8, 10, 12, and 13
psychoanalysis, 19
psychology, 51, 53, 54, 87, 177

quantum mechanics, 26, 125, 126, 152, 154, 160–64, 167, 168, 170–74, 176, 183, 185, 187, 201, 219, 221, 223–24, 235 n. 21, 236 n. 6, 237 nn. 7 and 10, 238 n. 31, 239 n. 11
Quechua, 61–62
Quevedo, Francisco de, 232 n. 8
Quiroga, Horacio, 98–100, 116–17, 146, 232 n. 3; *El hombre artificial*, 179

race: and mixing/assimilation, 79, 83, 91, 231 n. 25; in science fiction, 194–96; theories of, 84–85, 87, 89, 90, 93, 94, 100, 231 n. 2
Ramos-Izquierdo, Eduardo, 236 n. 1
Ramos Mejía, José María: *Las neurosis de los hombres célebres*, 53, 54, 66, 69, 230 n. 17
Ranquel Indians, 55–56, 62–63, 79, 81, 130
realism, 89, 184
relativity, 154, 157, 164
Rivadavia, Bernardino, 13, 31, 37, 41, 52–54, 162
Rivero-Potter, Alicia, 152–53, 235 n. 17
robotics, 13
Roca, Julio A., 55
Rock, David, 227 n. 11
Rodo, José Enrique: *Ariel*, 83
Rodríguez, Fermín, 228 n. 4
Roffé, Reina, 238 n. 4
Rojo, Alberto G., 152–53, 155, 235 n. 17
romanticism, 42–43, 48, 225, 238 n. 31

Rosas, Juan Manuel, 24, 30, 31, 32, 35, 48, 53, 57, 61, 66, 133, 171, 220, 226 n. 1 (intro.), 230 n. 17
Rosas, Mariano, 62
Roussel, Raymond, 185, 186
Rubino, Carl, 212
Rufinelli, Jorge, 232 nn. 2 and 9
Russell, Bertrand, 128–31, 133, 139, 235–36 n. 22
Rutherford, Ernest, 134–37

Sabato, Ernesto, 25, 97, 116–24, 126, 134, 158, 188, 190, 196, 220, 221, 233 nn. 15, 16, 18, and 19; *Abaddón el Exterminador*, 119, 120, 121, 233 n. 18; *Antes del fin*, 120–21; *Hombres y engranajes*, 121–23; *Sobre Héroes y Tumbas*, 116–17, 119, 233 nn. 16 and 17; *El túnel*, 116, 233 n. 16
Safir, Margery, 238 n. 22
Salazar, Béatrice, 237 n. 18
Salessi, Jorge, 231 n. 2
Sarlo, Beatriz, 98–99, 100, 102, 104
Sarmiento, Domingo, 229 n. 7; influence of, 28–29; journalistic writings of, 41, 27 n. 13; and the pampa, 43–46, 60, 64–65; and political power/attacks, 15, 17, 24, 30, 32, 44–45, 53, 56, 61, 65, 82–83, 88, 106, 108, 133, 171, 192, 197, 220, 226 nn. 1 and 5 (intro.); use of phrenology, physiognomy, or scientific discourse by, 15, 17, 24, 34, 35, 37–38, 41–48, 50, 53–54, 65, 67, 71–72, 80–81, 85, 89, 90, 96, 99, 101, 105, 111, 126, 134, 162, 218–20, 224, 226 n. 1 (intro.), 227 nn. 12 and 15, 228 n. 21 and 23, 228–29 n. 5. Works: "El diarismo," 227 n. 13; *Facundo*, 15, 17, 23–25, 27, 28–35, 37–38, 41–48, 50, 52–58, 63, 64–65, 80–81, 85, 87, 124, 131, 133, 138, 198, 202, 215, 217, 222, 226 nn. 1, 2, and 5 (intro.), 227 nn. 11 and 16, 228 n. 19, 20, 21 and 23, 228 n. 23, 228–29 n. 5
Scari, Robert M., 232 n. 2
Schade, George, 229 n. 12

Schmidt-Emans, Monika, 235 n. 16
Schopenhauer, Arthur, 142
Schreiber, Gabriel, 153, 235 n. 17
Schrödinger, Irwin, 167–70, 172, 237 n. 12
science: absence in Argentina of work in, 13–14; and cultural truth, 14, 21, 30–31, 35, 57, 96, 114–15, 124, 126, 131–32, 136, 146, 158, 163, 164, 202, 221, 222–23; and government, 31–32, 189–90; popularizations of, 13, 57, 98–99, 133, 140, 156, 162–64, 167, 170, 171, 173, 174, 176, 187, 188, 198, 200, 202, 212, 216, 239 n. 5, 239 n. 12; and power, 14–17, 19–22, 96, 102, 108, 123, 126–27, 147, 163, 187, 190–92, 195–97, 216, 220, 222–24; revolutions in, 173–74, 223; as type of knowledge, 17–19, 202. *See also individual fields of scientific inquiry*
science fiction, 23, 27, 99, 102, 146, 179, 189, 191–98, 232 n. 3, 238 n. 1
Selnes, Gisle, 234 nn. 10 and 11
Serres, Michel, 125, 155–56, 223, 233 n. 1
sexuality, 16–17, 88, 231 n. 2
Shaw, Donald L., 226 n. 3 (chap. 1), 228 n. 19, 232 n. 13, 234 n. 3, 234 n. 13, 238 n. 28
Showalter, Elaine, 197
Shua, Ana María, 26–27, 189, 192–94, 196, 197, 215, 216, 222, 238 n. 2; "Octavio el invasor," 193–94
Shumway, David, 16, 20
Shuttleworth, Sally, 36, 39, 226 n. 4 (chap. 1)
Silva Gruesz, Kirsten, 41, 44, 46, 226 n. 7, 227 n. 17, 228 n. 18
socialism, 231 n. 4
sociology, 51, 59
Sommer, Doris, 48, 88, 227 n. 11, 231 n. 1
Sorenson, Diana. *See* Goodrich, Diana Sorenson
Sosnowski, Saul, 170, 234 n. 13, 236 n. 4, 237 n. 16, 238 n. 23
Spencer, Baldwin, 59–60

Spurzheim, Johann, 40
Stark, John, 234 n. 13
Stengers, Isabelle, 200–202, 209, 212
Stepan, Nancy Leys, 100
Stern, Mirta, 228 n. 4, 229 n. 6
Stocking, George, 59, 60, 229 n. 13
Stonum, Gary, 184–85
structuralism, 184
surrealism, 116, 164

Taine, Hippolyte, 46, 228 n. 19
Taussig, Michael, 218
telluric novels, 217–18
thermodynamics, 25, 133, 139, 140, 141, 145, 200, 205, 208, 215, 221, 239 n. 8
Tocqueville, Alexis de, 47
Toeffler, Alvin, 200–201, 238 n. 9
travel writing, 23, 29–32, 54, 55–58, 63–64, 80–81, 82, 217–18, 229 n. 12, 230 n. 16
Tribuna, La, 55
Trigo, Benigni, 231 n. 2
Tylor, Edward Burnett, 60

ultraism, 164
Umansky, Roberto, 153, 235 n. 17
Unamuno, Miguel de, 137
Unitarios, 42, 43, 48, 50–53, 61, 227 n. 11, 228 n. 20, 230 n. 17, 231 n. 24
urban life, 97, 105, 111, 124, 220

Valenzuela, Luisa: *Novela negra con argentinos*, 197
Vasconcelos, José: *Raza cósmica*, 83
Verne, Jules, 160, 199, 205, 209, 210
Villalobos, Carlos Manuel, 233 n. 18

Weissert, Thomas, 155–56, 158, 197, 233 n. 1, 235 n. 17
Wheeler, John, 164, 237 n. 7
Whitman, Walt, 138
Wiener, Norbert, 177, 180, 183, 187, 188, 238 nn. 24 and 25
Wilde, Eduardo, 84
Williams, William Carlos, 184
women writers, 192–93, 197, 238 nn. 1 and 4
Woolf, Virginia, 210

World War I, 232 n. 4, 234 n. 6
World War II, 163
wormholes, 164

xenophobia, 25, 85, 86, 89–91. *See also* immigration

Yeats, William Butler, 224
Young, Richard, 237 n. 13

Yurkievich, Saúl, 236 n. 1

Zanelli, Jorge, 235 n. 17
Zeno, 128–29, 131–32, 136, 147, 157
Zola, Émile, 25, 84, 86–91, 93–96, 231 nn. 3, 4, and 5; "De la Moralité dans la Littérature," 87; *Le roman expérimental*, 87, 88, 179
Zubieta, Ana María, 232 n. 1